EXAM PREPARATION FOR RESIDENTIAL APPRAISER CERTIFICATION

APPRAISAL INSTITUTE
WILLIAM B. RAYBURN, SRPA
CONSULTING EDITOR

APPRAISAL INSTITUTE

Real Estate Education Company
a division of Dearborn Financial Publishing, Inc.

While a great deal of care has been taken to provide accurate and current information, the ideas, suggestions, general principles and conclusions presented in this text are subject to local, state and federal laws and regulations, court cases and any revisions of the same. The reader thus is urged to consult legal counsel regarding any points of law—this publication should not be used as a substitute for competent legal advice.

Publisher: Carol L. Luitjens
Acquisitions Editor: Margaret M. Maloney
Cover Design: Jody Leviton
Interior Design: Publishers Services, Inc.

© 1992 by Dearborn Financial Publishing, Inc. and the Appraisal Institute

Published by Real Estate Education Company/Chicago,
a division of Dearborn Financial Publishing, Inc.

All rights reserved. The text of this publication, or any part thereof, may not be reproduced in any manner whatsoever without written permission from the publisher.

Printed in the United States of America

92 93 94 10 9 8 7 6 5 4 3 2 1

Library of Congress Cataloging-in-Publication Data

Exam preparation for the residential appraiser certification exam / the Appraisal Institute : [edited by] William B. Rayburn.
      p.   cm.
  Includes index.
  ISBN 0-7931-0112-3
  1. Real Property—Valuation—United States—Examinations, questions, etc. I. Rayburn, William B. II. Appraisal Institute (U.S.)
HD1387.E93   1992
333.33'82'076—dc20   91-38470
                                                               CIP

Table of Contents

Preface — xi

Chapter 1: Introduction — 2
    Brief History of Appraiser Licensure/Certification — 4
    Test-Taking Strategies for Multiple-Choice Tests — 5
        Before the Exam
        During the Exam
    Exam Content Weights — 7

Chapter 2: Influences on Real Estate Value and Legal Considerations in Appraisal — 10
    Overview — 11
    Learning Objectives — 11
    Influences on Real Estate Value — 12
    Legal Considerations in Appraisal — 12
        Real Estate v. Real Property
        Real Property v. Personal Property
        Limitations on Real Estate Ownership
        Legal Rights and Interests
        Forms of Property Ownership
        Legal Descriptions
        Transfer of Title
    Endnotes — 22
    Key Terms and Concepts — 23
    Review Questions — 25

Chapter 3: Types of Value — 28
    Overview — 29
    Learning Objectives — 29
    Market Value — 30
        Market Value Assumptions
        Market Value Distinctions
    Other Types of Value — 33
        Value in Exchange
        Value in Use
        Investment Value
        Liquidation Value
        Insurable Value
        Assessed Value
        Going-Concern Value

Endnotes	35
Key Terms and Concepts	36
Review Questions	37

Chapter 4: Economic Principles — 40

Overview	41
Learning Objectives	41
Principles of Real Property Valuation	42
Anticipation	
Balance	
Change	
Consistent Use	
Competition	
Conformity	
Supply and Demand	
Highest and Best Use	
Substitution (Opportunity Cost)	
Contribution (Marginal Productivity)	
Variable Proportions and Increasing/Decreasing Returns	
Economic Characteristics of Value	46
Endnotes	46
Key Terms and Concepts	47
Review Questions	48

Chapter 5: Real Estate Markets and Analysis — 52

Overview	53
Learning Objectives	53
Market Analysis	54
Steps in Market Analysis	
Forecasts	
Neighborhoods and Neighborhood Analysis	
Characteristics of Real Estate Markets	56
Availability of Information	
Changes in Supply and Demand	
Immobility of Real Estate	
Segmented Markets	
Regulation	
Role of Money and Capital Markets	58
Monetary Policy	
Fiscal Policy	

   Competing Investments in U.S. Financial Markets
   Sources of Capital
  Real Estate Financing 60
   Mortgage Terms and Concepts
   Mortgage Payment Plans
   Types of Mortgages
  Endnotes 63
  Key Terms and Concepts 64
  Review Questions 66

Chapter 6: The Appraisal Process **70**
  Overview 71
  Learning Objectives 71
  The Appraisal Process 72
   Defining the Problem
   Collecting, Analyzing and Verifying Data
   Determining Highest and Best Use
   Analyzing Land or Site Value
   Applying the Approaches to Value
   Preparing Reconciliation and Final Value Estimate
   Submitting a Report
  Endnotes 76
  Key Terms and Concepts 77
  Review Questions 78

Chapter 7: Property Description **82**
  Overview 83
  Learning Objectives 83
  Site Description and Analysis 84
   Factors in Site Analysis
  Improvement Description 87
   Condition
   Market Standards
   Utility
  Basic Construction and Design 88
   Construction Terminology
   Techniques and Materials
  Endnotes 90
  Key Terms and Concepts 91
  Review Questions 92

Chapter 8: Highest and Best Use Analysis — **94**

- Overview — 95
- Learning Objectives — 95
- What is Highest and Best Use? — 96
  - *Traditional Tests (Constraints) of Highest and Best Use*
- Application of Highest and Best Use — 98
  - *Highest and Best Use of a Site as if Vacant*
  - *Highest and Best Use of Property as Improved*
- Other Related Highest and Best Use Topics — 100
  - *Special Purpose or Single-Use Properties*
  - *Interim Use Properties*
  - *Legally Nonconforming Use*
- Endnote — 100
- Key Terms and Concepts — 101
- Review Questions — 102

Chapter 9: Statistical Concepts in Appraisal — **104**

- Overview — 105
- Learning Objectives — 105
- Specific Quantitative Skills — 106
  - *Central Tendency*
  - *Measures of Dispersion*
- Regression Analysis — 109
- Basic Mathematical Skills — 111
  - *Parenthetical Equations*
  - *Percentage Change*
  - *Percentage Adjustments*
- Endnotes — 113
- Key Terms and Concepts — 114
- Review Questions — 115

Chapter 10: The Sales Comparison Approach — **118**

- Overview — 119
- Learning Objectives — 119
- Overview of the Process — 120
  - *Relationship to Underlying Valuation Principles*
  - *Research and Selection of Comparables*
  - *Steps in the Sales Comparison Approach*
- Key Terms and Concepts — 128
- Review Questions — 129

Chapter 11: Site Valuation — 134

- Overview — 135
- Learning Objectives — 135
- Techniques for Site Valuation — 136
    - *Sales Comparison*
    - *Allocation (Abstraction) Technique*
    - *Extraction Technique*
    - *Land Residual Technique*
    - *Capitalization of Ground Rents*
    - *Subdivision (Land Development)*
- Plottage Value and Assemblage — 138
- Endnotes — 139
- Key Terms and Concepts — 140
- Review Questions — 141

Chapter 12: The Cost Approach — 144

- Overview — 145
- Learning Objectives — 145
- Cost Approach — 146
    - *Rationale*
    - *Applications and Limitations of the Cost Approach*
    - *Valuation Principles*
    - *Steps in the Cost Approach*
    - *Estimating Cost New*
- Accrued Depreciation — 150
    - *Physical Deterioration*
    - *Functional Obsolescence*
    - *External Obsolescence*
    - *Techniques for Estimating Depreciation*
- Endnotes — 157
- Cost Approach Problem — 158
- Key Terms and Concepts — 162
- Review Questions — 163

Chapter 13: The Income Approach — 168

- Overview — 169
- Learning Objectives — 169
- The Income Approach — 170

Rationale
Estimation of Income and Expenses
Capitalization 173
Direct Capitalization
Yield Capitalization
Operating Ratios 175
Debt Service Ratio
Operating Expense Ratio
Break-Even Ratio
Equity Dividend Rate
Loan-to-Value Ratio
Gross Rent Multiplier 177
Requirements for Use of GRMs
Nature of Gross Rent Multipliers
Gross Rent Multiplier Procedure
Calculating Estimated Value
Gross Rent Multiplier Example 179
Endnotes 180
Key Terms and Concepts 181
Review Questions 182

Chapter 14: Valuation of Partial Interests, Reconciliation and Final Value Estimate — 186

Overview 187
Learning Objectives 187
Valuation of Partial Interests 188
Undivided Interests
Life Estates
Easements
Time-Shares
Cooperative
Leases
Financial Arrangements in Leases 190
Fixed or Gross Lease
Net Lease
Percentage Lease
Reappraisal Lease
Index Lease
Graduated Payment Lease

Sublease and Assignment	191
Sublease	
Assignment	
Reconciliation	191
Review	
Reconciliation	
Rounding	
Assumptions, Certification and Limiting Conditions	193
Assumptions	
Certification and Limiting Conditions	
Endnotes	194
Key Terms and Concepts	195
Review Questions	196

Chapter 15: Appraisal Standards and Ethics — **198**

Overview	199
Learning Objectives	199
Uniform Standards of Professional Appraisal Practice	200
State License Law	200
State Requirements for Licensure and/or Certification	
State Definitions	
Endnote	201
Excerpts from the Uniform Standards of Professional Appraisal Practice	202
Key Terms and Concepts	209
Review Questions	210

Chapter 16: Practice Examinations — **212**

Overview	213
Learning Objectives	213
Practice Exam I	214
Practice Exam II	232

Answer Key	**250**
Glossary	**268**
Index	**284**

Preface

Under the Financial Institutions Reform, Recovery and Enforcement Act (FIRREA) of 1989, states may require real estate appraisers to be licensed or certified. *Exam Preparation for Residential Appraiser Certification* represents the Appraisal Institute's response to the need for professional appraiser education as it relates to meeting the FIRREA requirement.

In their efforts to comply, many states now require two categories of state-licensed or state-certified appraisers for federally related transactions: residential and general. To obtain residential licensure/certification, an applicant must successfully complete a state exam that focuses primarily on residential real property. This book is intended to prepare students for that exam.

The text contains 16 chapters, each centering on appraisal principles, practices and theories and their applications to residential property. Although each chapter is designed to meet specific learning objectives, the overall objective of *Exam Preparation* is to provide the background a student needs to pass the state residential appraisal exam. Therefore the book culminates in Chapter 16 with two practice exams—a total of 200 questions—modeled on the "actual" state exam.

This book is not intended for use as a primary study guide for the general exam, which covers all types of valuation, with primary emphasis on income property appraisal. Even so, the reader probably will find this material helpful in the review of concepts, terminology and valuation theories. The detailed cost approach problem and the gross rent multiplier example, included as special features, may be of particular interest.

Appraisers of all levels of education and experience will find *Exam Preparation* to be a stepping-stone to their professional betterment. Without doubt, both the student and the seasoned appraiser will acknowledge the practical challenge that certification/licensure criteria have presented to the field of real property appraisal.

The content and organization of this book were reviewed extensively and I am indebted to the following colleagues for their comments and suggestions: Don Boyson, MAI, SRA, Columbia Savings; Douglas C. Brown, MAI, Appraisal Institute; Sandra Cece, Real Estate Coordinator, Triton College; Robert Chaapel, National College of Appraisal and Property Management; Joseph S. Durrer, Jr., MAI, SRPA; Alfred J. Ferrara, MAI, SRA, Appraisal Institute; Bernard J. Fountain, MAI, SRA, Vice-President, Appraisal Institute; George R. Harrison, Lincoln Graduate Center; Kenneth J. Longacre, J.D., University of Houston; David J. January, MAI, SRA, Frederick Realty, Inc.; Donald T. Keller, Anderson and Carr, Inc.; A. Scruggs Love, Jr., MAI, Real

Estate Consultants and Appraisers; C. David Matthews, MAI, SRA, David Matthews and Associates; Thomas P. Morlan, III, SRA, SREA, Appraisal Institute; Milton A. Morse, Jr., SRA, Appraisal Institute; Richard G. Pietrowitz, SRPA, SRA, President, 1991, Appraisal Institute; William L. Pittenger, Chief Appraiser, Barnett Banks, Inc.; William Pivar, J.D., College of the Desert; George C. Potter, Professor Emeritus, Western Illinois University; Donald E. Roach, SRA, St. Louis Appraisal Co.; Felice A. Rocca, Jr., MAI, Rocca Associates; Sara F. Schwarzentraub, SRA, Inter-State Appraisal Service; J. Donald Turner, SRPA, SRA.

I want to specifically thank Don Epley, Ph.D., MAI, for his excellent suggestions on the manuscript. Finally, two people have provided me inspiration and insight on this book. Dennis Tosh, Ph.D., a colleague at Ole Miss, served as an excellent mentor throughout this project; his thoughtful comments were very timely and deeply appreciated. My wife, Abi, contributed so much of her time, effort and encouragement to this project. Abi, I thank you so very much.

William B. Rayburn, D.B.A., CFA, SRPA

William B. Rayburn is a finance and real estate professor at the University of Mississippi in Oxford, Mississippi. He holds the Doctor of Business Administration (D.B.A.) degree in finance, the Charter Financial Analyst (CFA) and the Senior Real Property Appraiser (SRPA) designations. During 1991 he served as vice chair of the Appraisal Institute's Body of Knowledge and Residential Education committees. He is also president of Seminars for Real Estate and Financial Professionals.

1 Introduction

This book is designed to help you pass the appraisal examination(s) in your state. In addition, it is designed to serve as an appraisal reference. The outline for each chapter has been patterned after the Uniform Content Outlines developed by the Appraiser Qualifications Board of The Appraisal Foundation. These outlines must be followed by individual states when they develop content questions for their state examinations. For example, if a residential content outline states that 20 percent of the material should test the sales comparison approach, then approximately 20 percent of a state's content questions must be based on the sales comparison approach.

Most state examinations will be based on a common body of knowledge, including the Uniform Standards of Professional Appraisal Practice and the license law for that particular state. The common body of knowledge will consist of appraisal principles, practices, terms, theories, definitions and calculations. Therefore, the focus of this book is to provide you, the student, with a review of principles, practices, terms, theories, definitions and calculations. In addition, the text is designed to provide feedback through review questions on weak areas or areas where there are misunderstandings about certain topics. To supplement this text, the student should obtain a copy of the licensure/certification law for the state in which he or she will sit for the exam.

Brief History of Appraiser Licensure/Certification

Recently, due to perceived irregularities, the appraisal profession has come under close scrutiny. These irregularities have stemmed from financial institutions' losses on faulty appraisals. Lack of appraiser education and training have often been cited as contributing factors in faulty appraisals. In response to these and other problems in the savings and loan and financial services industry, Congress passed the Financial Institutions Reform, Recovery and Enforcement Act (FIRREA) of 1989. Part of this act, Title XI, specifies that either a state-certified or state-licensed appraiser must be used for a "federally related transaction," which is defined in Section 1121 as "any real estate related financial transaction which (a) a federal financial institution, regulatory agency or the Resolution Trust Corporation engages in, contracts for or regulates; and (b) requires the services of an appraiser." After December 31, 1991, the type of appraiser required—certified or licensed—is based on whether an appraisal is noncomplex or complex. A noncomplex appraisal has been defined by the Appraisal Subcommittee of the Federal Financial Institutions Examinations Council (FFIEC) as one whose subject is "typical of its market taking into account a list of factors." For a residential property (one- to four-family residential structure) whose transaction value is less than $1,000,000, the appraisal is assumed to be noncomplex. For transaction values exceeding $1,000,000, the appraisal is assumed to be complex. Transaction value is the amount of the mortgage for loan purposes. For purchases, sales or other conveyances, it is generally the price of the property. In general, state-certified appraisers must be used if the dollar amount is $1,000,000 or more; state-licensed appraisers may be used if the dollar amount is less than $1,000,000. However, a federal agency or federally related agency may require use of a certified appraiser. Members of FFIEC have stated that an appraisal is not required for those properties with a transaction value of less than $100,000.

Certification carries a higher requirement than does licensure. A state-certified appraiser generally will have taken the following steps:

1. obtained the necessary education to sit for the exam,
2. passed the state exam and
3. met the experience requirements.

Most states offer two types of certification—residential and general. The residential exam focuses on principles and practices related to residential properties, with minimal emphasis on income properties. The general exam focuses on principles and practices related to income properties.

There is a lesser requirement for licensure, but this is not specifically addressed by Title XI of FIRREA. Several states have opted to provide licensure based solely on passing the exam and certification based on licensure plus experience requirements.

The Appraiser Qualifications Board of the Appraisal Foundation recommended three experience classifications:

1. licensed appraisers,
2. certified residential appraisers and
3. certified general appraisers.

All appraisers, regardless of their training and experience, must pass an examination, for there is no provision in FIRREA to license current appraisers based exclusively on their experience (no grandfathering).

Test-Taking Strategies for Multiple-Choice Tests

Some experienced appraisers may feel that they lack the breadth or depth of knowledge needed to pass the exam. Although they may have extensive expertise in one small area (such as the appraisal of environmentally contaminated properties), they may have forgotten the definition of the principles of anticipation, supply and demand, contribution; the steps in the cost approach; or other topics related to appraisal principles. This text will provide that scope of knowledge necessary to pass the appraisal exam.

Many students are nervous about taking their state examination. Whereas a little nervousness can be positive, too much anxiety can lead to panic. To avoid a panic situation, consider the following suggestions.

Before the Exam

- After reading each chapter, work the problems and answer the questions. If you are unsure about certain subject matter, get an appraisal reference and find the answer. Two excellent references are The *Dictionary of Real Estate Appraisal*, 2nd ed. (1989) and *The Appraisal of Real Estate,* 9th ed. (1987), both published by the Appraisal Institute/Chicago.

- Get plenty of rest prior to the exam.

- Go through your normal morning routine the morning of the exam. If you usually have six cups of coffee before going to your office, then have six cups of coffee before the exam. If you have studied this text and can answer all questions at the end of each chapter, as well as all the questions in the practice exams at the end of the text, you should be sufficiently prepared.

- Bring the necessary materials to the exam center. For example, if an admissions ticket and a photo are required, lay these materials out the night before.

During the Exam

- RELAX before you begin the exam. Read the instructions on the exam itself, listen for special instructions from the exam proctor and make sure you follow these instructions.

- Be aware of time. If four hours are allowed for the residential exam and the exam has a total of 120 questions, you have two minutes for each question (4 hours × 60 minutes per hour = 240 total exam minutes ÷ 120 questions = 2 minutes per question). Each question should be equally weighted, so you should not spend 10 minutes on any one question. If you have trouble with a question, circle it and move on to the next one.

- Read the first question. If you are certain of the answer, then mark it on the answer sheet and "X out" question 1 on the answer sheet and on the test. If you are not certain of the answer to question 1, then circle question 1 on the answer sheet and on the test. Repeat this process for each question. In other words, the first pass through the exam should be to answer questions for which you are certain of the answer.

- Review answer choices carefully. There probably will be four possible choices for each question. Even though two or more answers may be partially correct or correct in unique situations, choose the **best** answer. As you read a question, look at answer "a." If "a" looks like a **possible** answer, then circle "a." If "a" is not a possible answer, then "X it out." Look at answers b, c and d. If these are possible answers, then circle them; if not, X them out. Once you have circled the possible answers, look at your circled choices and determine which of the circled possibilities is a probable answer. You may be left with only one choice at this point, and this usually will be the correct answer. However, if you can eliminate only two of the responses and are left with two good choices, you still have increased your odds of getting a correct answer from 25 percent (1 in 4) to 50 percent (1 in 2).

- Answer every question, even if you must guess. Leaving a question blank provides a zero percent probability of getting an answer correct, whereas a wild guess provides a 25 percent (1 in 4) probability. The computer used to grade a machine-graded test does not know whether you really knew the answer and rationale; it only knows whether the choice marked is correct.

- Make sure erasures are complete. Keep in mind that in many instances, your first impression is correct.

- Don't be obsessed with finishing first. Too many students think that those finishing first must really know the material and feel inferior about taking so long. In many instances, those finishing last or near the end tend to do better because they have checked and double-checked their answers.

In summary, every appraiser will probably be required to pass an appraisal test if he or she wants to perform appraisals on federally related transactions. This is especially true for complex appraisals.

Exam Content Weights

Chapter	Topic	Exam Content Weights
2	Influences on Real Estate Value	3–4% Conceptual
	Legal Considerations in Appraisal	6–8% Conceptual, Definitions
3	Types of Value	3–5% Conceptual, Definitions
4	Economic Principles	7–9% Conceptual, Definitions
5	Real Estate Markets and Analysis	5–7% Conceptual
6	The Appraisal Process	4–6% Conceptual
7	Property Description	2–4% Conceptual, Definitions
8	Highest and Best Use Analysis	5–7% Conceptual, Definitions, Analysis/Application
9	Statistical Concepts in Appraisal	1–3% Conceptual, Analysis/Application
10	The Sales Comparison Approach	21–24% Conceptual, Definitions
11	Site Valuation	4–6% Conceptual, Definitions, Analysis/Application

12	The Cost Approach	8–10% Conceptual, Definitions, Analysis/Application
13	The Income Approach	7–9% Conceptual, Definitions, Analysis/Application
14	Valuation of Partial Interests, Reconciliation and Final Value Estimate	1–3% Conceptual, Definitions
15	Appraisal Standards and Ethics	7–11% Conceptual, Definitions

2 Influences on Real Estate Value and Legal Considerations in Appraisal

Overview

This chapter summarizes the different influences on real estate values. Real property ownership can be thought of as a "bundle," or group, of rights; an owner of real property may own all or parts of the bundle. Restrictions on real estate ownership and the types of real property interests are discussed to provide background on the legal rights and interests that may be conveyed in real asset markets.

Learning Objectives

After completing this chapter, the student should be able to:

- Identify the four influences on real property values

- Identify and distinguish the different forms of legal ownership of real property

- Distinguish between the types of public and private restrictions on property ownership

- Identify and define the types of legal description

I. Influences on Real Estate Value

Four major forces influence property values: Physical or environmental forces, economic forces, governmental and legal forces, and social forces.

Physical or environmental forces include location, climate conditions, traffic arteries and contour of the land. **Economic forces** involve supply and demand for housing, income and employment levels and overall economic activity for an area. **Governmental and legal forces** include levels of public service, zoning and building code restrictions, and police and fire protection. **Social forces** include the rate of population growth, household size, and marriage and divorce rates.

II. Legal Considerations in Appraisal

A. Real Estate v. Real Property

The appraisal of real estate is concerned with the valuation of real property rights. **Real property** has been defined as "the interests, benefits and rights inherent in the ownership of real estate."[1] Real property represents the bundle of rights that an owner receives upon purchasing real estate. The tangible part of real property rights is real estate. Real estate can be touched (tangible). Real property includes the tangible and the intangible. For example, an easement cannot be touched (intangible), but the land on which an easement resides can be touched—as can the document granting the easement.

Real estate[2] is the land and all improvements on and to that parcel of land. Improvements may be *on* the land, such as buildings, or they may be *to* the land, such as grading for construction. Real estate has three physical characteristics: (1) it is immobile (cannot be moved); (2) it is durable (has a long life compared to other assets); and (3) it is heterogeneous (no two parcels are exactly alike).

B. Real Property v. Personal Property

The major difference between real and personal property is that real property is usually immobile or cannot be moved and **personal property** typically is movable. A second difference is how ownership is conveyed. Real property ownership is conveyed through a deed, whereas personal property ownership is conveyed through a bill of sale. It may not be clear whether an item is movable (personal property) or immobile (real property). For example, if a building contains a chalkboard, is this chalkboard real property or personal property? An item that was personal property but was attached in a permanent manner so as to become part of the property is considered a *fixture.* The courts use several tests to determine whether an item is a fixture: (1) Is the item attached in a permanent manner? (2) Is it used in a permanent manner? (3) What was the intent of the parties?

C. **Limitations on Real Estate Ownership**

Limitations on real estate ownership can be divided into two categories for purposes of analysis: private and public. **Private limitations** on real estate ownership include deed restrictions, leases, mortgages, easements, liens, encroachments, and adverse possession. Public limitations include police power, escheat, eminent domain and taxation.

1. Private Limitations

    a. A **deed** is "a written, legal instrument that conveys an estate or interest in real property when it is executed and delivered."[3] The party giving the deed is termed the *grantor* (the seller), and the party receiving the deed is termed the *grantee* (the purchaser). Does a purchaser of a house buy only the house and land, or are there other rights? The general rule is that a purchaser gets surface rights (the land and all improvements permanently attached to the land), subsurface rights (minerals) and suprasurface rights (air rights). Any of these rights may be restricted or limited through a deed restriction, "a limitation that passes with the land regardless of the owner; usually limits the real estate's type of use or intensity of use."[4] A seller of a parcel of property who wants to restrict certain items may state those restrictions in a deed. For example, a developer can restrict a purchaser on the size of a house or require a minimum size of 2,000 square feet of heated area in a subdivision.

    b. A **lease** is "a written (or oral) document in which the rights to use and occupancy of land or structures are transferred by the owner to another for a specified period of time in return for a specified rent."[5] A lease generally conveys only a right of possession or use, not ownership. Usually there are two parties to a lease agreement, each having a specified property interest. The owner of the unencumbered fee estate may give up a possessory interest in the property through a lease.

        1) Parties to a lease

            (a) The lessor, also known as the landlord, is the party who owns the fee estate prior to the lease (known as the unencumbered fee prior to the lease). A lessor has the right to receive rent from the tenant and the right to all property interests, including the reversionary right, at the expiration of the lease.[6] The lessor gives the lessee the right to use and occupy the premises during the term of the lease.

(b) The lessee, also known as the tenant, is the party who has the right to possession (use and occupancy) of the premises under the lease agreement. At the expiration of the lease term, the lessor regains possession. A lease will have value to the lessee if the amount of rent specified in the lease contract (the contract rent) is less than the current lease rate for similar space in the marketplace (market rent). In general, the lessee's rights to possession terminate at the end of the lease period, and any improvements made to the property accrue to the lessor.

2) Rights created by leases

(a) **Unencumbered fee estate** is the estate as if no lease exists. The lessor holds an unencumbered fee estate before a lease occurs and after a lease has expired.

(b) **Leased fee estate** is owned by the lessor during the term of the lease. The leased fee estate has the right to receive rents from the lessee during the term of the lease and to receive the reversionary right at the end of the lease period. The reversionary right is equal to the forecast net sales price at the end of the lease period.[7]

(c) **Leasehold estate** is held by the lessee and usually consists of a right to possession but no ownership. The lessee's right to possession generally ends at the expiration of the lease. A leasehold estate acquires value if the lease payments stated in the lease are less than the current market rent for similar property.

c. A **mortgage** is a loan or promissory note secured by real property.[8] Most real assets involve large dollar amounts, so real estate is characterized by a high degree of debt financing. Lenders who hold a properly executed mortgage generally have a high priority claim on mortgaged real estate if foreclosure is required.

d. **Easements** convey the right to use another's land.[9] Easements may be one of two types: easements in gross and easements appurtenant.

1) **Easements in gross** run with the person, whereas an easement appurtenant runs with the land. For example, if Sam gave Lorrie an easement in gross, that easement would only be good for Lorrie's use. Generally speaking, she cannot assign or convey this easement to another person.

2) **Easements appurtenant** run with the land and can be conveyed or assigned to other parties. For example, if Sam gave Lorrie an easement appurtenant, Lorrie could convey the easement. Suppose Lorrie owned parcel B (Figure 2.1) and sold parcel A to Sam. Sam gave Lorrie an easement appurtenant so she would have access. Sam's estate is the servient estate because the rights of his estate were second to Lorrie's right to use the area of property covered by the easement (burdened by the easement). Lorrie's estate is the dominant estate because her estate benefited from the easement.

e. **Liens** are "a charge against property in which the property is security for payment of a debt."[10] All mortgages are liens, but all liens are not mortgages. For example, a material lien might be placed on a new house for nonpayment of construction bills. This is not a mortgage because it was not coupled with a promissory note, even though there was an obligation to pay the contractor.

Figure 2.1
Easement Appurtenant

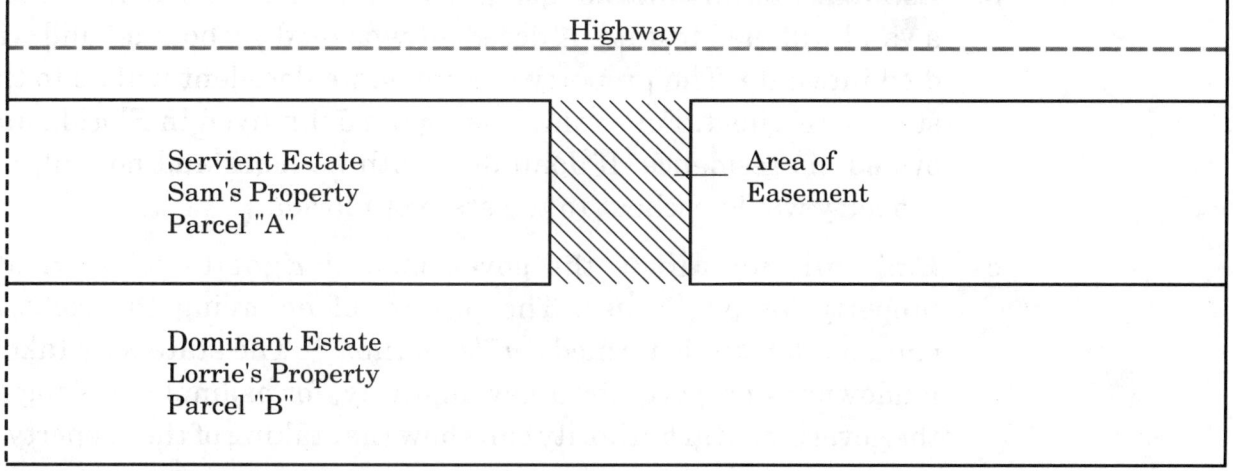

f. **Encroachments** are a trespass on another's land.[11] For example, if Joan built her house with the driveway extending 20 feet onto her neighbor's lot, the 20-foot extension would be an encroachment.

g. **Adverse possession** is a method of acquiring title to real property through possession. In some states, it is known as title by prescription. There are usually several requirements for adverse possession:

1) The possession must be open, visible and readily observed.

2) The possession must be continuous and uninterrupted for the statutory period (this period will vary by state).

3) The possession must be exclusive and with claim of right; the person in possession must believe that he or she has a claim to the property and make that claim to the public in general.

4) The possession must be hostile; this is denial or opposition to the true owner's title by the person in possession. If these conditions are satisfied, title is said to pass by adverse possession.

2. Public Limitations—**Public limitations** are those limitations placed on the private ownership of real property by governmental authorities.

    a. **Police power** is the right of the government to regulate land use for the public good. Examples of police power authority include zoning ordinances, building codes and environmental regulations. Zoning laws are designed to promote conformity in land use. Building codes are designed to promote a minimum standard and safety in construction. Environmental regulations are designed to protect the public from harmful environmental effects.

    b. **Escheat** literally means "going to the state." A decedent who left a valid will died testate. A decedent who died without a valid will died intestate. The property of a intestate decedent will go to the state, or escheat. For example, suppose John lived in Florida and owned his residence. If John died with no heirs and no will, his property would escheat to the state of Florida.

    c. **Eminent domain** is the governmental right to take private property for public use. The process of enforcing the right of eminent domain is termed *condemnation*.[12] The state may take a landowner's property for a new highway, for example. As long as the governmental authority can show that taking of the property is in the public good or will benefit the public as a whole, the only unresolved issue is the price to be paid. Eminent domain may also extend to other quasi-governmental entities such as utilities.

    d. **Taxation** is the right of governmental authorities to levy taxes on real property. Usually assessed by local governments, real property taxes are based on value and as such are ad valorem (as per value) taxes.

D. Legal Rights and Interests

There are several legal forms of ownership, and these vary from state to state. However, two categories are recognized in every state: fee simple estate and estates less than fee simple.

1. Fee Simple Estates—A **fee simple estate** is an absolute fee; a fee estate is inheritable without limitations to any particular heirs or restrictions.[13] It is the highest estate in land. However, it is subject to the governmental restrictions on private ownership discussed later in this chapter. In a fee simple estate, the bundle of rights generally have not been separated, or at least the owner was initially entitled to the full bundle of rights.

2. Estates Less Than Fee Simple

   a. A **life estate** is ownership interest giving the owner the right to use the property based on her life or the life of another.[14] For example, Mary might convey 20 acres "to Sue for life." When Sue dies, the life estate ends. Sue would be the grantee and the measuring life (also called the life tenant). There are two kinds of life estates.

       1) In a conventional life estate the grantee and the measuring life are the same person. "To Sue for life" means the grantee and the measuring life are the same person, so this is a conventional life estate.

       2) In a life estate pur autre vie, the measuring life and the grantee are two different people. For example, "to Sue for the life of John," is an example of a life estate pur autre vie in that the grantee and the measuring life are different persons. A person named to receive the property after termination of the life estate (death of measuring life), is a remainderman. This is true for both a conventional life estate and a life estate pur autre vie. For example, suppose Mary conveyed 20 acres in a life estate "to Sue for life, then to Jerry." This is a conventional

life estate (Sue is the grantee and the measuring life) and Jerry is the remainderman. Suppose Mary conveyed 20 acres "to Sue for the life of John, then to Jerry." Jerry is the remainderman, John is the measuring life, and Sue is the grantee.

b. A leasehold estate is an interest conveyed through a lease. If a landowner holds title to real property in fee simple, unencumbered by a lease, the landowner's interest is the unencumbered fee. If the landowner leased the property to a friend for one year, the landowner (also known as the lessor or landlord) would have a leased fee estate; fee ownership would remain intact, but it would be subject to the lease. The landlord would have the right to collect rent periodically and to receive the property at the end of the lease period. The tenant (also known as the lessee) would have a leasehold interest.

c. Leased fee estate is the landlord's (lessor's) estate under the lease. The lessor retains fee ownership, but that ownership is subject to the lease.

3. Other Legal Interests

   a. **Emblements** are crops that require annual planting. Typically these crops are deemed by the courts to be personal property. If a tenant fails to remove emblements before expiration of a lease, the tenant is allowed to remove them as they are considered to be personal property. However, if they are sold as part of an unencumbered fee estate, they generally pass with the title to the real property, unless the seller specifically reserves them from the transaction.

   b. **Profit** is the right to remove something, such as minerals, from another's land. A profit is generally considered a real property right.

   c. **License** is a right to enter another's land. A license is a personal property right and therefore runs with the person. It is usually granted for a specific purpose and is for a limited time.

E. **Forms of Property Ownership**

   1. Individual—In many cases, one person will own property alone. For example, Sue may own 40 acres by herself. If she owns a fee simple interest with no other owners, this is termed ownership in **severalty.**

2. Tenancies and Undivided Interests—More than one person may own the same piece of property. For example, suppose a married couple own a house together. This would be considered multiple ownership and could be any one of three forms: tenants in common, joint tenants or tenants by the entireties.

   a. **Tenants in common**—ownership gives an owner an undivided ownership interest in a parcel with one or more other owners, each with an equal right to possession. Upon the death of one tenant, that tenant's rights pass to his or her heirs. For example, if Bill and Marcy own 40 acres together as tenants in common, each of them owns an undivided interest in the 40 acres. However, at Bill's death the property does not automatically pass to Marcy but passes to Bill's heirs.

   b. **Joint tenants**—ownership occurs when two or more parties own inseparable property interests in a given parcel. At the death of one joint tenant, title automatically passes to the surviving co-owners; this is known as the right of survivorship. The only party that can pass title to their heirs is the last surviving joint tenant.

   c. **Tenants by the entireties**—ownership occurs when a "unit" owns the property and neither tenant may sell the property. The unit may sell it, but not the individual tenants. This form of multiple ownership is generally restricted to husband and wife. Neither the husband nor the wife is considered to be the owner. When one dies, title passes to the surviving spouse.

3. Special Ownership Forms—Some types of real estate ownership do not fit neatly into defined categories such as fee simple or less than fee simple. These special types of real estate ownership include condominiums, cooperatives and time-shares.

   a. A **condominium** is a form of ownership created by state legislatures. The owner of a condominium generally owns a fee simple interest in the actual unit but owns the common areas (such as the grounds and swimming pool) with the other residents of the complex as a tenant in common. For example, suppose there were 20 units in Abbey's complex and she lives in unit 10. Abbey would own a fee simple interest in unit 10 but would own the land, pool, parking and other common areas with the other 19 residents. Typically the common areas (all property owned by the group) are owned as tenants in common.[15]

b. A **cooperative** is a form of ownership in which a corporation owns the structure and residents of the building own stock in the corporation. Stock ownership gives the stockholder the right to reside in the building. Typically, the corporation signs a proprietary lease with the tenant stockholder. This lease requires the tenant to make a pro-rata share of the operating expenses and debt payments on the building.

c. A **time-share** may be a partial form of ownership or a lease for a specified period of time. The rights conveyed with the time-share will vary, depending on the time-share agreement. For example, a purchaser who bought a one-week time-share in Florida would receive the right to occupy that structure 1/52 of the time. In addition, the purchaser would own 1/52 of the property with the other time-share owners as tenants in common.

F. Legal Descriptions

A legal description is a technique used to describe real estate so as to distinguish one parcel from another easily. Four techniques of legal description are commonly accepted: metes and bounds, governmental (or rectangular) survey, lot and block, and monuments.

1. Metes and Bounds—In the **metes-and-bounds** method, metes denotes distance whereas bounds denotes direction. The key to a metes-and-bounds description is that it begins at a point of beginning (POB) and ends at the same POB.

2. Governmental (or Rectangular) Survey Method—**Governmental survey** utilizes township and range lines. A township (an area 6 miles by 6 miles, or 36 square miles) is formed by intersecting township (east-west) and range (north-south) lines. There are 36 sections in one township and 640 acres in each section. An acre contains 43,560 square feet. A legal description using the governmental survey method would read: NW1/4, NW1/4, NE1/4, S1/2 of Section 12, Township 5 North, Range 14 West, meaning: Northwest quarter of the Northwest quarter of the Northeast quarter of the South half of Section 12, Township 5 North, Range 14 West. This area would contain 5 acres. The amount of acreage could be calculated by taking the acres in one section and dividing by each of the denominators (640 ÷ 4 = 160 ÷ 4 = 40 ÷ 4 = 10 ÷ 2 = 5 acres) or by multiplying the denominators (4 × 4 × 4 × 2 = 128 and dividing 640 by 128 = 5 acres). A graph of the governmental survey method is shown in Figure 2.2.

Figure 2.2
Governmental (or Rectangular) Survey System

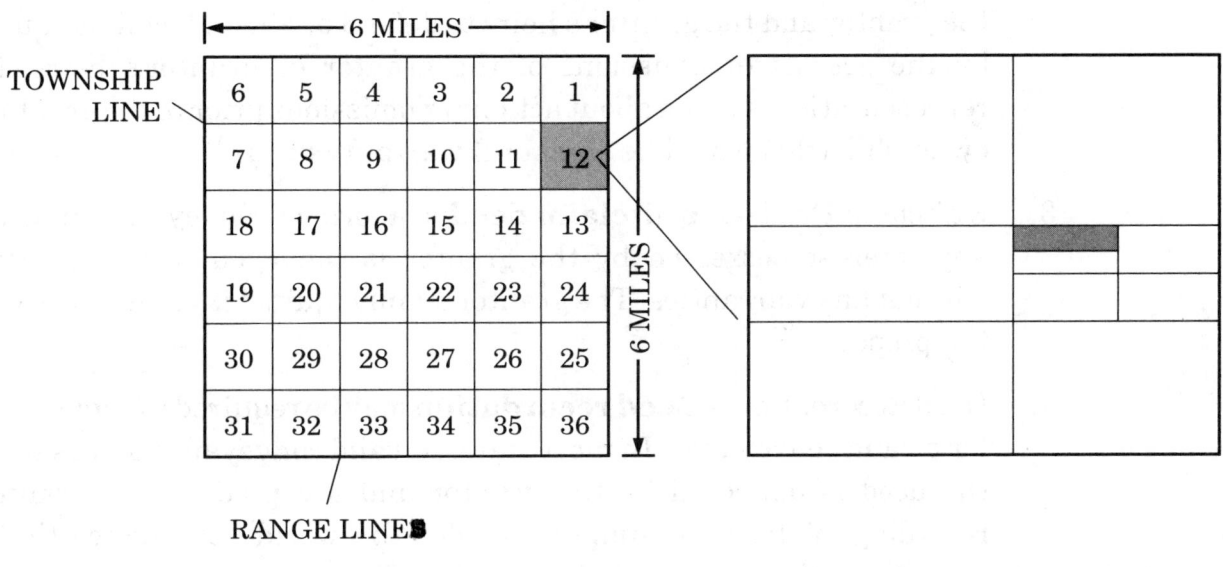

TOWNSHIP DIVIDED INTO SECTIONS   NW 1/4, NW 1/4, NE 1/4, S 1/2

3. Lot and Block—The **lot and block** method is used in subdivisions. Suppose a developer purchases 40 acres with the intention of dividing them into smaller parcels. The developer would file a plat or subdivided plat in the county courthouse in which the property is located. This plat would stipulate a subdivision name and show all the dimensions of each lot along with any easements, street right of ways, and other encroachments. Each lot and block in the subdivision would be numbered or labeled alphabetically. Any lot could then be described by reference to a lot and block number and the name of the subdivision.

4. Monuments—There are two kinds of **monuments:** natural and man-made.[16] An example of a monuments description is "proceed 200 feet South to the eastern shore of the Blue River."

G. Transfer of Title

Title to real property is conveyed by a deed, defined earlier in this chapter. The basic types of deeds include general warranty deeds, special warranty deeds and quitclaim deeds.

1. General Warranty (or Warranty) Deed—**General warranty deeds** convey a covenant of warranty, which binds the grantor and all heirs to

defend the title conveyed to the grantee and heirs against lawful claims of all persons.[17]

2. Special Warranty Deed—**Special warranty deeds** are warranties by the grantor and the grantor's heirs to defend against all claims caused by the actions or omissions of the grantor or grantor's heirs. No representation is made about actions or omissions prior to the grantor's ownership (this would be a general warranty deed).[18]

3. Quitclaim Deed—A **quitclaim deed** is a form of conveyance in which any interest possessed by the grantor is conveyed to the grantee, without any warranties. The grantor simply "quits his claim," if any, in the property.[19]

4. Deed Recordation—**Deed recordation** may be required in some states for a valid conveyance. In most states, a valid conveyance occurs when the deed is delivered by the grantor and accepted by the grantee; recording of the deed simply provides the world with notice that a conveyance has occurred. However, a few states recognize a valid conveyance only after recordation.

Endnotes

1. Appraisal Institute, *The Dictionary of Real Estate Appraisal,* 2nd ed. (1989), p. 248.
2. Realty is an outdated name for real estate; it has the same meaning.
3. Appraisal Institute, *The Dictionary of Real Estate Appraisal,* 2nd ed. (1989), p. 83.
4. Ibid., p. 84.
5. Ibid. p. 177.
6. Ibid., p. 259. The right to repossess and resume full and sole use and ownership of the real property . . ., is called the reversionary right.
7. Ibid., p. 259.
8. Ibid., p. 202. There are also chattel mortgages, which are secured by personal property.
9. Ibid., p. 99.
10. Ibid., p. 180.
11. Ibid., p. 103. An encroachment is also the partial or gradual displacement of an existing use by another use.
12. Ibid., p. 63.
13. Ibid., p. 120.
14. Ibid., p. 181. The grantee of a life estate is the life tenant.
15. Ibid., p. 63. Tenants in common are discussed earlier in this chapter.
16. This method of legal description is outdated but may appear on some state examinations.
17. Appraisal Institute, *The Dictionary of Real Estate Appraisal,* 2nd ed. (1989), p. 135.
18. Ibid., p. 283.
19. Ibid., p. 243.

Key Terms and Concepts

Influences on real estate:
    physical or environmental forces
    economic forces
    governmental and legal forces
    social forces
Legal considerations in appraisal:
    real property
    real estate
    personal property
Limitations on real estate ownership:
    private limitations:
        deeds
        leases
        mortgages
        easements
        liens
        encroachments
        adverse possession
    public limitations:
        police power
        escheat
        eminent domain
        taxation
Types of easements:
    in gross
    appurtenant
Interest in a lease:
    unencumbered fee estate
    leased fee estate—lessor
    leasehold estate—lessee
Legal forms of ownership:
    fee simple estates
    life estates
    emblements
    profits
    licenses
Multiple forms of ownership:
    severalty

        tenants in common
        joint tenants
        tenants by the entireties
Special forms of ownership:
        condominium
        cooperative
        time-share
Legal descriptions:
        metes and bounds
        governmental (or rectangular) survey
        lot and block
        monuments
Transfer of title:
        general warranty deed
        special warranty deed
        quitclaim deed
        deed recordation

Review Questions

1. The highest or fullest estate in land is the:
   a. fee tail.
   b. fee simple.
   c. fee simple determinable.
   d. life estate.

2. Ownership of real estate by only one owner is called:
   a. joint tenancy.
   b. tenant by the entireties.
   c. sole proprietorship.
   d. ownership in severalty.

3. Four governmental restrictions on private ownership rights include:
   a. escheat, police power, zoning and building codes.
   b. escheat, police power, zoning and taxation.
   c. escheat, police power, eminent domain, and taxation.
   d. escheat, police power, eminent domain and zoning.

4. Parties to a deed are called:
   a. testator and testatrix.
   b. mortgagor and mortgagee.
   c. grantor and grantee.
   d. buyer and purchaser.

5. A _____ is a contract for the use of specified premises in exchange for payments.
   a. listing agreement
   b. lease
   c. option
   d. offer

6. Four factors influencing real property value are:
   a. legal, social, economic and environmental.
   b. social, legal, financial and international.
   c. regional, international, local and city.
   d. physical, economic/financial, legal/governmental and social.

7. If a landowner leased a site to a tenant, the owner's interest would be called a:
   a. tenant.
   b. linkage.
   c. leasehold.
   d. leased fee.

8. In a condominium, the homeowner typically owns a particular unit in _____ and the common areas as a tenant in common.

   a. fee simple
   b. tenants in common
   c. joint tenants
   d. tenants by the entireties

9. In a cooperative, the owner actually owns:

   a. stock in a corporation.
   b. land.
   c. the actual unit.
   d. a ground rent.

10. Which of the following is NOT a form of ownership in real property?

    a. Time-share
    b. Condominium
    c. Cotenancy
    d. Cooperative

11. Joint ownership with right of survivorship by two or more parties describes:

    a. tenancy in common.
    b. ownership in severalty.
    c. joint tenancy.
    d. sole proprietorship.

12. In most states, title generally passes to real property with:

    a. passage of the bill of sale.
    b. recording of the deed.
    c. delivery and acceptance of the deed.
    d. passage of the license.

13. The conveyance "To John for life" is an example of a(an):

    a. fee simple estate.
    b. life estate.
    c. fee conditional.
    d. lease.

3 Types of Value

Overview

This chapter provides information on the major types of value that may be estimated in an appraisal report. Some common types are market value, value in exchange, value in use, investment value, liquidation value, insurable value, assessed value, and going-concern value. In most appraisal assignments, the appraiser will be estimating market value.

Learning Objectives

After completing this chapter, the student should be able to:

- Define and discuss the concept of market value

- Understand the differences between market value, most probable sales price, market price, and cost

- Define and discuss seven other types of value

- Compute assessed value, annual property tax and the effective property tax rate

I. Market Value

Market value is the most probable price an informed purchaser will pay on a given date, with buyer and seller being typically motivated and the property having sufficient market exposure. Sale is based on cash to the seller or financing terms generally available in the marketplace (cash equivalent) and an arm's-length transaction, not a distorted sale. A distorted sale is not arm's length; a purchaser is not acting in their best financial interest. Most appraisals seek to estimate market value. Market value is **not cost,** for cost is related to production. Market value is **not price,** for an uninformed purchaser could pay too much for a property. Market value is the most probable price to a typically informed purchaser. The Uniform Standards of Professional Appraisal Practice (USPAP) defines market value as follows:

> The most probable price which a property should bring in a competitive and open market under all conditions requisite to a fair sale, the buyer and seller each acting prudently and knowledgeably, and assuming the price is not affected by undue stimulus. Implicit in this definition is the consummation of a sale as of a specified date and the passing of title from seller to buyer under conditions whereby: (1) the buyer and seller are typically motivated; (2) both parties are well informed or well advised, and acting in what they consider their best interests; (3) a reasonable time is allowed for exposure in the open market; (4) payment is made in terms of cash in United States dollars or in terms of financial arrangements comparable thereto; and (5) the price represents the normal consideration for the property sold unaffected by special or creative financing or sales concessions granted by anyone associated with the sale.[1]

In some states, market value is defined by statute and therefore is different and in contrast to the definition in USPAP. If a state has a different definition, the appraiser should cite the Jurisdictional Exception to USPAP, and use that state's definition of market value.[2]

A. Market Value Assumptions

1. Buyer and Seller Are Typically Motivated—Market participants should act in their own best self-interests. They should prefer more wealth to less. For example, a seller would desire to obtain the maximum possible amount for his property, whereas the buyer would seek to pay the minimum possible amount.

2. Both Parties Are Well Informed or Well Advised, Acting in What They Consider To Be Their Best Interests—This assumption is based on believing that market participants have obtained sufficient market information to make informed decisions. For example, suppose a house was listed for $200,000 in an oversupplied local housing market. At the request of a new employer, a potential purchaser came to town for a short time on a house-hunting trip in this market. Because of time pressures of moving and transferral to a new position, the purchaser offered $230,000 for the house listed at $200,000. The sales (market) price would be $230,000 and would include participants that had not sought market information. Market value would assume that sufficient research was accomplished to obtain market information.

3. A Reasonable Time is Allowed for Exposure in the Open Market—A reasonable time for exposure addresses the illiquid nature of real estate. This assumption differentiates market value from liquidation value. Unlike market value, liquidation value does not provide for a reasonable time for exposure—it assumes a quick sale must occur.

4. Payment is Made in Terms of Cash in United States Dollars or in Terms of Financial Arrangements Comparable Thereto—This assumption assumes the seller is provided with cash or item equivalent to cash.

5. The Price Represents the Normal Consideration for the Property Sold Unaffected by Special or Creative Financing or Sales Concessions Granted by Anyone Associated with the Sale—This assumption also addresses the notion of cash to the seller and special sales concessions. For example, a seller may include an automobile in the garage as part of the package if the buyer will take the house. The appraiser should adjust the sales price to reflect the sales concession provided by the seller, because market value assumes there are no special financing or sales concessions.

B. Market Value Distinctions

Certain subtle distinctions between terms relating to value are more difficult for the client to understand and may need special clarification.

1. Market Value v. Most Probable Sales Price

    a. Because market value is a price that tends to prevail under specified market conditions, it is possible to estimate the most probable selling price (the use of statistical techniques may be particularly appropriate) provided sufficient market data are available.

b. The most probable sales price is that price at which a property would most probably sell if exposed to the market for a reasonable time, under market conditions prevailing as of the date of the appraisal.[3]

c. Thus, most probable selling price is virtually synonymous with market value in that it emphasizes what is most likely to occur, given available data on market conditions and market sales. It is useful primarily as an antidote to highly legalistic and special definitions of market value used in the past (especially by courts), since it places emphasis on the influence of the market.

2. Market Value v. Market Price

a. Market price is an historic fact. It does not look to the future as market value does and is usually an actual transaction or sales price. Market price is an accomplished fact; market value is an estimate.

b. Market price is "the amount actually paid, for a property in a particular transaction."[4]

c. The parties are not necessarily informed in an actual sales transaction; nor do they act rationally, free from pressure, or always independently (at arm's length). Market price does not have to be justified, as does market value. The financing or other terms of sale may be unique or may vary widely from typical market. The entire transaction need not be "typical."

d. Market price may be greater than, less than or, possibly, equal to market value in any given transaction.

3. Market Value v. Cost

a. Cost does not create value; cost is not value. However, under given conditions, cost may be an appropriate measure of value.

b. As used in appraising, cost is the outlay of capital (including financing and selling expenses) for supervision, land, materials and labor sufficient to bring an improvement into existence. The amount of capital required depends on economic conditions at the time. The important point is that the term *cost*, as used in appraising, refers to the total cost to produce.

II. Other Types of Value

A. Value in Exchange

Value in exchange, synonymous with market value, can be defined as the amount of one good that can be exchanged for that of another (or the ratio of exchange).

B. Value in Use

Value in use is the value to a particular user. A swimming pool that costs $25,000 to build and install obviously is worth $25,000 to the owner who had it installed. However, other prospective purchasers may be willing to pay only an additional $7,000 for a house with a pool. The $25,000, then, would be the pool's value in use whereas the $7,000 would be its market value.

C. Investment Value

Investment value is the value to a particular investor. A typically informed purchaser might be willing to pay one price for a parcel, but a given investor might be willing to pay more if he or she owned the adjoining parcel.

D. Liquidation Value

Liquidation value is the value of the subject if liquidation (conversion to cash) is required. For example, if a financial institution foreclosed on a property and wanted to sell it immediately, it would probably be interested in liquidation value.

E. Insurable Value

Insurable value is the value of property for insurance purposes.[5]

F. Assessed Value

Assessed value is the value for taxation purposes.[6] It is computed by multiplying the market value (as estimated by the local government) by the assessment ratio. Assessment ratios are established by state or local governments for certain classes of property. For example, all residential property in a state may have an assessment ratio of 10 percent of market value. If a residence has a market value of $100,000 and a 10 percent assessment ratio, the assessed value is $10,000 ($100,000 × .10 = $10,000).

G. Going-Concern Value

Going-concern value is the value that is attributable to an operating business. This value assumes that the business entity will continue operat-

Figure 3.1
Computation of Assessed Value, Property Tax, and Effective Tax Rates

Assessed Value

Market Value for Tax Purposes × Assessment Ratio = Assessed Value
$100,000 × .10 = $10,000

Assessed Value × Millage Rate
(1 Mill = .001 or 90 Mills = .090) = Annual Property Tax
$10,000 × .090 = $900

Effective Tax Rate

Assessment Ratio × Millage Rate = Effective Tax Rate
.100 × .090 = 0.009 or 0.09 percent

or

Annual Property Tax ÷ "Market Value" = Effective Tax Rate
$900 ÷ $100,000 = 0.009 or 0.09 percent

---

ing as a viable, competitive firm in the marketplace. Going-concern value includes a value for the real property plus a business value. For example, suppose you were hired to appraise an automobile auction. Part of the value of the automobile auction could be attributable to the real estate itself; part could also be attributable to the value of the business. The value of the whole as an operating entity would be termed going-concern value.

The student should know how to compute assessed value, property taxes and the effective property tax rate. As shown in Figure 3.1, **assessed value** can be computed by multiplying the estimated market value times the assessment ratio. From above, the assessed value is $10,000. Annual property taxes can be computed by multiplying the assessed value by the appropriate millage rate. Millage rates usually are set by local governments and differ from city to city and state to state. One mill is equal to .001.[7] If a county charged 90 mills, this would be equal to .090 (.001 × 90 = .090). Millage rates may also be quoted per hundred dollars—a millage rate of .090 could be quoted as $9.00/$100. Annual property taxes would be $900 (assessed value times millage rate, or $10,000 × .090 = $900).

The effective tax rate[8] is the amount of property taxes divided by the amount subject to tax (assessed value). In this example, it is $900 divided by 100,000 or .009 ($900 ÷ $100,000 = .009). The effective tax rate can also be computed by multiplying the assessment ratio by the millage rate (.10 × .090 = .009).

Endnotes

1. Definitions Section, Uniform Standards of Professional Appraisal Practice, The Appraisal Foundation, April 20, 1990, p. I–7.
2. Jurisdictional Exception, Uniform Standards of Professional Appraisal Practice, The Appraisal Foundation, p. I–6.
3. Appraisal Institute, *The Dictionary of Real Estate Appraisal,* 2nd ed. (1989), p. 204.
4. Ibid., p. 234. See the definition of *price,* p. 234. *See also* Appraisal Institute, *Appraising Residential Properties* (1988), pp. 20–22.
5. Ibid., p. 160. Insurable value has also been defined as "that portion of the value of an asset or asset group that is acknowledged or recognized under the provisions of an applicable loss insurance policy."
6. Ibid., p. 18.
7. Ibid., p. 197.
8. Ibid., p. 101.

Key Terms and Concepts

Market value:
    not cost
    not price
Other types of value:
    value in exchange
    value in use
    investment value
    liquidation value
    insurable value
    assessed value
    going-concern value
Assessed value
Property taxes
Effective tax rate for property taxes

Review Questions

1. Most appraisals seek to:
   a. set or establish value.
   b. set or establish price.
   c. estimate market price.
   d. estimate market value.

2. The type of value typically sought in an appraisal is:
   a. value in use.
   b. investment value.
   c. market value.
   d. cost of production.

3. When estimating market value, the appraiser takes the viewpoint of:
   a. any buyer.
   b. any seller.
   c. typically informed buyers.
   d. typically informed sellers.

4. Market value typically is based on:
   a. highest price paid by any purchaser.
   b. lowest price paid by any purchaser.
   c. most probable price paid by any purchaser.
   d. most probable price paid by a typically informed purchaser.

5. Market value is synonymous with (similar to):
   a. liquidation value.
   b. value in use.
   c. value in exchange.
   d. cost of production.

6. The value of a property to a particular owner/user is termed:
   a. market value.
   b. value in exchange.
   c. value in use.
   d. value in earnest.

7. If a parcel of land has a market value of $2,000,000 for assessment purposes and the assessment ratio is 50 percent, what is the property tax assuming the millage rate is 70 mills ($7 per $100)?
   a. $1,000,000
   b. $70,000
   c. $7,000
   d. $700,000

8. If a municipality has an assessment ratio of 40 percent and a taxing or millage rate of 80 mills ($8 per $100), what is the effective tax rate? .40 × .080 = .032

    a. 80 percent
    b. 40 percent
    c. 32 percent
    ✓d. 3.2 percent

9. The value of an operating entity or business enterprise is:

    a. value in use.
    ✓c. going-concern value.
    b. investment value.
    d. value in exchange.

10. The value of a particular property to a given investor is:

    a. value in use.
    ✓b. investment value.
    c. value in exchange.
    d. vaue of production.

11. _____ is the value of a property if it had to be converted to cash immediately.

    a. Value in use
    ✓b. Liquidation value
    c. Market value
    d. Value in exchange

12. Market value _____ the same as cost.

    a. is
    ✓b. is not
    c. is always
    d. is never

13. Which of the following statements is NOT true about market value assumptions?

    a. Buyers and sellers are typically motivated.
    ✓b. A reasonable time is allowed for market exposure.
    c. Financing is cash or cash equivalent.
    d. Only the seller is well informed.

14. Market value _____ market price:

    ✓a. may or may not be
    b. is always
    c. is never
    d. is always based on

4 Economic Principles

Overview

This chapter introduces the student to the economic principles that affect real property values. Moreover, relevance of each principle to appraisal theory and practice will be addressed. To the extent that application of the appraisal practices is predicated on these economic principles, this chapter provides background material for understanding later chapters.

Learning Objectives

After completing this chapter, the student should be able to:

- Define and discuss the economic principles of value

- Name the four facts of production and give a brief definition of each

- List the economic characteristics of value

I. Principles of Real Property Valuation

The valuation of real estate is based on a set of general economic principles. These principles are continuously at work in the determination of dynamic real property value, and they apply to every type of real estate and value to be estimated. They influence what an appraiser does (or should do) in every appraisal assignment.

A. Anticipation

The principle of **anticipation** states that value is a function of expected benefits to be derived from ownership in realty.[1] Buyers are influenced by two types of anticipation: (1) the utility they expect to receive from property and (2) their belief of what the property will bring if it is sold. Expectations of buyers or sellers can have a direct effect on market value—what people expect naturally influences what they are willing to pay for a property and, thus, its value. For example, if a highway is proposed for a given area, there is normally a dampening effect on property values in the path of the highway right-of-way, as well as significant lessening of market activity because of the expected public taking. At the same time, commercial properties that will remain in the vicinity of an interchange are often bid up speculatively in anticipation of changed use patterns and increased demand.

B. Balance

The point of maximum productivity, and hence of maximum value, is achieved when all factors of production are in balance with one another.[2] The factors of production are those inputs necessary to produce any item—**capital, labor, land** and **entrepreneurship** (also known as **coordination**). For example, when a building is constructed, capital (money)—called debt capital—is needed for construction and permanent financing. Funds provided by investors are equity capital. Labor is needed to perform the actual construction. Land is needed for placement of the structure. Entrepreneurship (management ability or coordination) is required for successful completion of the structure.

The principle of **balance** applies to a development program for a parcel of land; it also applies to maximizing the amenities of a neighborhood. The point of maximum productivity, or balance, is known in economic analysis as the point of diminishing returns. Beyond this point, successive increments of the variable factors of production result in less than proportionate increase in productivity, and hence in value. This could apply to putting more and more improvements on a single site.

C. Change

Because of marketplace dynamics, which depend on the forces of supply and demand, the principle of **change** is a continuous force in the real estate market. Value, therefore, is subject to change as market conditions change.[3] For this reason, every value estimate must be made "as of" a given date. This is also why the appraiser must forecast market conditions and the reactions of the typical purchaser to expected future market conditions. For example, the appraiser must observe and estimate the life cycle stage of the neighborhood in which the appraisal property is located.

D. Consistent Use

Land and improvements should be valued based on **consistent use.** For example, it would be incorrect to value the land based on a commercial use and the structure based on a residential use. The property could be valued with both land and building based on a residential use or with both land and building based on a commercial use. That is, both must be valued on the same use.

E. Competition

The principle of **competition** holds that profits bring more competition into the marketplace. Furthermore, excess profits lead to too much competition, forcing some firms to leave the marketplace. For example, if it appears that residential builders are making large profits, other individuals in the marketplace will enter the residential construction business. This creates an oversupply, which will force some builders to exit the market.

F. Conformity

The principle of **conformity** asserts that value is enhanced if adjacent land uses are similar. Suppose a purchaser recently bought a house in a nice subdivision. If a chemical company locates a plant next to this house, the effect on value could be disastrous. The principle of conformity is a major factor for zoning ordinances.

G. Supply and Demand

Market value is determined by the interaction of supply and demand in the marketplace as of the appraisal date.[4] **Supply** is the quantity of a good offered by producers at a given price. **Demand** is the quantity of a good that purchasers desire to buy at a given price. In purely competitive markets, market participants determine how much to produce or purchase based on one factor—price of the good. Value does not exist intrinsically in a good, only in the minds of individuals. For example, a house does not intrinsically have value in its bricks and mortar; it has value because people believe it to be a good place to live and are willing to pay other goods or assets to obtain it.

H. Highest and Best Use

Real estate is valued in terms of its highest and best use. The highest and best use of the land (or site) if vacant and available for use may be different from the highest and best use of the improved property. This will be true even if the improvement is not an appropriate use yet makes a contribution to total property value in excess of the site value.

1. Highest and Best Use—**Highest and best use** (most profitable use or optimum use) is that reasonable and probable use that will support the highest present value as defined, as of the effective date of the appraisal.[5] Alternatively, it is the most profitable likely use to which a property can be put. It may be measured in terms of the present worth of the highest net return that the property can be expected to produce over a stipulated period of time. The principle holds that urban space (land or improved properties) tends to be put to its highest and best use in a competitive market over the long run. This is the basis for decision making about the allocation of urban space among alternative competing uses. Because the owner, user or potential buyer is presumed to plan to put real estate to its highest and best use, it is the basis for valuation. As long as the buildings on an improved property contribute to total property value in excess of the value of the vacant site, it would be in the owner's best interest to continue that use.

I. Substitution (Opportunity Cost)

The principle of **substitution** holds that a prudent purchaser would pay no more than the cost of acquiring (either through purchasing or building) such a substitute on the open market.[6] Application of the principle of substitution operates on two presumptions:

1. The purchaser will consider the available alternatives and will act "rationally" or "prudently" on the basis of information about those alternatives. Time or speed of acquisition is not a factor.

2. Acquiring an equally desirable substitute means obtaining one of equal utility. Considering the alternatives involves applying the concept of opportunity cost. Three alternative means of acquiring a substitute are available to purchasers:

   a. Buying an existing property that is a substitute for the one being appraised—this is the basis for sales comparison analysis in value estimation.

   b. Producing a substitute with the same utility—this is the basis of cost analysis in value estimation.

   c. Acquiring an investment that will produce an income stream of the same size with the same risk as that involved in the property being appraised—this is the basis of income capitalization analysis in value estimation.

J. Contribution (Marginal Productivity)

The principle of **contribution** states that the value of an agent of production or of a component part of a property depends on how much it contributes to the value of the whole.[7] Its contribution is a measure of its marginal productivity—how much it adds to the total productivity of the property. The principle is the basis for three approaches:

1. Estimating accrued depreciation because of deficiencies or superadequacies in cost analysis.

2. Measuring differences between the subject property and comparable properties in the adjustment process of direct sales comparison analysis.

3. Valuing component parts of the real estate in the residual techniques of income capitalization analysis.

K. Variable Proportions and Increasing/Decreasing Returns

Income (in dollars, benefits or amenities) first increases at an increasing rate, then at a decreasing rate, and finally decreases absolutely, when successive increments of one or more factors of production are added to fixed amounts of the other factors.[8] This is an important principle in comparing alternative use patterns and intensities of use to reach a conclusion as to highest and best use. In such analysis, the amount of land is typically the fixed factor and alternative improvement programs represent the variable factors. A house, for example, may be an overimprovement or underimprovement of its site.

II. Economic Characteristics of Value

For a good to have value, it must possess four economic characteristics: demand, utility, scarcity, and transferability. Purchasers' desire to obtain an item must be accompanied by their ability to pay for it; this is effective **demand,** which is required for an item to have value. **Utility** is the ability of an item to satisfy wants and desires and is necessary for an item to have value in the minds of individuals. **Scarcity** relates to the amount of supply relative to demand. When demand exceeds supply, price (and usually value) generally increases as more potential purchasers desire the item. When supply exceeds demand, price (and usually value) generally decreases. For transactions to occur in the marketplace, an item must be **transferable,** that is, sellers must be able to convey ownership to purchasers.

Therefore, the appropriate market forces must be analyzed and evaluated carefully in terms of their impact on the value of the property in question. For example, a sudden influx of new workers into a market area will increase demand and result in an increase in market prices and market values for the type of housing sought. A sharp increase in mortgage interest rates will increase housing costs and tend to lessen demand and, hence, values in the market area.

Endnotes

1. Appraisal Institute, *The Dictionary of Real Estate Appraisal,* 2nd ed. (1989), p. 14.
2. Ibid., p. 23.
3. Ibid., p. 49.
4. Ibid., p. 295.
5. Ibid., p. 149.
6. Ibid., p. 293.
7. Ibid., p. 68.
8. Ibid., p. 157.

Key Terms and Concepts

Economic principles:
- anticipation
- balance
- change
- consistent use
- competition
- conformity
- supply and demand
- highest and best use
- substitution (opportunity cost)
- contribution (marginal productivity)
- variable proportions and increasing/decreasing returns

Four factors of production:
- capital
- labor
- land
- entrepreneurship (or coordination)

Four economic characteristics of value:
- demand (effective)
- utility
- scarcity
- transferability

Review Questions

1. Three distinguishing physical characteristics of real estate are:
    a. homogeneity, immobility and durability.
    b. heterogeneity, mobility and durability.
    c. durability, heterogeneity and immobility.
    d. appreciation, location and long-life.

2. Real estate is:
    a. rights in realty.
    b. land and all the improvements on and to land.
    c. land only.
    d. the intangible part of real property.

3. Real property can be defined as:
    a. movable property.
    b. rights in real estate.
    c. land.
    d. land and all the improvements on and to land.

4. Tangible and intangible benefits generated by a property that are not typically received in money are called:
    a. pleasantries.
    b. niceties.
    c. bonuses.
    d. amenities.

5. Title to real property is transferred with a:
    a. bill of sale.
    b. mortgage.
    c. deed.
    d. contract.

6. Title to personal property is transferred by a:
    a. deed.
    b. bill of sale.
    c. mortgage.
    d. chattel mortgage.

7. The factors of production are:
   a. land, labor, capital and money.
   b. land, labor, capital and coordination or entrepreneurship.
   c. escheat, police power, eminent domain, and taxation.
   d. escheat, police power, eminent domain and zoning.

8. In a purely competitive market, all participants make decisions on the basis of:
   a. price.
   b. supply.
   c. demand.
   d. shortage.

9. The principle of _____ holds that a purchaser is buying the right to receive future benefits.
   a. substitution
   b. supply and demand
   c. change
   d. anticipation

10. In residential properties, expected future benefits are called:
    a. quiet enjoyment.
    b. income.
    c. leased fee.
    d. amenities.

11. To have value, an item must possess which economic characteristics?
    a. Land, labor, capital and entrepreneurship
    b. Social, legal/political, environmental and economic
    c. A viable marketplace
    d. Utility, scarcity, demand and transferability

12. The reasonable and probable use that supports highest present value is termed:
    a. highest and best use.
    b. change.
    c. marginal productivity.
    d. substitution.

13. The added value of a pool to a residence can be estimated using the economic principle of:
    a. change.
    b. supply and demand.
    c. marginal productivity.
    d. regression analysis.

14. A good's capacity to satisfy human desires or needs is termed:
    a. usefulness.
    b. utility.
    c. functional obsolescence.
    d. external utility.

5 Real Estate Markets and Analysis

Overview

This chapter provides background information on real estate markets and market analysis and financial and quantitative applications in residential appraisal. In addition, a summary of the U.S. financial system is presented, with emphasis on understanding the interrelationships between the financial and real estate markets.

Learning Objectives

After completing this chapter, the student should be able to:

- Comprehend general real estate markets

- Understand what a neighborhood is and how to delineate neighborhood boundaries

- Name and define the four stages in the neighborhood life cycle

- Understand the U.S. financial system, including monetary and fiscal policy

- Discuss basic mortgage terms and concepts

I. Market Analysis

Market analysis is the study of an identified market for a specific type of property.[1] Its focus is on demand and supply interactions within the identified market area. Market analysis differs from feasibility analysis in that a **feasibility analysis** (or study) attempts to determine a "go" or "no go" decision for a specific project or proposal. Moreover, feasibility analysis examines the cost-benefit relationships for a given project.[2] Market analysis for residential properties achieves four goals: identification of the market, analysis of demand factors, analysis of supply factors and analysis of absorption rates. In many instances, marketability of a given property or type of property is the thrust of market analysis.[3]

A. Steps in Market Analysis

1. Identification of the Market—A market may be very localized, such as a neighborhood within a city, or it may be international in scope. For example, the market for most houses is very localized. However, the former Post Mansion (owned by Donald Trump as of this writing) in South Florida had an international market. Market analysis usually begins by identifying the market on the highest, general level (such as the international or national real estate market) and proceeds to a lower, specific level (such as the local neighborhood). Ultimately, market analysis will focus on supply and demand relationships as they affect the subject property.

2. Analysis of Demand Factors—**Demand** for real estate, and especially residential properties, is influenced by several factors including levels and types of employment, population trends, household size, income levels and other demographic factors. Demographics is the study of population characteristics—income, employment, age, preferences, and such. Psychographic data describe group life-style preferences.

3. Analysis of Supply Factors—Several **supply factors** influence real estate and these factors should be considered in market analysis. These include current levels of completed space on the market, new construction underway but not yet completed, the possibility of new construction and the influence of external factors—such as level and direction of interest rates and availability and cost of credit.

4. Rates of Absorption—New developments are very concerned with the interaction of supply and demand as it relates to absorption. **Absorption** is the rate at which a particular property or type of property will be sold

or leased in the marketplace during a specified period of time (usually one year). It is usually expressed as number of units per year.

B. Forecasts

Forecasts utilize analytical judgment and past trends to predict a future happening or occurrence.[4] An appraisal is one type of forecast since the appraiser uses past market trends, market perceptions, and well-reasoned judgment.

C. Neighborhoods and Neighborhood Analysis

A neighborhood is a set of complementary land uses.[5] It consists of those properties that affect the value of one another. Because neighborhoods are constantly changing, they all (residential, commercial, agricultural and others) exhibit a life cycle.[6] The neighborhood life cycle is characterized by four progressive and distinct stages: (1) growth, (2) maturity or stability, (3) decline and (4) revitalization or renewal.

1. Stages in a Neighborhood Life Cycle

    a. **Growth** is characterized by rising property prices and values. Demand exceeds supply in a growth neighborhood.

    b. **Maturity** is characterized by stable property values and an environment in which demand is nearly equal to supply.

    c. Neighborhood **decline** is evidenced by slumping property values. Supply typically exceeds demand during this stage.

    d. During **revitalization** or **renewal,** the life cycle begins again. A new growth stage emerges and property values begin to increase.

2. Neighborhood Boundaries—One of the appraiser's most difficult problems in neighborhood analysis is determining **neighborhood boundaries,** which define the neighborhood. Boundaries may be natural or artificial (man-made). To determine a neighborhood boundary, the appraiser should obtain a map of the area and draw tentative boundaries (a major highway or natural barrier such as a river) on the map. Then the tentative boundaries should be tested against demographic data in the defined area. Revisions based on demographic data may be necessary.

II. Characteristics of Real Estate Markets

In simple terms, a market is where buyers and sellers interact to carry out sales transactions.[7] Title is transferred from sellers to buyers in a market. Some markets are very centralized, such as the New York Stock Exchange, because trading occurs in one central location. Other markets, such as local residential real estate markets, are not very centralized. Markets can be distinguished by type of product, number of participants and access to information in the marketplace. Some markets are termed *efficient markets* because they exhibit certain characteristics, whereas others are termed *inefficient* because they lack these features. For example, in an efficient market, current prices reflect all information. The implication is that purchasers cannot, on average, "beat the market." Investors' strategy in an efficient market should be a "buy and hold" strategy if they cannot consistently outperform the market. However, in an efficient market, an investor who performs superior market analysis should achieve superior returns. Real estate has been perceived to be an inefficient market due to unavailability of information, changes in supply and demand, immobility of real estate, segmented markets, and regulations.

A. Availability of Information

Market participants do not have equal access to information in real estate markets, nor do they interpret a given set of information equally. In an efficient market, participants tend to have equal or similar access to information and to have equal or similar interpretation of that information. This is certainly not true in real estate markets.

B. Changes in Supply and Demand

Real estate tends to be supply constrained; that is, the supply of real estate (improved properties) is fixed in the short run and cannot be changed. In an efficient market, market prices move very quickly to a new equilibrium. Equilibrium occurs (theoretically) when supply is just equal to demand. In real estate markets, supply is constrained, which forces a slower, more gradual move to a new equilibrium. Changes in supply and demand is another reason for the perception of inefficiency in real estate markets.

C. Immobility of Real Estate

Because real estate is immovable, its location plays a very important role in its value; it is the only asset that is so location-dependent. Consequently, two properties may not be (and usually are not) substitutes for each other. The importance of location contributes to the concept of segmented markets.

D. Segmented Markets

Some markets trade homogeneous products; that is, every product is identical or very similar, every good traded is similar to other goods. For example, a share of common stock represents similar interests to other shares of common stock. One share of common stock traditionally represents one vote on corporate matters. It also represents one share of equity ownership. Trading on the stock exchanges is somewhat standardized—buyers and sellers usually trade in round lots (trades of 100 shares each). In real estate markets, the product traded is not homogenous but heterogeneous (every product is unique). Because of this heterogeneous product, real estate markets are perceived to be inefficient. Moreover, all real estate transactions are financed differently, in contrast to stock transactions, which are financed under prescribed rules (everyone trades according to the same initial financing requirements—called the initial maintenance margin—on the organized stock exchanges). Because of heterogeneous products and different financing packages, real estate typically is traded in local, segmented markets as opposed to a national market. Market segmentation is also exacerbated by the number of market participants—for a market to be efficient, there must be a sufficient number of participants so as to provide quick price adjustment to new information as information hits the marketplace. For example, if the President of the United States were shot, the stock markets would react to the news quickly (within hours on the same trading day). Could real estate markets react that quickly? Because real estate markets are characterized by a small number of participants in any one local market, transaction time is often very slow relative to other markets. Therefore, adjustment of prices to new information is slower.

E. Regulation

The use of a given property in a given location has a direct impact on value. Generally the use of real estate is highly regulated through police power, eminent domain, escheat and taxation. Police power regulations—zoning laws, building codes and environmental regulations—are the primary controls on the use of a given location. Regulation of use increases the perception that real estate markets are inefficient.

Based on all of these factors, then, real estate markets are perceived to be inefficient. This means that asset prices do not reflect all information and superior investors can achieve superior returns. Superior market analysis should pay off or provide superior rewards in real estate markets.

III. Role of Money and Capital Markets

The financial system and currency in the United States is based on one element—confidence in the government. Formerly, U.S. dollars were backed by gold and silver, but today, after years of repaying government obligations, the dollar is backed only by confidence in the government. Because the U.S. government has never defaulted on (failed to repay) a loan, because of its perceived stability worldwide, the dollar is held by foreigners to be the safest currency. This is why in times of global armed conflict, there is a "flight to quality" or a "flight to safety" (in financial terms) and foreign investors want to hold dollar-denominated assets.

The U.S. banking system operates based on **fractional reserve banking.** This means that a depositor's money placed in a U.S. bank does not remain in the bank but is lent to borrowers. The bank retains a small reserve (a small fraction) of the actual deposit should some borrowers desire their money.

The U.S. government attempts to manage the economy through fiscal and monetary policies. Although the U.S. economy is a free-market, capitalistic economy, the government exercises control through these fiscal and monetary policies.

A. Monetary Policy

Monetary policy guides control of the money supply in the economy. The **Federal Reserve (the Fed)** system is charged with regulating the money supply. The Fed comprises 12 Federal Reserve districts, each with its own Federal Reserve bank. More particularly, the Federal Reserve Board of Governors is charged with establishing and regulating monetary policy. The seven-member Board of Governors has three policy vehicles for regulating the money supply. First, they can raise or lower the federal discount rate, the rate the Fed charges member banks to borrow from the Fed, usually on a very short term basis (generally overnight). Many other interest rates are pegged to this rate. Raising the discount rate has the effect of raising other rates in the economy. Increased interest rates means that fewer borrowers will borrow money and the money supply will be reduced.

A second policy vehicle available to the Fed is raising or lowering the reserve requirement on time deposits (savings accounts) and/or demand deposits (checking accounts). Raising the reserve requirement requires financial institutions to retain more of their deposits in the institution and not lend them to borrowers. It also has the effect of reducing the money supply.

A third policy vehicle is buying and selling U.S. Treasury securities. This is usually done through the Federal Open Market Committee (FOMC), a 12-member committee[8] of the Federal Reserve system charged with "fine-tuning" monetary policy. The FOMC's perspective is short-term and it implements many tactical decisions of the Board of Governors.

B. **Fiscal Policy**

Fiscal policy is the management of government receipts and expenditures. The executive branch of government is charged with the planning and maintenance of fiscal policy. Overall budgetary planning is performed through the Office of Management and Budget (OMB) and through each department in the executive branch. Collection of revenues is primarily the responsibility of the Treasury Department. If budget expenditures exceed collections, the government encounters a budget deficit. If revenues exceed expenditures, the government encounters a surplus. If revenues are equal to expenditures, a balanced budget exists.

C. **Competing Investments in U.S. Financial Markets**

Financial markets in the U.S. can be divided into several categories, one of which is by the type of instrument traded. Two types of markets are money markets and capital markets. **Money markets** generally involve financial instruments with maturities of one year or less (Treasury securities, notes and bonds). **Capital markets** generally involve financial instruments with maturities of more than one year (most mortgages). Other examples of capital markets include stock markets, bond markets and mortgage markets.

1. Mortgage Markets—Mortgage markets trade only mortgage or mortgage-related financial instruments. A mortgage is a loan secured by real property.[9] There are two general types of mortgage markets:

    a. Mortgage loans are originated in **primary mortgage markets.** For example, to purchase a house, John and Sue may obtain a mortgage loan from a local lender. This original mortgage is considered to be in the primary mortgage market. Local mortgage lenders are competitors in the primary mortgage markets.

b. In the **secondary mortgage markets** a borrower (the *mortgagor*) signs a mortgage and receives cash from the lender (the *mortgagee*). In return, the borrower is obligated to repay the loan in a series of installments. The lender has the right to a stream of cash inflows and can sell this right in the secondary mortgage market. The major participants in the secondary mortgage market include the Federal National Mortgage Association (Fannie Mae), the Government National Mortgage Association (Ginnie Mae), the Federal Home Loan Mortgage Corporation (Freddie Mac) and other large insurance companies and mortgage bankers.

D. **Sources of Capital**

There are several sources of real estate capital in the primary mortgage markets. These include commercial banks, savings and loan associations, insurance companies, pension funds, mortgage brokers and mortgage bankers. **Commercial banks** generally make short-term loans. Traditionally they have provided construction financing, but recently banks have entered the traditional mortgage arena through operating subsidiaries and holding companies. Historically, **savings and loan associations (S&Ls)** and banks for savings have been residential mortgage lenders, but recently they have made commercial loans and acquisition and development loans. However, due to their current problems, S&Ls now command a smaller market share. **Insurance companies** traditionally have made commercial loans on very large projects. **Pension funds** make very large commercial loans, such as for shopping malls or major office buildings. **Mortgage brokers** are similar to real estate brokers in that they arrange mortgage loans. Mortgage brokers generally do not use their own money, they simply originate mortgages by bringing together, for a fee, a seller of funds (lender) and a purchaser of funds (borrower). **Mortgage bankers** arrange mortgage loans but generally use their own supply of money. Each of these sources of real estate capital may also provide equity capital for real estate investments by purchasing an equity position.

IV. Real Estate Financing

A. **Mortgage Terms and Concepts**

1. Principal—**Principal** is the amount of money borrowed from the lender/mortgagee. It is also the amount of money in each payment,

which is credited by the lender toward repayment of the amount borrowed. Principal is also called *return OF capital* to the lender. On a mortgage, the systematic process of repayment of principal is called **amortization**. However, there are two components to each payment—principal and interest—and the interest portion is assumed to be paid first, with the remaining money applied to principal. If there is insufficient money to meet even the interest portion, the deficiency is "added back" to the original principal, a process referred to as **negative amortization.** In a negatively amortized loan, the borrower would owe more on the mortgage in the future than he or she owes today.

2. Interest—**Interest** is the cost or price paid for borrowing money. It is usually quoted as an annual percentage, for example, a 12 percent mortgage loan would have a cost (or price) of 12 percent per year on the outstanding balance. Interest is termed *return ON capital* to the lender.

B. Mortgage Payment Plans

1. Fixed Rate, Level Payment—**Fixed-rate mortgages** have a constant, or fixed, interest rate over the term of the loan. Some mortgages do not have fixed rates. Most fixed-rate, level-payment mortgages are also fully amortized. A **fully amortized mortgage** has a systematic repayment of principal and interest over a specified time period so as to fully repay or amortize the principal with the last payment; no principal remains unpaid after the final payment. In a **partially amortized mortgage,** on the other hand, a portion of the principal remains unpaid at the end of the mortgage term (balloon payment).

2. Adjustable Rate—With an **adjustable-rate loan** the interest rate changes over the term of the loan. As a result of the interest rate change, the payment or term also changes; usually, however, only the payment changes. Most adjustable-rate loans are adjusted annually.

3. Buydown—Sometimes, in an effort to sell a property, sellers may pay part of the interest rate for a given period of time (**buydown**). For example, suppose the going market interest rate for a 30-year fixed-rate mortgage is 15 percent. The seller may tell the buyer that he or she (the seller) will "buy down" the mortgage to 12 percent for the first three years. The buyer still owes the lender a 15 percent mortgage for 30 years. However, the seller pays the lender or the buyer enough cash at the loan closing to make the buyer's payments equal to what they would have been on a 12 percent loan for the first three years. During years

4 through 30, the buyer's payments are based on a 15 percent rate. The buyer pays a rate of 12 percent for the first three years because the seller has "bought down" the loan to 12 percent for the first three years.

4. Other Mortgage Terminology

   a. **Leverage** is the use of debt to finance an asset, such as real estate. Positive leverage is earning more return on the asset than the cost of debt. Negative leverage is earning less on the asset than the cost of debt. Neutral leverage is earning the same rate of return of the asset as the cost of debt.

   b. The **loan-to-value ratio** is the mortgage amount divided by the value of the property. For example, if a lender lends $80,000 on a house valued at $100,000, the loan-to-value ratio would be $80,000 ÷ $100,000, or .80. Many lenders use loan-to-value ratios to determine the maximum amount they will lend on a given property or type of property.

C. **Types of Mortgages**

1. Conventional—Conventional loans carry no guarantee or insurance by a federal agency. However, most lenders insist on private mortgage insurance.[10] This type of insurance, with premiums paid by the borrower, would pay the lender if the borrower defaulted.

2. Insured—Some mortgages include insurance or a guarantee to protect the lender in case of borrower default.[11] The Federal Housing Authority (FHA) insures loans against default. The mortgagor pays an insurance premium for the benefit of the mortgagee (the lender) for this protection. The Veterans Administration (VA) guarantees loans to veterans. In the event of default, the VA or FHA would assume much if not all of the loss.

3. Blanket Mortgages—**Blanket mortgages** cover more than one parcel in the same loan package. For example, suppose a developer wanted a development loan on 20 acres with the intention of selling one-acre lots. The developer could obtain one loan from the lender and obtain a partial release on each lot as it was sold.

4. Purchase Money Mortgages—**Purchase money mortgages** are mortgages taken back by the seller and provide part of the purchase price. For example, John and Mary want to purchase a new home from Sue for $100,000. If Sue had a large equity position in the house, John

and Mary might give her a down payment of $10,000 and ask to sign a $90,000 mortgage for the balance. If Sue agreed, she would be providing part of the funds by taking back a purchase-money mortgage.

5. Chattel Mortgages—**Chattel mortgages** generally cover personal property and are secured by personal property. A rancher, for example, might use his cattle to secure a chattel mortgage.

6. Package Mortgages—**Package mortgages** generally cover both real and personal property.

Endnotes

1. See the Definitions Section, Uniform Standards of Professional Appraisal Practice, p. I–8.
2. Ibid., p. ?.
3. Appraisal Institute, The Dictionary of Real Estate Appraisal, 2nd ed. (1989), p. 191. Marketability refers to the salability of a property.
4. Ibid., p. 129.
5. Ibid., p. 207. There are many definitions of a neighborhood, but this one is easy to understand and use.
6. Ibid., p. 208.
7. Ibid., p. 191.
8. The FOMC's membership is made up of the seven members of the Board of Governors and five elected members from the 12 presidents of the Federal Reserve banks. However, the president of the Federal Reserve Bank of New York is always one of the five because the Fed implements its decisions through the New York Federal Reserve Bank.
9. There are also chattel mortgages, which are secured by personal property.
10. Private mortgage insurance may not be required if the loan-to-value ratio is below a certain percentage. Most lenders will not require it if the loan-to-value ratio is less than 70 or 80 percent, but this varies by lender.
11. Obviously, the most common cause of default is nonpayment.

Key Terms and Concepts

Market analysis:
    feasibility analysis
    identification of the market
    identification of demand factors
    identification of supply factors
    absorption
Neighborhood analysis:
    stages in life cycle:
        growth
        maturity or stability
        decline
        revitalization or renewal
    neighborhood boundaries
Characteristics of real estate markets:
    availability of information
    changes in supply and demand
    immobility of real estate
    segmented markets
    regulation
    monetary policy
    fiscal policy
    Federal Reserve (the Fed)
    fractional reserve banking
General financial markets:
    money markets
    capital markets
Types of mortgage markets:
    primary mortgage market
    secondary mortgage market
Sources of real estate capital:
    commercial banks
    savings and loan associations (S&Ls)
    insurance companies
    pension funds
    mortgage brokers
    mortgage bankers

Mortgage terminology:
- principal
- amortization
- interest
- fully amortized mortgage
- negative amortization
- partially amortized mortgage
- fixed-rate mortgage
- adjustable-rate mortgage
- buydown
- leverage
- loan-to-value ratio
- blanket mortgages
- purchase-money mortgages
- chattel mortgages
- package mortgages

Review Questions

1. In financial terms, interest is:
   a. what financial institutions charge to keep a borrower broke.
   b. the price or rent for the use of money.
   c. the payment on a typical mortgage.
   d. the exchange rate.

2. In the U.S., the _____ has responsibility for monetary policy.
   a. the president
   b. Congress
   c. Office of Management and Budget
   d. Federal Reserve system

3. Banks retain only a small portion of actual deposits. The majority of funds are invested (loaned to customers). Such a banking system is termed:
   a. fractional reserve banking.
   b. speculative.
   c. unsound.
   d. total dollar banking.

4. The use of debt to finance an asset is termed:
   a. chattel.
   b. leverage.
   c. blanket financing.
   d. joint venture financing.

5. Sometimes a seller will take back a mortgage as part of the purchase price. Such a mortgage is called a:
   a. blanket mortgage.
   b. purchase-money mortgage.
   c. bad deal.
   d. chattel mortgage.

6. Two components of a mortgage payment are:
   a. principal and time.
   b. interest and time.
   c. principal and interest.
   d. interest and term.

7. Holding all other factors constant, increasing the term on a mortgage will:
   a. lower the monthly payment.
   b. raise the monthly payment.
   c. have no effect on the monthly payment.
   d. lower the interest rate.

8. The process of systematic repayment of principal is referred to as:
   a. payoff.
   b. balance outstanding.
   c. amortization.
   d. negative amortization.

9. In a fully amortized mortgage, which component is satisfied first from each payment?
   a. Principal
   b. Interest
   c. Term
   d. Amortization

10. If a borrower fails to meet the interest component of the payment, the lender typically adds this deficiency to the original loan amount. This amortization process is described as:
    a. positive amortization.
    b. fully amortized.
    c. partially amortized.
    d. negative amortization.

11. In a partially amortized loan, the amount remaining at the end of the loan term is referred to as the:
    a. interest due.
    b. principal paid.
    c. balloon payment.
    d. annuity due.

12. Real estate is characterized by a high degree of _____ financing.
    a. equity
    b. debt
    c. illiquid
    d. nonmarket

13. A mortgage secured by both real and personal property is termed a _____ mortgage.
    a. blanket
    b. personal
    c. package
    d. fixture

14. The study of a local market for a given type of property is termed:
    a. market analysis.
    b. feasibility analysis.
    c. investment analysis.
    d. financial analysis.

15. All of the following are sources of real estate capital EXCEPT:
    a. commercial banks.
    b. pension funds.
    c. insurance companies.
    d. appraisal firms.

6 The Appraisal Process

Overview

This chapter presents the appraisal or valuation process—a logical, step-by-step framework for handling any appraisal problem. The focus of the chapter will be to provide an overview of the process itself with a concentration on each step.

Learning Objectives

After completing this chapter, the student should be able to:

- Name and discuss the steps in the appraisal process

- Name and describe briefly the various types of appraisal reports

- Discuss the four forces that influence value

- Name the three approaches to value

I. The Appraisal Process

The **appraisal process** (also known as the **valuation process**) consists of several steps that provide the appraiser with a logical approach to solving a valuation problem. The process, which should be followed regardless of the nature of the appraisal assignment, includes these steps: (1) defining the problem; (2) collecting, analyzing and verifying data; (3) determining highest and best use; (4) analyzing land or site value; (5) applying the approaches to value; (6) preparing reconciliation and final value estimate; and (7) submitting a report.

A. Defining the Problem

Defining the problem includes specifying the legal property interests to be valued. Is the legal interest in the property to be appraised (the *subject*) a fee simple interest, a leasehold interest or some other interest? The appraiser should provide a physical and legal identification of the subject as part of defining the problem.

In performing an appraisal appraisers must rely on attorneys and surveyors for pertinent information. Assumptions and limiting conditions are also included in the definition of the problem (see Figure 6.1). Any value estimate is based on assumptions shown in the appraiser's report. Moreover, certain market conditions serve to limit any value estimate.

An appraiser should define the type of value—market value, liquidation value or assessed value for example—to be estimated. The date of the value estimate should also be included in this step. Usually this is the date of the final inspection of the subject, and it identifies the market and environmental conditions for the value estimate. In some appraisal assignments, the date of the value estimate will be in the distant past. For example, an appraiser may be engaged to perform an appraisal as of the date of a tax return, say ten years ago. The date of the value estimate also may be as of a future date, as in the case of a proposed structure. Definition of the problem also includes the purpose of the appraisal, which for most assignments is to estimate defined value.

B. Collecting, Analyzing and Verifying Data

Data collection and analysis involves collection of two types of data: primary data and secondary data. Primary data are those collected for the first time directly by the appraiser, for example, market information. Secondary data, on the other hand, have been collected previously. These include demographic data already collected by the U.S. Census Bureau.

Figure 6.1
Market Value

DEFINITION OF MARKET VALUE: The most probable price which a property should bring in a competitive and open market under all conditions requisite to a fair sale, the buyer and seller, each acting prudently, knowledgeably and assuming the price is not affected by undue stimulus. Implicit in this definition is the consummation of a sale as of a specified date and the passing of title from seller to buyer under conditions whereby: (1) buyer and seller are typically motivated; (2) both parties are well informed or well advised, and each acting in what he considers his own best interest; (3) a reasonable time is allowed for exposure in the open market; (4) payment is made in terms of cash in U.S. dollars or in terms of financial arrangements comparable thereto; and (5) the price represents the normal consideration for the property sold unaffected by special or creative financing or sales concessions* granted by anyone associated with the sale.

*Adjustments to the comparables must be made for special or creative financing or sales concessions. No adjustments are necessary for those costs which are normally paid by sellers as a result of tradition or law in a market area; these costs are readily identifiable since the seller pays these costs in virtually all sales transactions. Special or creative financing adjustments can be made to the comparable property by comparisons to financing terms offered by a third party institutional lender that is not already involved in the property or transaction. Any adjustment should not be calculated on a mechanical dollar for dollar cost of the financing or concession but the dollar amount of any adjustment should approximate the market's reaction to the financing or concessions based on the appraiser's judgment.

CERTIFICATION AND STATEMENT OF LIMITING CONDITIONS

CERTIFICATION: The Appraiser certifies and agrees that:

1. The Appraiser has no present or contemplated future interest in the property appraised; and neither the employment to make the appraisal, nor the compensation for it, is contingent upon the appraised value of the property.

2. The Appraiser has no personal interest in or bias with respect to the subject matter of the appraisal report or the participants to the sale. The "Estimate of Market Value" in the appraisal report is not based in whole or in part upon the race, color, or national origin of the prospective owners or occupants of the property appraised, or upon the race, color or national origin of the present owners or occupants of the properties in the vicinity of the property appraised.

3. The Appraiser has personally inspected the property, both inside and out, and has made an exterior inspection of all comparable sales listed in the report. To the best of the Appraiser's knowledge and belief, all statements and information in this report are true and correct, and the Appraiser has not knowingly withheld any significant information.

4. All contingent and limiting conditions are contained herein (imposed by the terms of the assignment or by the undersigned affecting the analyses, opinions, and conclusions contained in the report).

5. This appraisal report has been made in conformity with and is subject to the requirements of the Code of Professional Ethics and Standards of Professional Conduct of the appraisal organizations with which the Appraiser is affiliated.

6. All conclusions and opinions concerning the real estate that are set forth in the appraisal report were prepared by the Appraiser whose signature appears on the appraisal report, unless indicated as "Review Appraiser." No change of any item in the appraisal report shall be made by anyone other than the Appraiser, and the Appraiser shall have no responsibility for any such unauthorized change.

CONTINGENT AND LIMITING CONDITIONS: The certification of the Appraiser appearing in the appraisal report is subject to the following conditions and to such other specific and limiting conditions as are set forth by the Appraiser in the report.

1. The Appraiser assumes no responsibility for matters of a legal nature affecting the property appraised or the title thereto, nor does the Appraiser render any opinion as to the title, which is assumed to be good and marketable. The property is appraised as though under responsible ownership.

2. Any sketch in the report may show approximate dimensions and is included to assist the reader in visualizing the property. The Appraiser has made no survey of the property.

3. The Appraiser is not required to give testimony or appear in court because of having made the appraisal with reference to the property in question, unless arrangements have been previously made therefor.

Figure 6.1 Continued

---

4. Any distribution of the valuation in the report between land and improvements applies only under the existing program of utilization. The separate valuations for land and building must not be used in conjunction with any other appraisal and are invalid if so used.

5. The Appraiser assumes that there are no hidden or unapparent conditions of the property, subsoil, or structures, which would render it more or less valuable. The Appraiser assumes no responsibility for such conditions, or for engineering which might be required to discover such factors.

6. Information, estimates, and opinions furnished to the Appraiser, and contained in the report, were obtained from sources considered reliable and believed to be true and correct. However, no responsibility for accuracy of such items furnished the Appraiser can be assumed by the Appraiser.

7. Disclosure of the contents of the appraisal report is governed by the Bylaws and Regulations of the professional appraisal organizations with which the Appraiser is affiliated.

8. Neither all, nor any part of the content of the report, or copy thereof (including conclusions as to the property value, the identity of the Appraiser, professional designations, reference to any professional appraisal organizations, or the firm with which the Appraiser is connected), shall be used for any purposes by anyone but the client specified in the report, the borrower if appraisal fee paid by same, the mortgagee or its successors and assigns, mortgage insurers, consultants, professional appraisal organizations, any state or federally approved financial institution, any department, agency, or instrumentality of the United States or any state or the District of Columbia, without the previous written consent of the Appraiser; nor shall it be conveyed by anyone to the public through advertising, public relations, news, sales, or other media, without the written consent and approval of the Appraiser.

9. On all appraisals, subject to satisfactory completion, repairs, or alterations, the appraisal report and value conclusion are contingent upon completion of the improvements in a workmanlike manner.

Date:................   Appraiser(s) ....

Freddie Mac
Form 439   JUL 86

Fannie Mae
Form 1004B   JUL 86

Data collection also should involve information about the four forces that influence value: **social forces, governmental and legal forces, economic forces** and **physical and environmental forces.** To be useful, data must be verified in the marketplace.

C. Determining Highest and Best Use

Highest and best use has been defined as the "perfect" use for a given property, or that use that provides the highest land value.

D. Analyzing Land or Site Value

Land is raw or in a natural state, whereas a site is land that is ready for its intended use.

E. Applying the Approaches to Value

Traditionally, appraisers have used three **approaches to value—sales comparison approach, cost approach** and **income approach**.[1] An appraiser may not be able to use all of these approaches in any one appraisal, but each approach should be considered for every appraisal.

F. Preparing Reconciliation and Final Value Estimate

After considering each approach to value, the appraiser must prepare a **final value estimate** for the subject, to be reported to the client. The process of developing a final value estimate (or range of values) is known as **reconciliation.**

G. Submitting a Report

An appraisal report may take several forms. Clients may request a specific type of appraisal report, but appraisers should follow the appraisal process regardless of the form of the report. Types of appraisal reports include letter reports, form reports, narrative reports and oral reports. A **letter report** contains a defined value estimate or range of value for the subject, but in letter format. Supporting material for a letter report is placed in the appraiser's files. **Form reports,** such as the Uniform Residential Appraisal Report (URAR), also contain a final estimate or range of defined value and are presented on a preprinted URAR appraisal form. **Narrative reports** are very detailed and thorough presentations of data, analyses and conclusions that contain a final estimate or range of defined value. Narrative reports are usually required for demonstration appraisal reports, which are a requirement to obtain an MAI or SRA appraisal designation. An **oral report** is presented directly (in person or by phone) to the client. It contains the minimum requirements for an appraisal, including an estimate of defined value. Supporting material for an oral report is placed in the appraiser's files.

A **letter of opinion** may or may not be considered an appraisal report. It is a preliminary investigation of market information and activity. A letter of opinion usually results in a broad price estimate, but not a value conclusion.[2]

1. Report Components—At a minimum, certain items are required by the Uniform Standards of Professional Practice to be included in an appraisal, regardless of the form of the report. These items are:

a. Identification (physical and legal) of the real estate and property rights to be valued

b. Definition of purpose and description of use of the appraisal

c. Specification of date of the value estimate, the date of report completion and definition of value

d. Determination of highest and best use of the property

e. Description of the appraisal procedures used

f. Description of supporting data and methodology used to reach conclusions and opinions

g. Explanation of assumptions of limiting conditions and certification of value

Endnotes

1. The sales comparison is also known as the direct sales comparison approach, and the income approach is also known as the income capitalization approach.
2. Appraisal Institute, *The Appraisal of Real Estate,* 9th ed. (1987), Chicago: pp. 573–574. The assumption is that a letter of opinion is a report in letter format.

Key Terms and Concepts

Appraisal (or valuation) process:
    defining the problem
    collecting, analyzing, verifying data
    determining highest and best use
    analyzing land or site value
    applying the approaches to value
    preparing reconciliation and final value estimate
    submitting a report
Types of appraisal reports:
    letter report
    form report
    narrative report
    oral report
    letter of opinion
Three approaches to value:
    sales comparison
    cost
    income

Review Questions

1. The _____ establishes the market conditions for the value estimate.

    a. amount of the fee
    b. date of the value estimate ✓
    c. date of first inspection
    d. date of contract signing

2. Every appraisal should _____ the three approaches to value.

    a. use
    b. employ
    c. consider ✓
    d. evaluate

3. When estimating market value, an appraiser typically will value the:

    a. land.
    b. site. ✓
    c. open areas.
    d. vacant space.

4. Description of the real estate occurs during which part of the appraisal process?

    a. Definition of the problem ✓
    b. Data collection and analysis
    c. Highest and best use analysis
    d. Application of the approaches to value

5. Identification of the property interests to be appraised occurs during which part of the appraisal process?

    a. Definition of the problem ✓
    b. Data collection and analysis
    c. Highest and best use analysis
    d. Application of the approaches to value

6. The first step in the appraisal process is to:

    a. define the fee arrangement.
    b. collect the fee before starting.
    c. define the problem. ✓
    d. identify the property.

7. The final step in the appraisal process is to:

    a. prepare reconciliation and final value estimate.
    b. write report and provide report and findings to client. ✓
    c. collect the fee.
    d. develop an indication of value.

8. Reconciliation is performed:

    a. throughout the appraisal process.
    b. throughout the review process.
    c. after application of the approaches to value.
    d. as the final step in the appraisal process.

9. The final value estimate is rounded to:

    a. come up with the "right" number.
    b. show a precise calculation.
    c. show that the number is an estimate and not a precise mathematical calculation.
    d. help the three approaches derive similar value estimates.

10. The _____ identifies the market and environmental conditions in effect at the time of the value estimate.

    a. date of the report
    b. date of report completion
    c. date of the value estimate
    d. date of first inspection

11. A detailed appraisal report showing the appraiser's analyses, opinions and conclusions is a _____ report.

    a. letter
    b. form
    c. oral
    d. narrative

12. Expert testimony in the courtroom is an example of a(an) _____ report.

    a. letter
    b. form
    c. oral
    d. narrative

13. Assumptions and limiting conditions typically are addressed during:

    a. definition of the problem.
    b. data collection and analysis.
    c. application of the approaches.
    d. reconciliation.

14. Certification of value typically is addressed during which stage in the process?

    a. Definition of the problem
    b. Data collection and analysis
    c. Application of the approaches
    d. Reconciliation

15. Data verification typically is addressed during which section of the appraisal process?

   a. Definition of the problem
   b. Data collection and analysis
   c. Application of the approaches
   d. Reconciliation

7 Property Description

Overview

This chapter identifies and analyzes factors involved in site analysis and valuation. Methods of site valuation will be compared and contrasted, and basic construction techniques will be discussed.

Learning Objectives

After completing this chapter, the student should be able to:

- Discuss the factors identified and analyzed in estimating site value

- Evaluate site characteristics in relation to market standards

- Explain the methods of site valuation and compare and contrast them

- List the major types of construction techniques

I. Site Description and Analysis

Land is unimproved real estate; it is raw or undeveloped. A **site,** however, is land that has been improved for the use for which it was intended. There are two types of improvements—improvements *to* the land and improvements *on* the land. Improvements to the land are those necessary to support the intended land use; examples include grading and utilities. Improvements on the land are those structures, such as buildings, situated on the land. The site is valued as if vacant and available to be put to its highest and best use. This generally includes improvements to the land but does not include improvements on the land.

The site is analyzed separately for several reasons. Before a site can be valued, significant characteristics must be identified and evaluated so that the site may be compared to others in the marketplace. Its value, general acceptability and marketability are part of the site and improvement package. Site characteristics influence the value of the package as well as its contribution to the package. Site analysis is part of analyzing the suitability of present improvements. **Site analysis** is the identification and analysis of the characteristics that create, enhance or detract from utility, desirability, marketability and thus value of the site. The site should be evaluated and valued separately, as if vacant.

A. Factors in Site Analysis

Factors in site analysis can be divided into two broad categories: legal/governmental and physical. These factors interact to enhance or detract from the site and the property as improved. The focus of site analysis should be market oriented, that is, the identification of those market-determined factors that affect the marketability, appeal, general acceptability and value of the site. Several factors are included in site analysis:

1. Legal/Governmental—**Legal and governmental** factors in site analysis include title data, zoning and other governmental use restrictions. Title data are necessary to identify what rights are being appraised. Zoning and other use restrictions may restrict use of the site and limit its marketability, appeal and value. This factor involves identification of permitted and prohibited uses, setback requirements, nonconforming uses and violations that may affect value.

2. Physical—**Physical factors** include such items as utilities, access, topography, size, and site improvements. Economic and locational factors also are included in the category.

    a. **Utilities** at the site may be public and/or private. The type and availability of utilities is important for residential sites, as are cost and stability of the services. Typical utilities for sites include water, sewer, storm water and surface water disposal, electricity and gas.

b. **Access** to the site is also important. Access is the means of physical entrance into or upon a property.[1]

c. **Topography** refers to the contour of the site. It also includes the site's slope (grade), drainage, landscaping, building capabilities and load-bearing capabilities. Drainage refers to how water runoff is accomplished at the site—if water runoff is excellent, so is drainage. Building capabilities include the site's ability to support intended improvements and possible alternate uses of the site. Load-bearing capabilities of the site relate to sinking and shifting of the soil and subsoil and the site's ability to support a structure.

d. The **size** dimension of a site may encompass several factors including area, effective area, frontage, depth and shape. Area[2] may be measured in terms of a common unit of measure (square footage, cubic footage or number of acres). However, the entire area of a site may not be available for improvements. Area available to support improvements is known as the effective area. The local market or neighborhood will determine the appropriate or "ideal" size of a site for a given use. Additional land in excess of this ideal size is surplus land. Frontage is the distance—usually measured in feet—abutting a street or public way.[3] Depth is the distance from the front to rear of the site.[4] Shape refers to the diagram formed by the perimeter boundaries of the property.

e. **Site improvements** include sidewalks, curbs, streetlights, alleys and easements for access. Because these improvements may affect site value, marketability and appeal, they should be addressed during site analysis. Finally, the orientation of the site with respect to the elements (sun and wind) may affect site value.

f. **Economic considerations** include prices of comparable sites, site-to-building ratios and the tax burden. Prices of similar (comparable) sales are used to estimate how the market prices a similar bundle of goods. Site to property ratios provide the appraiser with a market-determined estimate of how much land the local market perceives is necessary for a given use. For example, if most residential properties in a local market have a site-to-building ratio of 10 to 1, then given a 2,000-square-foot house, the site should be 10 times this size, or 20,000 square feet. A site with 60,000 square feet of site and 2,000 square feet of house, would have a site that is too large

(40,000 square feet too much). In this example, the additional 40,000 square feet would be termed excess land (more than is required by the market standard).

The tax burden of the site should be compared to the tax burden of competing properties in the local market. The dollar amount of the tax and the relative tax burden should be considered. Special assessments and fees for private services (such as garbage collection) should be considered also.

g. **Locational factors,** which should be considered and analyzed during site analysis, include the relation of the site to the local general land use pattern, degree of conformity, neighborhood and market area reputation, amenities of the neighborhood, neighborhood hazards and nuisances.

Local land-use patterns may provide the appraiser with an indication of a market preference for certain neighborhoods. For example, some properties may be situated on a lake. If the market deems lake access a desirable quality, these sites would have higher market preference. Access to shopping, schools and employment centers may be better for some neighborhoods than others.

In addition, the degree of conformity within the neighborhood should be considered. Generally, value is enhanced given a higher degree of conformity within the neighborhood. Some neighborhoods enjoy an excellent reputation in the minds of market participants, whereas others do not. The appraiser must attempt to measure the market's perception of a neighborhood in an objective and systematic fashion.

Amenities are the tangible and intangible benefits of ownership. Usually these benefits are nonmonetary. Amenities are those attractions and benefits that accrue to the owners.[5] They include such things as satisfaction of being in a particular location, quiet enjoyment and pride of ownership. The appraiser must ascertain the general tastes and standards of typical buyers in the local market area. Certain neighborhoods may have more (or less) amenities—for example, a neighborhood may have a swimming pool for residents of that neighborhood. Finally, some neighborhoods may have hazards or nuisances, or a site may have a hazard or nuisance.

h. **Environmental factors** play an increasingly important role in site valuation, so the appraiser should analyze the interrelationships between the subject and neighboring properties. Hazards, nuisances and safety should be considered.

II. Improvement Description

The size, condition and functional utility of the improvements combine to influence acceptability, desirability and, hence, the marketability and value of the property. The ultimate test of adequacy of the improvements is how they perform in relation to the market standard.

A. Condition

The ultimate objectives of improvement analysis are (1) to establish the basis for highest and best use (or most probable use) of the improved property (site and buildings) and (2) to provide the basis for estimating the contribution of the improvements to total property value.

1. Establishing Highest and Best Use—To achieve this objective, the appraiser must reach judgments or conclusions about the following items:

    a. Functional utility of the improvements

    b. Market acceptability of the improvements

    c. Actual and effective age of improvements

2. Estimating Contribution—Completeness and accuracy of the property improvement description is the basis for:

    a. Selection of comparable sales of properties that are structurally similar

    b. Quality and quantity of items included in reproduction cost new

    c. Estimates of accrued physical deterioration and functional obsolescence

B. Market Standards

The "good" and "bad" found in the material, condition and utility of the improvements are in terms of local market standards. These standards may vary over time and change as market conditions change. It is important that the analysis be both current and local. At least three criteria are to be considered in analyzing acceptability of improvements:

C. Utility

1. Functional Utility—**Functional utility** is defined as "the sum of the attractiveness and usefulness of the property. It is the ability of the property to perform the function for which it is intended in terms of current market tastes and standards."[6] Not only is value influenced by external factors—bricks and sticks—but also by buying habits, social traits, living habits and life-styles of potential purchasers. The function of a residence is simply to provide the amenities of living and shelter as efficiently and as economically as possible, applying proper use of the following:

    a. Construction materials

    b. Design and layout, traffic pattern

    c. Architecture

    d. Room size, type, utility

    e. Performance standards (equipment, including kitchen and bath fixtures, heating and cooling systems, electrical service and fixtures, laundry, plumbing, water heater and such)

2. Marketability—This is the ultimate test of functional utility. Marketability is the state of being salable.[7]

3. Functional Adequacy—"Adequacy" depends to a considerable extent on the current local market (the local current submarket specifically). **Functional adequacy** addresses the question, "Does the subject perform the function for which it was intended given current market standards?"

III. Basic Construction and Design

A. Construction Terminology

The student should understand the terms *modernization, rehabilitation* and *remodeling*.

1. Modernization—**Modernization** refers to bringing a property up to current market standards and demands. The changes may be to the

exterior, the interior, or they may involve an addition.

2. Rehabilitation—**Rehabilitation** involves repair; the property is restored to a suitable condition without changing its basic form or style.

3. Remodeling—**Remodeling** applies to changing a structure's form or style to correct functional or other types of deficiencies.

B. **Techniques and Materials**

1. Foundation—The **foundation,** also referred to as the substructure, is typically below grade (or below ground) and serves as a support base for the structure. A foundation may consist of a slab, pilings, columns or other support structures.

2. Frame—The **frame** is the skeleton of the building. Generally, the frame consists of load-bearing walls. The frame is part of the area above grade (above ground) and is considered part of the superstructure.[8] Most houses have a wooden frame. If the residence is multistory, the frame is one of three types: post and beam, platform or balloon.

   a. In a **post and beam** frame, the structure of the frame is constructed on beams. These beams are supported by posts, which may be concrete, brick, or some other strong support material.

   b. In a **platform** frame each story is constructed separately and serves as a "platform" for the next higher story.

   c. In a **balloon** frame, the frame supports (the studs) extend from the floor to the ceiling of the highest story. A horizontal timber (joist) is attached at each floor level.

3. Finish—In simple terms, the **finish** of a residence is the portion of the house seen by the eye. The finish represents the covering, exterior and interior, on the frame.

Endnotes

1. Appraisal Institute, *The Dictionary of Real Estate Appraisal,* 2nd ed. (1989), p. 3.
2. Ibid., p. 16.
3. Ibid., p. 132.
4. The effect of depth on site value may be expressed in percentage terms in standard depth tables. However, these tables may bear little resemblance to actual market behavior.
5. Appraisal Institute, *The Dictionary of Real Estate Appraisal,* 2nd ed. (1989), p. 11.
6. Ibid., p. 134.
7. Ibid., p. 191.
8. Technically, the superstructure is the area of the structure above grade.

Key Terms and Concepts

Site description and analysis:
    land
    site
    site analysis
Factors in site analysis:
    legal/governmental
    physical
        utilities
        access
        topography
        size
        site improvements
        economic considerations
        locational factors
            amenities
        environmental factors
Condition
Market standards:
    functional utility
    functional adequacy
Basic construction and design:
    modernization
    rehabilitation
    remodeling
    foundation (substructure)
    frame
        post and beam
        platform
        balloon
    finish

Review Questions

1. The standard lot size in a local market is one acre. If a subject parcel contains five acres, the additional four acres are considered:

   a. waste.
   b. functional obsolescence (superadequacy).
   c. excess land.
   d. highest and best use.

2. A site is not just land, because:

   a. land never appreciates.
   b. sites include land and any improvements to the land necessary for construction.
   c. of location.
   d. sites are larger.

3. The sum of the attractiveness and usefulness of a property is its:

   a. functional utility.
   b. marketability.
   c. market standard.
   d. exterior depreciation.

4. A type of construction in which each floor supports itself and not other floors is called:

   a. balloon.
   b. post and beam.
   c. platform.
   d. stick built.

5. The nonmonetary pleasantries of ownership are:

   a. benefits.
   b. luxuries.
   c. amenities.
   d. quiet enjoyment.

6. The adequacy of a structure is measured in terms of:

   a. seller responses.
   b. number of prospective purchasers.
   c. price.
   d. market standards.

7. Usually, if the appraiser is seeking market value, the _____ value is estimated.
   - ✓a. site
   - b. land
   - c. location
   - d. externalities

8. The distance abutting a street or public way is measured in:
   - a. cubic feet.
   - ✓b. front feet or frontage.
   - c. depth.
   - d. length.

9. The distance from the front to rear of a site is measured by:
   - a. cubic feet.
   - b. front feet or frontage.
   - ✓c. depth.
   - d. length.

10. The _____ is the major part of the structure below grade.
    - a. frame
    - b. basement
    - ✓c. foundation
    - d. floor

11. Bringing a property up to current market standards is called:
    - a. repair.
    - ✓b. modernization.
    - c. remodeling.
    - d. rehabilitation.

12. _____ is changing a structure's form or style to correct functional deficiencies.
    - a. Repair
    - b. Modernization
    - c. Remodeling
    - ✓d. Rehabilitation

13. _____ is altering a property to a suitable condition.
    - ✓a. Repair
    - b. Modernization
    - c. Remodeling
    - d. Rehabilitation

14. The skeleton of a structure is its:
    - a. foundation.
    - b. finish.
    - ✓c. frame.
    - d. substructure.

8 Highest and Best Use Analysis

Overview

This chapter discusses highest and best use, along with typical constraints on the application of the concept. Highest and best use is an integral part of the appraisal process. Most definitions of market value assume that the subject is used as its highest and best use.

Learning Objectives

After completing this chapter, the student should be able to:

- Define highest and best use

- Discuss the traditional tests that are commonly used to estimate highest and best use

- Discuss the highest and best use of the site, as if vacant

- Discuss the highest and best use of the property, as improved

I. What is Highest and Best Use?

Highest and best use is "The reasonably probable and legal use of vacant land or an improved property, which is physically possible, appropriately supported, financially feasible, and that results in the highest value."[1] Highest and best use may be (and usually is) the present use.

For most appraisal assignments, an appraiser attempts to estimate market value. Most definitions of market value assume that the property being appraised (the subject) is at its highest and best use or will be converted to its highest and best use. Therefore, to better understand market value and the appraisal process in general, the appraiser must understand highest and best use. A second reason for highest and best use analysis is that it assists the appraiser in identifying similar sales (comparables), which may be needed in the application of the three approaches to value.

Highest and best use asks the question, "What is the perfect use for a parcel?" There may be many alternative uses, but there is one use which is theoretically "perfect." Highest and best use is, in a practical sense, the **most probable use** for a parcel. Highest and best use is based on the principle of conformity and the interaction of market forces in the marketplace. The principle of conformity holds that value is created, enhanced and sustained when a property conforms to market forces and market demands.

A. Traditional Tests (Constraints) of Highest and Best Use

1. Physically Possible—To be the highest and best use a use must be **physically possible** for that site and for that use. Some questions the appraiser should address include:

    a. Will the site support the current or intended use based on soil, subsoil and topographical conditions?

    b. Will the site accommodate the size of structure intended? This should be determined through an examination of competing properties.

    c. What utilities are offered at the site? Some uses require certain utilities; for example, some manufacturing facilities require natural gas at the site.

    d. What are the means of access to the site? Will convenient access be critical for a given use? What is the traffic flow at the site?

    e. What are the physical qualities of the site with respect to size, frontage and depth? Size generally refers to area. For example, how many square feet or acres does the site contain? Frontage generally refers to the distance abutting a street or public way. It is usually measured in front feet, a lineal measurement. Depth is the distance from the front of the site to the rear of the site.

2. Legally Permissible—Several legal constraints are addressed with respect to possible uses for the site. To determine whether the use is **legally possible,** ask these questions:

   a. Is the use permissible based on current zoning regulations? In some situations, especially proposed construction, the proposed use may not be in conformity with existing zoning regulations. However, if it is reasonable and probable to obtain an amendment to the zoning regulations or to obtain a variance to current regulations, then the appraiser may conclude a certain highest and best use subject to these zoning changes. A **zoning variance** is the legal authority to construct a structure that does not conform to existing zoning regulations. For example, a zoning ordinance might require a maximum density of use of 3.5 houses per acre. A variance to the density restriction might allow a subdivision to have 4.0 houses per acre.

   b. Is the use permissible based on current building codes? This issue is usually applied only to new or proposed projects. For example, suppose a property is located on the coast in an area where there have been numerous hurricanes. Local building codes might require construction of a building that can withstand sustained high winds. If the proposed structure could not do so, it would not be in conformity with the building codes.

   c. Is the use permissible based on current deed restrictions? Deed restrictions are those private limitations that are placed in the deed itself and limit the purchaser's (grantee's) use of the property. Typically, deed restrictions are more restrictive than zoning ordinances or building codes. In addition, deed restrictions, unlike subdivision restrictive covenants, do not necessarily apply to each property owner in a subdivision. Deed restrictions usually apply only to a specific grantee.

   d. Is the use permissible based on current subdivision restrictive covenants? Restrictive covenants generally apply to all purchasers in a given subdivision. These covenants are more restrictive, in most instances, than local zoning ordinances or building codes.

   e. Does the use conform to existing environmental regulations? This area has become more and more important in recent years. The appraiser should make every attempt to determine compliance with existing environmental laws at the site.

3. Financially or Economically Feasible—To be **financially or economically feasible** the use must produce some net return or a positive net present value to the owner: Which use(s) does the market indicate as most likely, based on market area properties, market conditions and economic factors?

4. Most Profitable Use or Maximally Productive Use—The remaining uses are analyzed to determine which use is most profitable. There are four factors of production: labor, capital, entrepreneurship (coordination or management ability) and land. The **most profitable use** is the use that returns the highest cash to the land after satisfying labor, capital and coordination requirements.

II. Application of Highest and Best Use

The theory of highest and best use implies that there is a perfect use for the site, with application of the principle focusing on two scenarios: highest and best use of the site "as if vacant" and highest and best use of the property "as improved." Some appraisers have considered highest and best use in appraisal reports by reciting the definition and the four constraints. However, to provide the client with a thorough appraisal report, the appraiser should follow a logical and systematic sequence in determining highest and best use.

A. **Highest and Best Use of a Site as if Vacant**

1. *The site is always valued as if vacant and available to be put to its highest and best use.* Land is raw or unimproved, but a site has been improved for its intended use. Some improvements to the land include grading, preparation for construction, and improvements for utilities. Alternate uses (those uses other than the present use) must also be considered. The appraiser must discover that use which is most probable in the mind of the typically informed buyer: the market and its participants tend to put property to its highest and best use.

2. Questions that should be answered include:

   a. For which use is the site best suited?

   b. What is permitted on the site?

   c. What uses are limited by the physical characteristics of the site?

   d. What would current buyers have in mind in bidding for the site?

3. The appraiser will probably consider several possible uses for any given site, with each possible use subjected to the four tests for highest and best use. Some uses will be eliminated because they are not physically possible. Others will be eliminated because they are not legally permissible or because they are not economically viable. Usually, only one or two uses will satisfy the first three tests. If only one use remains, that use is probably the highest and best use of the site as if vacant. If two or more uses remain after the first three tests, the remaining use that is most profitable is the highest and best use of the site as if vacant.

B. **Highest and Best Use of Property as Improved**

1. This concept always considers the existing or proposed improvements. The appraiser should identify the "ideal" improvements for the site. If there are existing improvements, any deviation from the ideal improvements is functional obsolescence. If there are existing improvements, as is the case with most appraisals for single-family dwellings, the highest and best use of the site may be different from that of the property improved.

2. For total property valuation, the applicable highest and best use is that of the total improved property. This includes retention and use of the existing improvements, provided the existing improvements represent the highest and best use of the property as improved.

3. Even when the present use differs from highest and best use of the site, the existing use will continue until site value in the highest and best use of the site exceeds the total value of the property in the existing use. Simply stated, the highest and best use will continue to be as currently improved until the current improvements do not add to the value of the site as if vacant.

4. The present use of an improved property is presumed to be the highest and best use (or most probable use) unless it is demonstrated that change is imminent and/or value as vacant land exceeds value in present use. This is important in situations of improper improvements, or houses in business and commercial areas. For example, suppose that a site being valued was initially zoned residential but has been rezoned commercial. The site has a single-family residence on it with an estimated value of $35,000 as a residence. However, if the site were vacant and used as a commercial site, it would have an estimated value of $50,000, less a demolition cost of $5,000 for the residence. The improvements do not add to value. The value of the site as if vacant

($50,000 − $5,000 = $45,000) is greater than the value of the site as currently improved ($35,000). In this example, the highest and best use of the property is use as a commercial site.

III. Other Related Highest and Best Use Topics

Some properties do not "fit" traditional highest and best use analysis. These nontraditional categories include special purpose (or single-use) properties, interim use properties and legally nonconforming–use properties.

A. Special Purpose or Single-Use Properties

Special purpose or single-use properties usually serve only one use, such as an automobile auction, a museum or a theme park. Generally speaking, the highest and best use of a special purpose property is its current use.

B. Interim Use Properties

Interim use properties are expected to undergo change in highest and best use in the near future but have not done so as of today. The highest and best use of an interim use property is generally its current use, but this current use is not expected to remain as the highest and best use.

C. Legally Nonconforming Use

If a property conformed to legal restrictions in the past but does not currently conform, it is considered to be a **legally nonconforming use.** For example, if a parcel was zoned for residential property and has a house built on it but has been rezoned for commercial property, the use as a residence is a legally nonconforming use. Although most legally nonconforming uses are caused by zoning changes, they also can result from legislative enactment, such as environmental laws.

Endnote

1. Appraisal Institute, *The Dictionary of Real Estate Appraisal,* 2nd ed. (1989), p. 149.

Key Terms and Concepts

Highest and best use
Most probable use
Tests (Constraints) for Highest and Best Use:
    physically possible
    legally permissible
        variance (zoning variance)
    financially (or economically) feasible
    most profitable (maximally productive)
Highest and Best Use Is Analyzed from Two Perspectives:
    highest and best use of a site as if vacant
    highest and best use of property as improved
Nontraditional property analysis:
    special purpose or single use
    interim use
    legally nonconforming use

Review Questions

1. When seeking market value, the site is valued:
   a. as improved.
   b. as if vacant and available to be put to its highest and best use.
   c. as currently improved.
   d. as currently improved and available to be put to its highest and best use.

2. When there are existing improvements, the highest and best use of the site _____ the highest and best use of the property as improved.
   a. is the same as
   b. is similar to
   c. may be different from
   d. may not be different from

3. Four tests, or constraints, on highest and best use are:
   a. physically possible, legally permissible, financially feasible and most profitable.
   b. legally possible, economically permissible, financially feasible and most profitable.
   c. financially feasible, not legally possible, physically permissible and most profitable.
   d. least profitable, financially feasible, legally possible and physically possible.

4. In a practical sense, highest and best use is based on the:
   a. perfect use.
   b. least probable use.
   c. ideal use.
   d. most realistic use.

5. Nonconformity with zoning regulations might require the appraiser to discard a potential use for a site. This use would fail which test for highest and best use?
   a. Financially feasible
   b. Physically possible
   c. Legally permissible
   d. Most profitable

6. An improvement that conformed to existing laws and ordinances when constructed originally but that does not conform at present describes:

   a. special purpose property.
   b. variance.
   c. legally nonconforming use.
   d. interim use.

7. If the highest and best use of a property is expected to change from its current use to some other use in the near future, this would describe:

   a. special purpose property.
   b. variance.
   c. legally nonconforming use.
   d. interim use.

8. Sometimes a building is constructed that is not in conformity with existing zoning regulations at the time of its construction. However, municipal authorities permit its construction as a(an):

   a. special purpose property.
   b. variance.
   c. legally nonconforming use.
   d. interim use.

9. Any deviation from the "ideal" improvements in existing or proposed improvements will result in:

   a. an alternate highest and best use.
   b. interim use.
   c. legally nonconforming use.
   d. functional obsolescence.

10. To be the most profitable use, a site must:

    a. provide the highest cash to the land.
    b. provide the highest cash to the improvements.
    c. be a special purpose property.
    d. have the same use as currently improved.

9
Statistical Concepts in Appraisal

Overview

This chapter reviews basic statistical concepts that may be used in appraising and that may be tested on a residential licensure/certification examination. In addition, basic mathematical skills are reviewed.

Learning Objectives

After completing this chapter, the student should be able to:

- Compute the mean, median, mode and range of a sample

- Define standard deviation, correlation coefficient, coefficient of determination and coefficient of variation

- Compute basic mathematical problems faced by appraisers

I. Specific Quantitative Skills

Appraisers should have sufficient quantitative skills to handle the most complex of appraisal assignments.[1] In recent years, statistical analysis has been applied to the appraisal of real estate. Such "number crunching" should assist and supplement the appraiser's judgment and training—although it is not meant to, nor will it ever, replace sound, well-reasoned appraiser judgment. However, every appraiser should have a basic understanding of statistical concepts as they relate to real estate appraisal.

Statistics can be used for two purposes—description and inference. They can be used to examine the past (description) and to forecast the future (inference). Most statistics are based on a set of data called a sample, which is any data set that is less than total population. For example, if an appraiser knew all possible house sales since houses were sold in an area, he or she would know the population of house sales for that area. A data set with fewer sales than the population is a sample. Suppose 2,000 houses sold locally last year. If the appraiser had 500 sales during that year, this data set would be a sample. Most appraisers use sample data and sample statistics to describe a population. Statistics from the 500 observations would be used to describe the population of sales in the local market area.

A. Central Tendency

Central tendency is a measure how observations tend to group together toward the middle. Three measures of central tendency are commonplace: mean[2], median and mode.

1. Mean—The **mean** is the average of a set of data. Data may be presented or collected in an ungrouped or grouped format.[3] The data may have been classified, or grouped by a particular characteristic (price for example). The formula for the arithmetic mean for grouped data is

$$\overline{X} = \frac{\sum_{i=1}^{N} f X_i}{N}$$

where $\overline{X}$ is the arithmetic mean, $\sum_{F_i}^{N} X_i$ is the sum of the frequency of observations, and f is the frequency, or number in each group.

Suppose you have three houses for $70,000, five houses for $80,000 and two houses for $100,000.

$$\overline{X} = \frac{(3 \times 70{,}000) + (5 \times 80{,}000) + (2 \times 100{,}000)}{10}$$

$$\overline{X} = 81{,}000$$

The formula for the arithmetic mean for ungrouped data is the sum of observations divided by number of observations, or

$$\overline{X} = \frac{\sum_{i=1}^{N} X_i}{N}$$

where $\overline{X}$ is the arithmetic mean for ungrouped data; $\sum_{i=1}^{N} X$ is the sum of observations as X goes from 1 to N; and N is the number of oberservations.

Suppose there are four house sales:

Sale No.	Sale Price
1	$60,000
2	$70,000
3	$80,000
4	$85,000

The mean of this sample is ($60,000 + $70,000 + $80,000 + $85,000) ÷ 4 = $73,750.

2. Median—The **median** is the 50th percentile, or the "one in the middle." To find the median, first, array ("line up") the observations in ascending or descending order. If you have an odd number of observations, the observation in the middle is the median. If there's an even number of observations, take the two observations in the middle, add them together and divide by two.[4] This will be the median. There is a more complicated formula, but this should be sufficient. For example, suppose an appraiser was faced with the following sales information:

Sale No.	Sale Price
1	$50,000
2	$65,000
3	$70,000
4	$72,000
5	$80,000
6	$90,000

Because the six sales in this example comprise an even number, the appraiser should take the two in the middle (sales 3 and 4), add them together, and divide by 2. The median is $71,000 ($70,000 + $72,000 = $142,000 ÷ 2 = $71,000). Suppose only the first five sales had been observed in the marketplace. Because five is an odd number of observations, the median would be $70,000.

3. Mode—The **mode** is the most frequently occurring observation. Suppose the appraiser noticed the following sales in the marketplace:

Sale No.	Sale Price
1	$60,000
2	$75,000
3	$60,000
4	$72,000
5	$75,000
6	$60,000
7	$73,000

In this example, $60,000 is the mode because it is the most frequently occurring observation.

B. **Measures of Dispersion**

In general, measures of dispersion measure how data are distributed around a certain central tendency. The most common measures of dispersion include the range, the standard deviation, the variance and the coefficient of variation.

1. Range—The **range** is the difference between the high and low observations (values). For example, for the following data the formula is:

$$R = H - L$$

where R is the range, H is the highest observation and L is the lowest observation.

Suppose there are four house sales:

Sale No.	Sale Price
1	$60,000
2	$70,000
3	$80,000
4	$85,000

The range is $85,000 − $60,000, or $25,000.

2. Standard Deviation—Generally, the **standard deviation** is the distance from the mean. For a normally distributed population, we can expect 68.26 percent of the possible observations to fall between the mean and plus or minus (±) one standard deviation. In addition, we can expect 95.44 percent of the possible observations to fall between the mean and plus or minus two standard deviations; 99.74 percent between the mean and plus or minus three standard deviations.[5]

3. Variance—The **variance** is the standard deviation squared (the standard deviation times itself, or standard deviation times standard deviation). For example, suppose the standard deviation was $500. The variance would be $500 ¥ $500 or $25,000. Likewise, the standard deviation can be computed if the variance is known: the standard deviation is the square root of the variance.

4. Coefficient of Variation—The **coefficient of variation** is a measure of dispersion adjusted for the size of the mean. The standard deviation is an absolute measure of dispersion, whereas the coefficient of variation is a relative measure; its value depends on the size of the mean. The formula is the standard deviation divided by the mean, or

$$C.V. = \frac{C}{\overline{X}}$$

II. Regression Analysis

Regression analysis is another appraisal tool.[6] **Regression analysis** attempts to determine the relationship between variables, for example, the relationship between sales price and square footage in a given market.

There are three major limitations to using regression analysis. First, it assumes that every relationship is linear—that every important variable is related to other important variables in a linear relationship, a relationship that may or may not be true. Second, regression analysis assumes that relationships are constant over time, which is not necessarily true. Finally, for regression analysis to provide meaningful relationships for use in appraisal analysis, there should be a sufficient number of observations from which to draw meaningful conclusions. Whereas an appraiser may use regression analysis with only a small number of sales, the results will be less conclusive than an analysis with many sales.

Two terms common to regression analysis are simple regression and multiple regression. *Simple regression* describes a single independent variable that is used in a regression equation. *Multiple regression* describes two or more independent variables that are used in a regression equation. A typical simple regression equation is:

$$Y = a + BX$$

where, Y is the dependent variable, so named because its value depends on the right side of the equation; a is the intercept, where the line crosses the Y axis; B is the slope of the line, the rise of the line divided by the run of the line (or how fast the line goes up or down as it goes out from the origin); X is the independent variable whose value is derived from the local marketplace.[7]

This equation could be rewritten using the actual variables in an appraisal assignment. For example, suppose the appraiser was attempting to estimate the relationship between sales price and square footage. The equation would be:

$$\text{Sale Price} = a + B \text{ (square footage)}$$

Actual data from sales in the local marketplace would be entered into the equation. Suppose, for example, that a regression equation produced the following results for houses in the East neighborhood in City, USA:

$$Y = 21{,}000 + 23.5\,X$$

The appraiser could insert the square footage (the variable X) into the equation to estimate a value for any house in the East neighborhood. If a house had 2,000 square feet, the estimated sales price should be $68,000 (68,000 = 21,000 + 23.5 × 2,000). A major problem with this example is that variables other than square footage may affect sales price. The coefficient of determination, denoted R^2 or r^2, is a measure of how well the left-hand side of the equation (the Y or sales price) is explained by the right-hand side of the equation. The value of R^2 may take on a value from 0 to 1. The higher the number (closer to 1), the more of Y is explained by the right-hand side of the equation. An R^2 of .70 implies that 70 percent of the variation in Y is explained by the right-hand side of the equation.

A concept related to the coefficient of determination is the correlation coefficient, which is denoted as R or r. The correlation coefficient measures how two variables move together. It may take on a value from −1.0 to +1.0. A correlation coefficient of −1.0 implies that two variables are perfectly correlated negatively (when one variable increases 10 percent, the other variable decreases 10 percent). A correlation coefficient of +1.0 implies that the two variables are perfectly correlated positively.

III. Basic Mathematical Skills

Appraisers use basic mathematical skills in completing appraisal assignments. Some of these skills include the proper order for multiplication, division, addition and subtraction; how to calculate the percentage change or rates of change; how to solve basic algebraic expressions.

There are two levels of mathematical operations: (1) **multiplication and division** and (2) **addition and subtraction**. Either multiplication or division is performed first, and addition or subtraction is performed next. For example: Suppose an appraiser faced the following problem:

$$7 + 3 - 3 = ?$$

The answer is 7. The example should be worked from left to right because there is no multiplication or division: $7 + 3 - 3 = 7$.

Suppose the following problem was presented:

$$7 - 3 + 3 \times 12 = ?$$

The correct answer is 40 ($3 \times 12 = 36 + 4$). Multiplication or division was performed before addition or subtraction; then addition or subtraction was performed, working from left to right.

A. Parenthetical Equations

The general rule for working with parenthetical equations is to solve inside the parentheses first, then work outside the parentheses. For example,

$$7 + (3 - 7) + 2 = ?$$

The correct answer is 5 ($3 - 7 = -4 + 7 = 3 + 2 = 5$). If more than one set of parentheses is involved (one set of parentheses inside another set), the general rule is to work the *innermost* set first and work outward until all terms inside all parentheses have been addressed; then work the remainder of the equation. This rule also holds if parentheses are included inside brackets or braces.[8]

B. Percentage Change

Many appraisal assignments require the appraiser to use **percentage change.** For example, if a time adjustment is required, it is usually first estimated in percentage terms and then converted into a dollar amount. The formula for percentage change is:

$$\text{(Ending Price} - \text{Beginning Price)} \div \text{Beginning Price}^9$$

For example, assume that the average price per square foot in the local market was $35 one year ago and today is $40. The percentage change in price per square foot for the year would be $(40 - 35) \div 35 = 5 \div 35 = .1429$, or 14.29 percent. The percentage change for the year is 14.29 percent.

The answer .1429 is stated as a decimal. To convert from a decimal to a percentage, move the decimal point two places to the right (.1429 becomes 14.29 percent, or 14.29%). If a percentage is given and a decimal is desired, move the decimal point two places to the left.[10]

C. Percentage Adjustments

Basic algebraic expressions present a problem for many appraisers. For example, a comparable was 10 percent better than the subject on one item and this was the only difference based on market facts. The comparable sold for $100,000. What should be the adjustment to the comparable for this difference? (The lesson presented in this example is *not* how to make adjustments but how important algebraic expressions are to the appraiser.) Many appraisers would conclude that the comparable was 10 percent better so 10 percent should be subtracted from the comparable ($100,000 − 10% = 10,000). However, this is technically incorrect. The subject is the standard, and the comparables are adjusted to the standard. Therefore the comparable is 110 percent of the standard (if the subject is the standard, it represents 100 percent). This relationship can be stated mathematically as:

$$\$100,000 = 1.10Z$$

where Z is the adjusted sales price of the comparable adjusted to the subject. The expression $1.10Z$ is 110% (1.10) times Z. The goal of the math is to isolate Z on one side of the equal sign. This can be accomplished by dividing both sides by 1.10. Dividing $1.10Z$ by 1.10 equals Z. Dividing $100,000 by 1.10 equals $90,909.09:

$$\frac{\$100,000}{1.10} = \frac{1.10Z}{1.10}$$
$$\$90,909.09 = Z$$

If the adjusted sales price should be $90,909.09, the dollar amount of the adjustment should be $9,090.91 ($100,000 − $90,909.09 = $9,090.09).

Endnotes

1. The student should not get "bogged down" in the computation of statistical formulas. The focus should be on understanding and interpretation of the numbers.
2. Technically, this is the arithmetic mean.
3. An arithmetic mean or expected value also may be computed based on probabilities. Multiply the sum of the probabilities times their respective outcomes, or notationally,

$$\text{Expected value or } \bar{X} = \sum_{i=1}^{N} P_i \times X_i$$

4. An even number of observations occurs when the number of observations divided by 2 does not result in a remainder. For example, suppose an appraiser collected 20 similar sales. Twenty divided by 2 is 10.0, with no remainder. However, suppose there were 21 sales. Twenty-one divided by 2 is 10.5—the .5 is a remainder. Simply put, if a number can be divided by 2 without a remainder, that number is an even number.
5. Appraisal Institute, *The Appraisal of Real Estate,* 4th ed. (1987), pp. 640–647.
6. The regression explanation provided in this section is designed to provide the reader with a basic understanding of regression analysis to assist in passing the residential appraisal examination. It is not intended to make the reader an "expert" in regression analysis. The focus is to provide sufficient knowledge to pass the exam.
7. Technically,, the equation is $Y = a + BX + e$, where e is the error term. However, for simplicity the error term was omitted here.
8. Some students may be puzzled by the treatment of negative and positive signs. The general rule is two positives result in a positive; one negative and one positive result in a negative; two negatives result in a positive.
9. This could also be stated as (new price − old price) ÷ old price.
10. This is equivalent to division by 100.

Key Terms and Concepts

Measures of central tendency:
- mean
- median
- mode

Measures of dispersion:
- range
- standard deviation
- variance
- coefficient of variation

Regression analysis

Basic mathematical skills:
- sequence for calculations:
  - multiplication and division
  - addition and subtraction
- parenthetical equations
- percentage change
- percentage adjustments

Review Questions

1. The most frequently occurring value in a distribution or a sample is the:
   a. mean.
   b. median.
   c. mode.
   d. standard deviation.

2. The measure of central tendency, which can be defined as the 50th percentile or "the one in the middle," is the:
   a. mean.
   b. median.
   c. mode.
   d. standard deviation.

3. A measure of dispersion, which is computed by taking the difference between the high and low values, is the:
   a. mean.
   b. range.
   c. coefficient of variation.
   d. standard deviation.

4. Two uses of statistics are _____ and _____.
   a. to impress, to show off
   b. description, inference
   c. description, demographics
   d. inference, prediction

Refer to the following data to answer questions 5–7.

Suppose you are appraising a house with three bedrooms and two bathrooms. Analysis of the market reveals ten similar sales. These sales and their sales prices are as follows:

Number of Sales	Sale Price
1	$55,000
2	$60,000
3	$57,000
2	$58,000
2	$62,000

5. What is the median sale price?
   a. $55,000
   b. $60,000
   c. $57,000
   d. $58,000

6. What is the mean sale price?

   a. $55,000
   b. $60,000
   c. $57,000
   ✓d. $58,600

7. What is the range of sale prices? 55-62=7

   a. $55,000 to $62,000
   b. $60,000 to $60,000
   ✓c. $7,000
   d. $58,000

8. Suppose we have the following regression equation: $Yc = a + BX$. What does a represent?

   a. Independent variable
   b. Dependent variable
   c. Slope of the line
   ✓d. Intercept of the line with the Y axis

9. In equation shown in question 11, what does B represent?

   a. Independent variable
   b. Dependent variable
   ✓c. Slope of the line
   d. Intercept of the line with the Y axis

10. In a normal distribution, _____ percent of the observations lie between the mean and plus or minus one standard deviation.

    a. 34.13
    b. 95.44
    ✓c. 68.26
    d. 99.74

11. In a normal distribution, _____ percent of the observations lie between the mean and plus or minus two standard deviations.

    a. 34.13
    ✓b. 95.44
    c. 68.26
    d. 99.74

10 The Sales Comparison Approach

Overview

This chapter provides the rationale and background for the sales comparison approach, one of three generally accepted approaches to real property valuation. (The two other approaches are the cost approach and the income approach, discussed in Chapters 12 and 13 respectively.) For most residential appraisals, sales comparison is the most applicable approach. The chapter also provides "how to" steps to lead the student through this approach. Adjustments are presented in their proper sequence and based on the elements of comparison. Finally, a reconciled value estimate is developed.

Learning Objectives

After completing this chapter, the student should be able to:

- Explain the rationale of the sales comparison approach
- List the economic principles underlying the sales comparison approach and understand why each principle is important
- Outline the requirements of the sales comparison approach
- Explain the issues in selecting appropriate comparable properties
- Describe the steps in the adjustment process
- Develop an estimate of value using the sales comparison approach, including reconciliation

I. Overview of the Process

A. Relationship to Underlying Valuation Principles

The sales comparison approach is based on several economic principles. These include the principles of substitution, balance, supply and demand, and externalities. The principle of substitution holds that a typically informed purchaser would not be willing to pay more for a property than the cost of acquiring an equally desirable substitute, assuming that no excess waiting time was required. Thus the substitute may be an existing property or construction of a new one, assuming no undue cost or delay.

The principle of supply and demand asserts that the interaction of supply and demand has an effect on price. The desire by potential purchasers for a given area affects prices in that area. Likewise, the amount of space offered for sale in an area also affects prices. Balance also affects prices. Supply and demand tend to move toward a market clearing point (equilibrium) where quantity supplied equals quantity demanded. However, this point of balance is constantly changing. Externalities also affect prices and, hence, the sales comparison approach. External forces have positive and negative impacts on property values and sales prices.

B. Research and Selection of Comparables

The sales comparison approach is most applicable when there is an active market of recent, similar sales. As already mentioned, this approach usually is most applicable for residential properties. Sometimes, however—even with residential appraisal assignments—this approach may be inappropriate or may have limited application. For example, if there are no sales of similar, competing properties, this approach has limited (if any) application.

The sales comparison approach is used to estimate the market value of the property being appraised (the **subject property** or, simply, the subject) by comparing it to properties that are considered similar (called **comparables** or **comps**) with respect to physical, environmental and economic characteristics. In other words, the subject is compared to properties that are considered comparable in the mind of a hypothetical, typically informed potential purchaser. Comparables also must be considered competitive. That is, some comparables may be quite similar, others may have offsetting features and still others may be superior (or inferior) overall.

Because properties vary in their characteristics, **adjustments** are made to compensate for these differences. It is important to emphasize that the *local* market sets the standard for adjustments. Adjustments are always made to the comparables based on market evidence. Neither the appraiser's personal preferences (bias) nor the cost of the item should be a factor for making adjustments.

The subject is never adjusted; the comparables are adjusted to the subject. Comparable properties are adjusted to the subject in an effort to estimate what the comparable would have sold for if it had the characteristics of the subject that materially influence value.

Adjustments are made for key points of significant difference between the comparable sale and the subject. Occasionally an appraiser will be faced with an assignment where there have been no confirmed sales of similar properties. If this happens, the appraiser should consider pending contracts, offers and listings of similar property. A *pending contract* is one for which a sales contract has been signed by all parties to the transaction but the deed has not been conveyed from the seller to the purchaser. The "closing" has not occurred. A *closed sale* is one for which a deed or land contract has been delivered to the grantee (purchaser) by the grantor (seller).

1. Data Sources—Sources of comparable sales data (**data sources**) include data from the appraiser's files as well as data from other appraisers, real estate brokers, mortgage lenders, attorneys and title insurance companies.

2. Verification—Regardless of the data source, the appraiser should document each comparable sale. This **verification** is required to ensure the validity of the data used in the appraisal report.

C. Steps in the Sales Comparison Approach

Primarily an application of the principle of substitution, the sales comparison approach is essentially used to discover what competitive properties have sold for recently on the local market and, through an appropriate adjustment process, to indicate what they would have sold for had they possessed all the pertinent physical and economic characteristics of the subject property. Indications of such adjusted sales prices are developed for several comparable sales. When appropriately rounded, these indications should fall into a clustered pattern to provide an indication of the market value of the subject property as of the appraisal date. The appraiser should follow five steps in the sales comparison approach to develop a value estimate. These five steps are outlined through the end of this chapter.

1. Research Market for Comparables—There is no set rule for selection of comparable properties; the critical component here is the appraiser's judgment. Selection of similar closed sales, pending sales or offers and listings should be based on sound reasoning and supported with appropriate documentation. The ideal situation is to have several identical comparables, but this may not be possible if data are unavailable. In most appraisal assignments, therefore, comparisons and decisions must be made and conclusions drawn with less information than desired. The question often arises as to whether to select comps primarily on the basis of geographic proximity (hopefully within the immediate area and set of neighborhood influences) or from properties some distance away but having greater physical similarity. The general rule, again, is to use comparables that would be considered by the typical buyer of the subject in the search process; if the buyer would consider the property along with the subject in making a buy decision, the comparable may be considered suitable. The appraiser must rely on his or her knowledge of the marketplace and personal judgment as the basis for selection of comparables.

    As for relying on geographic proximity versus physical similarity, then, it is usually wise to do both: some comps in geographic proximity reflect locational influences and others reflect precise physical similarities.

    For effective comparisons, detailed information must be obtained about each of the comparable sales properties. This requires a systematic data program whereby pertinent characteristics of the subject property can be itemized—for example, size, age, location and overall competitiveness of properties. Those same points should then be covered consistently for each comparable sales property.

    Not every residential property that has recently sold on the local market is a comparable sale. Physical characteristics, market conditions and terms of sale must be investigated. Again, the appraiser's judgment comes into play. The basic test of whether the selection is appropriate is to ask, "Is the comp sale competitive with the subject property in the mind of the typical informed purchaser?"

2. Verify Data for Comparables—All transaction data (especially sales price, date, terms of sale and financing, and motivating forces) must be verified by the appraiser with the buyer or the seller, or with an

authorized agent of either. Failure to do so can result in distortion, misinterpretation or misrepresentation by the appraiser. Common deviations from bona fide arm's-length transactions in residential sales include: (1) liquidation from inheritance tax or other pressing reasons (no "reasonable" market exposure); (2) tax gain or tax considerations in the sale; (3) transactions between related or affiliated parties under non-market conditions—(for example, sale of a residence to a son or daughter); (4) superior bargaining power on the part of one party to the transaction—(for example, if the buyer owns part of the property and needs to acquire the remaining interests in the property, the seller might have a superior bargaining position).

a. In verifying transactions data, the appraiser must pay particular attention to the terms of financing and to **conditions of sale** (motivating forces) in selecting and analyzing comparable sales properties. Physical and locational characteristics should, of course, be carefully and accurately identified and analyzed.

b. There is no preset minimum number of comparable sales that must be obtained by the appraiser to perform an appropriate sales comparison analysis. However, the appraiser should use as many comparable sales as he or she can identify and verify. Conventional wisdom dictates that three to four "good" comparable sales transactions are sufficient to represent the competitive market. This view has been reinforced by the fact that most appraisal report forms (such as the Uniform Residential Appraisal Report) require only three comparable sales transactions.

3. Develop Appropriate Units of Comparison and Analyze Each Relevant Unit—Several units of comparison are appropriate in an appraisal so as to compare different properties, yet standardize the comparison. For example, a common unit of comparison for residential properties is *price per square foot* (of heated area). This standardized unit of comparison allows appraisers to account for some price differences based on size. Moreover, the chosen unit (or units) of comparison should be market-based and a function of the appraisal problem. If many market participants use this as a unit of comparison, appraisers should use this as a unit of comparison.

Some standard units of comparison include **price per acre, price per square foot, price per cubic foot, price per front foot, price per room, price per bed** and **price per gross rent.** The most common unit of comparison for residential properties is price per square foot, whereas the most common unit of comparison for farmland is price per acre. Commercial lots may be appraised using a price per front foot as a unit of comparison; however, local market participants may price commercial lots on the price per square foot of land area. Apartments may be analyzed and compared on the basis of price per room, price per unit or price per square foot. Gross rent per unit also may be used as a unit of comparison of residential property, especially for apartments.

Knowledge of the local marketplace and an accurate definition of the appraisal problem are two critical elements of successful appraising. Selection of the appropriate unit of comparison will depend on the appraiser's judgment and experience and on the local market standard.

4. Compare Each Comparable Sale, and Adjust Each Comparable to the Subject Using the Elements of Comparison in Proper Sequence—As already noted, sales prices of comparable sales are adjusted to the subject, not vice versa. The subject is, in effect, 100 percent (the base) of an index.

   a. In estimating the adjustment to make for the presence or lack of salient factor, the only valid measure is evidence of market reactions of buyers to such a difference. These reactions are reflected in varying sales prices of otherwise identical properties with and without the factor in question (if such evidence is available). Cost is not the appropriate measure of the difference, for cost to install may or may not equal the sales price differential reflected in market behavior of buyers. *Every adjustment should be justified by market evidence.* Examination of market behavior of typical buyers may reveal that a particular deficiency or superiority is not reflected in a sales price differential, even though the appraiser believes that it "should be." If the market does not recognize a difference, the appraiser should not recognize it in the adjustment process.

   b. The types of adjustment are dollar adjustments and percentage adjustments.

      1) **Dollar adjustments** are the differences between the comparables and the subject, stated in dollar amounts.

      2) **Percentage adjustments** are the differences between the comparables and the subject, stated in percentages with the subject representing 100 percent. For example, if a comparable is 10 percent *better than* the subject, the comparable is 110 percent of the subject; if the comparable is 10 percent *worse than* the subject, the comparable is 90 percent of the subject.

c. **Elements of comparison** are those items for which market participants perceive differences, thus causing real estate prices to vary. (Specific elements of comparison have been listed under d., "sequence of adjustments.") **Property rights** should be similar for both the subject and comparables. For example, if the subject is a fee simple interest, the comps also should be fee simple.

The type and term of **financing** may also be important to market participants. For example, a potential purchaser would be willing to pay more for a 6 percent loan if the market rate were 14 percent.

Market conditions generally mandate adjustments for price differences that arise over time. However, changing economic conditions in the marketplace are also included in this element of comparison.

Location adjustments are made to comparable sales to adjust them to the subject's location. Generally, **location adjustments** are required when sales (or the subject) are in different neighborhoods.

Physical differences between comparables and the subject may also require adjustment. Differences such as building size, quality of construction and age are some physical differences that require adjustment; other differences include income differences, quality of tenants (tenant mix) and quality of management.

d. **Sequence of adjustments** refers to the proper prioritizing for making adjustments. If dollar adjustments are used, the sequence of adjustments does not affect the final adjusted sales prices of the comparables, nor does it affect the estimated value of the subject. However, if percentage adjustments or cumulative percentage adjustments are used, the sequence of adjustments may affect both the adjusted sales prices of comparables and the estimated value of the subject. Therefore, as a matter of good appraisal practice, the appraiser should follow a logical priority sequence in every appraisal assignment, defined in the following sections.

1) Did the comparables convey the same property rights as the subject? For example, if the subject involves conveyance of a fee simple ownership interest, do the comparables also convey a fee simple interest? If not, the comparables must be adjusted or eliminated from consideration.

2) Is financing on the comparables at cash or cash equivalent terms or as defined in the appraisal report? If not, the comparables must be adjusted or eliminated from consideration.

3) Were the conditions of sale distorted or did the sale represent a bona fide, arm's-length transaction? In most situations, the sale must be eliminated from consideration as a possible comparable sale.

4) Market conditions may be related to time or to general economic conditions. Were the comp sales made under similar market conditions prevailing at the date of the value estimate, or have the market conditions changed? If market conditions were not similar, the comparables must be adjusted or eliminated from consideration.

5) Are there locational differences between the subject and comparables? If yes, the comparables must be adjusted or eliminated from consideration.

6) Are there physical differences between the subject and comparables? If yes, the comparables must be adjusted or eliminated from consideration.

e. In calculating adjustments, the objective is to measure what difference the presence, absence or variation in an element of comparison makes to sales price. The adjustment process is based on the principle of contribution, which states that the value of an item is the value that the item contributes to value by virtue of its presence or detracts from value by virtue of its absence. The amounts and directions of adjustments are determined by, and derived from, the market behavior of buyers, as reflected in sales price differentials.

The process of making adjustments is usually accomplished through **paired sales** (or **paired data**) **analysis.** Ideally, two similar sales are identified and verified, except for the item being valued. For example, suppose an appraiser was estimating the value of a swimming pool in the local marketplace. Two houses that were very similar—except one had a swimming pool—were identified and verified in the marketplace. Suppose the house with the pool sold for $225,000 and the house without the pool sold for $200,000. The adjustment for a swimming pool for that neighborhood would be the difference of $25,000 ($225,000 − $200,000 = $25,000).

Whether the adjustment is negative (−) or positive (+) is determined by the relationship between the comparable to be adjusted and the subject. First, a specified dollar or percentage is estimated for an element of comparison (for example, the $25,000 for the swimming pool shown above). Second, each comparable sale is compared to the subject for that element. If the comparable is better than the subject, then subtract the amount that is better from the sales price of the comparable ("comp better subtract"). If the comparable is poorer than the subject, then add the amount to the comparable sales price ("comp poorer add").

After each element of comparison has been addressed, the adjustments for each comparable should be summarized into total net adjustments. For example, suppose a comparable had a +$3,000 adjustment for market conditions and a –$2,000 adjustment for location. The net adjustment would be +$1,000 (+3,000 – 2,000 = $1,000). This net adjustment is then added or subtracted (depending on the sign) to the sales price of the comparable to arrive at an adjusted sales price for the comparable. For example, if the sales price for a comparable was $100,000 and the total net adjustment was $1,000, the adjusted sales price would be $101,000 ($100,000 + $1,000 = $101,000).

5. Reconcile the Adjusted Sales Prices into a Single Estimate of Value (or Range of Values)—After each comparable sale has been adjusted and an adjusted sales price estimated, the appraiser will be faced with several similar sales with different indicated sales prices. These should fall within a relatively reasonable range, if the comparable sales data are truly comparable and competitive with the subject and if the proper adjustments have been made. Appraisers should use individual judgment to estimate which comparable sale is *most* similar to the subject. Generally those comparable sales that require the least adjustment receive greatest emphasis as the best indicators of the subject's market value—provided the proper adjustments have been made; judgment, experience, logic and analysis are all required. The appraiser must then select the most appropriate indicated market value of the subject site, based on the estimate of the quality and quantity of data utilized and the justification for each adjustment. Once similar sales have been identified and verified, they should be eliminated based on noncomparability, or compared to the subject based on units of comparison.

Key Terms and Concepts

Subject property (subject)
Comparables (comps)
Adjustments:
    data sources
    verification
Steps in sales comparison approach:
    units of comparison
        price per acre
        price per square foot
        price per cubic foot
        price per front foot
        price per room
        price per bed
        price per gross rent
Dollar adjustments
Percentage adjustments
Elements of comparison:
    property rights
    financing
    conditions of sale
    market conditions
    locational differences
    physical differences
Sequence of adjustments
Paired sales (paired data) analysis

Review Questions

1. For residential properties, the sales comparison approach is primarily based on the principle of:

   a. change.
   b. conformity.
   c. externalities.
   d. substitution.

2. Market value estimates in the sales comparison approach are through the eyes of:

   a. typically informed purchasers.
   b. typically informed sellers.
   c. typically informed brokers.
   d. uninformed buyers.

3. One major constraint of the sales comparison approach is that it requires:

   a. several new constructions.
   b. an active market of competitive properties.
   c. accurate cost information.
   d. accurate information on investor expectations.

4. When the appraiser researches the market for data not previously collected, such data are called:

   a. secondary data.
   b. primary data.
   c. useful data.
   d. quantitative data.

5. Adjustments are made to the:

   a. subject to make it like the comparables.
   b. comparables to make them like the subject.
   c. subject to make it like the market.
   d. comparables to make them like the market.

6. One technique used for making adjustments is based on estimating the amount of adjustment for the presence or absence of a factor. This technique is called:

   a. regression analysis.
   b. grid analysis.
   c. paired sales analysis.
   d. cost analysis.

7. Which approach is usually the MOST applicable approach for appraising residential properties?

    a. Cost
    b. Sales comparison
    c. Income
    d. Cost and income

8. Types of adjustments include:

    a. percentage.
    b. comps to subject.
    c. subject to comps.
    d. dollar and percentage.

9. The proper order of adjustments is referred to as the:

    a. elements of comparison.
    b. sequence of adjustments.
    c. types of adjustments.
    d. reconciliation.

10. Adjustments using paired sales analysis in the sales comparison approach should be:

    a. direct.
    b. market-justified.
    c. dollar amounts.
    d. indirect.

11. The objective of any appraisal is to:

    a. collect the fee.
    b. estimate market value.
    c. estimate value as defined.
    d. estimate value in exchange.

12. The sales comparison approach requires what minimum number of sales?

    a. Three
    b. Six
    c. Four
    d. No set minimum number

Refer to the following data to answer questions 13–20.

The subject is a single-family residence that contains 2,000 square feet of living area. Constructed 10 years ago, the subject has 4 bedrooms and 2 bathrooms. Other amenities include a 2-car garage and a basement. The seller has agreed to provide a special financing package on the house worth $4,000. Examination of the market has revealed several sales of competitive properties:

Comparable 1 has 1,800 square feet of living area with 3 bedrooms and 2 bathrooms. It has a 1-car garage but no basement. It sold approximately one year ago for $175,000 at financing terms typical of the market.

Comparable 2 has 2,000 square feet of living area with a 2-car garage, 4 bedrooms and 2 bathrooms. It sold one year ago for $180,000 at terms generally available in the marketplace. In addition, the comparable had a 2-car garage but no basement.

Comparable 3 has 2,000 square feet of living area, 4 bedrooms and 2 bathrooms. It also has a 2-car garage, and a basement. It sold one week ago for $200,000 at financing terms typical of the market.

13. What should be the magnitude, sign and sequence of the adjustment to the comparables for financing?

    a. 0, 0, 0
    b. +4,000, +4,000, +4,000
    c. −4,000, −4,000, −4,000
    d. +2,000, +2,000, +2,000

14. What should be the magnitude, sign and sequence of the adjustment to the subject for financing?

    a. 0, 0, 0
    b. +4,000, +4,000, +4,000
    c. −4,000, −4,000, −4,000
    d. The subject should not be adjusted.

15. Further research reveals that an additional comparable (comparable 4), similar to comparable 3, sold one year ago for $190,500. Also, two other sales (comparables 5 and 6) in the same neighborhood were discovered to be the same as the other comparables, and similar to each other, except for the date of sale. Comparable 5 sold six months ago for $175,600 and comparable 6 sold last week for $180,000. What should be the magnitude, sign and sequence of the adjustments for comparables 1, 2 and 3 for time?

    a. 0, 0, 0
    b. +8,750, +9,000, +10,000
    c. −8,750, −9,000, −10,000
    d. +8,750, +9,000, +0

16. What should be the magnitude, sign and sequence of the adjustments for comparables 1, 2 and 3 for basement?   180,000 + 9,000 = 189,000

    a. +21,000, +21,000, +21,000
    b. +11,000, +11,000, 0
    c. −21,000, −21,000, −21,000
    d. +20,000, +20,000, +20,000

17. In the appraiser's research efforts in the subject's neighborhood, a 2-car garage is discovered to carry a $3,000 premium over a 1-car garage. The magnitude, sign and sequence of the adjustments for comparables 1, 2 and 3 for garage are:

    a. 0, 0, 0.
    b. 0, as no adjustment is necessary.
    c. +6,000, 0, 0.
    d. +3,000, 0, 0.

18. What should be the magnitude, sign and sequence of the adjustments for comparables 1, 2 and 3 for square footage including extra rooms?

    a. 0, 0, 0   c. +2,250, +2,250, +2,250
    b. +2,250, +2,250, 0   d. +2,250, 0, 0

19. What are the total adjustments for comparables 1, 2 and 3?

    a. 0, 0, 0   c. +25,000, +20,000, +0
    b. +39,000, +34,000, +14,000   d. −39,000, −34,000, −14,000

20. What is the adjusted sales prices of comparables 1, 2 and 3?

    a. $175,000, $180,000, $200,000
    b. $214,000, $214,000, $214,000
    c. $210,000, $210,000, $210,000
    d. $200,000, $200,000, $200,000

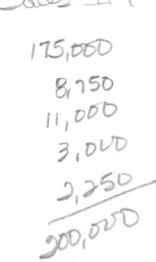

11 Site Valuation

Overview

This chapter reviews site valuation, along with the techniques for site valuation, plottage and assemblage.

Learning Objectives

After completing this chapter, the student should be able to:

- Describe the different techniques for site valuation

- Work a site valuation problem

I. Techniques for Site Valuation

Site valuation, usually performed as a separate step in the appraisal, is the process of estimating the value of a site as if vacant and available to be put to its highest and best use. No one method of site valuation is preferable in every situation. Several techniques are available, each with its own merits and limitations. The techniques commonly used for site valuation include sales comparison, allocation or abstraction, extraction, land residual, capitalization of ground rents, and subdivision or development.

A. Sales Comparison

Valuation of the site using the sales comparison approach assumes that an active market of similar site sales exists. Whenever sales data of adequate quantity and sufficient quality are available, sales comparison is the preferred method to employ in site valuation (particularly for residential site valuation). The underlying presumption is that recent sales transactions of comparable sites competitive with the subject site on the local market are the best guide to the most probable current market behavior and reactions of typically informed purchasers. There is no fundamental difference between the valuation process of improved properties and vacant sites using sales comparisons.

1. Rationale—Sales comparison analysis for site valuation basically applies the principle of substitution: a typically informed and prudent purchaser will pay no more for a residential site than the cost of acquiring a substitute site with the same or similar amenities and utility.

2. Requirements—The criteria for applying sales comparison analysis to residential site valuation include complete and detailed site description, an active market to provide sales transaction data on competitive (comparable) sites, sufficient quality and quantity of data and verification of data.

3. Units of Comparison—Frequently it is desirable to account for minor physical variations in lot size by reducing the valuation analysis to a unit basis. This makes it possible to directly compare sites that vary in size or shape. Selection of the appropriate unit of comparison will depend on the appraiser's judgment and experience and the local market standard. Some common units of comparison in residential properties follow.

a. *Price per front foot* is frequently measured in terms of a standard depth. Front-foot measures are generally applicable in built-up areas, often for relatively small lots.

b. *Price per square foot* is frequently used for expensive residential sites and for large and/or irregularly shaped lots.

c. *Price per lot or building site* accommodates minor variations in lot sizes that may not significantly or measurably influence value. The unit of measure is simply the standard one-unit building lot.

d. *Price per acre* is utilized more for raw land valuation than for building site valuation, except in rural areas or large lot developments where prices vary widely with size differences.

B. Allocation (Abstraction) Technique

The **allocation technique**, also known as the **abstraction technique,** involves allocating the total property value into a site value and a building value. Typically a ratio of site value to total property value is used. This ratio may be determined from the appraiser's experience in the local market area. Based on experience, an appraiser may have prior knowledge that, historically, sites in a given neighborhood sell for 35 percent of total sales price. In addition, an appraiser may utilize assessors' site to total property value ratios for a given area. Use of a constant ratio assumes that the relationship is constant over time—a questionable assumption at best. However, this technique may be useful in situations where there are no vacant site sales, such as well-developed subdivisions or rural areas with few transactions.

The allocation method has limited applicability as an indicator of value. The appraiser must be able to justify a division of value or sales price of improved residential properties between the site and the buildings. It should be applied only if there are no current sales data for vacant sites.

C. Extraction Technique

The **extraction technique**, a variation of the allocation technique, involves estimating site value by taking the sale price of the total property and subtracting the depreciated cost of the improvements. For example, suppose a comparable residence recently sold for $58,500. The site is highly competitive with the subject site in all respects. The building is a "typical" improvement, estimated to have a depreciated present worth of $42,000. The site is worth $16,500 ($58,500 − $42,000 = $16,500). Thus the site is 28 percent of sales

Figure 11.1 Plottage and Assemblage

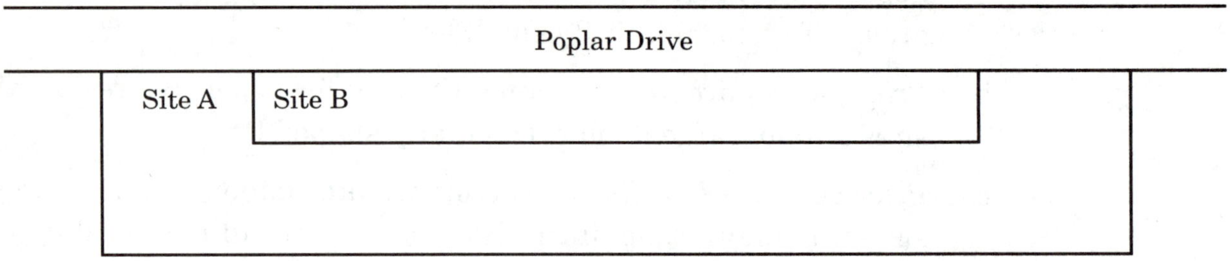

```
                           Poplar Drive
        ┌──────┬─────────────────────────────────────┐
        │Site A│ Site B                              │
        │      └──────────────────────────────┐      │
        │                                     │      │
        └─────────────────────────────────────┘──────┘
```

price ($16,500 ÷ $58,500 = .28), and the building represents 72 percent of sales price ($42,000 ÷ $58,500 = .72).

D. Land Residual Technique

The **land residual technique** is most applicable for the valuation of income-producing sites. The method is beyond the scope of the residential examination; however, it is included in the Uniform Content Outline for the General Exam.

E. Capitalization of Ground Rents

Capitalization of ground rental streams may be useful for the valuation of income-producing properties. (Residential properties usually do not have income streams attached to them.) This technique is not included on the Residential Exam Uniform Content Outline prepared by the Appraiser Qualifications Board of The Appraisal Foundation. However, this topic appears on the Uniform Content Outline for the General Exam.

F. Subdivision (Land Development)

The **subdivision method** is most applicable for the valuation of sites in new residential developments. However, because this technique is beyond the scope of the residential examination it is not addressed here.

II. Plottage Value and Assemblage

Sometimes an appraisal assignment may uncover market data that support the conclusion that two sites, when combined, have a greater value than the sum of the two individual sites. For example, in Figure 11.1 sites A and B are located on Poplar Drive. Site A has 20 feet of frontage but is a deep lot; site B has 200 feet of frontage but is very narrow. Site A has a value of $5,000, whereas site B has a value of $10,000. The sum of their individual values is $15,000. However, when combined, sites A and B have a value of $20,000 because of the increased frontage and added depth. Additional value from combining parcels A and B (plottage value) is $5,000.

The added value from combining two or more sites into a single parcel[1] having greater utility than the smaller, individual sites is termed **plottage value.**[2] **Assemblage** is the combining of two or more parcels into one ownership.[3]

Endnotes

1. Technically, the combination does not have to be two or more sites into a larger single site. The technical requirement is that two or more sites must be combined under a single ownership. The sites do not have to be contiguous, but in most cases they are. Plottage value can also be *negative;* the value of one larger parcel can be less than the combined values of the individual parcels.
2. Appraisal Institute, *The Dictionary of Real Estate Appraisal,* 2nd ed. (1989), p. 229.
3. Ibid., p. 18.

Key Terms and Concepts

Site valuation
Allocation (abstraction) technique
Extraction technique
Land residual technique
Capitalization of ground rents
Subdivision (development) method
Plottage value
Assemblage

Review Questions

1. The added utility (added value) from combining two or more sites into one larger parcel is:

    a. assemblage.
    b. plottage.
    c. plottage value.
    d. added cost.

2. The process of combining two or more parcels into one ownership is:

    a. assemblage.
    b. plottage.
    c. plottage value.
    d. added cost.

3. The technique for site valuation in which the depreciated reproduction cost of improvements is deducted from sales prices of comparable improved properties is:

    a. sales comparison.
    b. allocation.
    c. extraction.
    d. land residual.

4. One technique for site valuation for new developments is:

    a. land residual.
    b. extraction.
    c. subdivision (development).
    d. allocation (abstraction).

5. Site value is typically estimated as if:

    a. vacant.
    b. vacant and available to be put to highest and best use.
    c. improved and available to be put to highest and best use.
    d. improved.

6. If similar sales of vacant sites are available, the _____ technique for site valuation is preferred.

    a. allocation
    b. abstraction
    c. extraction
    d. sales comparison

Refer to the following data to answer questions 7-9.

Sales Comparison Approach Problem—Site Valuation

The subject is a residential lot located on the interior portion of the street. Rectangular in shape, it measures 150' × 100'. The site is level with good drainage and adequate public utilities for the marketplace. In fact, the subject has drainage, topography and view equivalent to competing parcels. The date of the value estimate is July 1, 1990. Several similar vacant lot sales have been noted in the marketplace.

Comparable 1 sold July 1, 1989, for $30,000. It was in a square shape, of 140' × 140'. The comparable was located on the interior of a residential street.

Comparable 2 sold JULY 1, 1989 for $22,000. It was in a rectangular shape, of 125' × 110'. It was located on the corner of two residential streets. The appraiser noted that comp 2 was generally similar to the subject in all other aspects.

Comparable 3 sold one week ago for $20,000. It was rectangular in shape and measured 150' × 100'. It was located on a corner lot at the intersection of two residential streets. All other aspects were similar to the subject.

Comparables 4 and *5* were similar to each other except for date of sale. Comparable 4 sold one year ago for $1.50 per square foot, and comparable 5 sold yesterday for $1.59 per square foot. Additional market evidence indicates that corner lots sell for $.05 more per square foot than interior lots.

7. What are the indicated units of comparision for the comparables?
   a. Price per acre or price per front foot
   b. Price per front foot or price per cubic foot
   c. Price per square foot or price per acre
   d. Price per cubic foot or price per square foot

8. What are the indicated sales prices of comparables 1, 2 and 3, stated in an appropriate unit of comparison?
   a. $1.53, $1.60, $1.33 per square foot
   b. $66,667, $69,690, $82,600 per hectare.
   c. $1.25, $1.23, $1.18 per cubic foot
   d. $12.59, $13.22, $11.27 per front foot

9. What is the indicated dollar adjustment to comparables 1, 2 and 3 for market conditions?

   a. +$1,800, +$1,320, +$1,200
   b. +6%, +6%, 0
   c. +$1,800, +$1,320, +0
   d. +.09, +.05, +0

12 The Cost Approach

Overview

This chapter examines the cost approach, one of three approaches to value as applied to new or relatively new structures. In addition, the cost approach has application to "no market" appraisals.

Learning Objectives

After completing this chapter and working the sample cost approach problem, the student should be able to:

- Identify the steps in the cost approach

- List the economic principles underlying the cost approach

- List and define the types of costs

- List and define the types of accrued depreciation

- Define the differences between long-lived and short-lived items

- Define the differences between curable and incurable items of depreciation

- Use the different methods for estimating depreciation

- Define the concepts of total economic life, remaining economic life, actual age and effective age

I. Cost Approach

A. Rationale

The basic premise of the **cost approach** is that total property value is equal to the sum of site value plus contribution of improvements. The value of the site is estimated as if vacant and available to be put to its highest and best use. The depreciated value (contribution) of the improvements is added to site value to estimate value by the cost approach. Cost estimates for the improvements are derived from interviews with contractors, building supply houses, professional cost estimators, engineers' estimates, and from published cost services.

The cost approach assumes a hypothetical buyer considers producing a substitute residence that has the same utility as the subject property. The measure of value by this approach is the cost to this informed and rational purchaser (not the cost to a builder/contractor). The approach is based on the concept that value is evidenced by the cost to the purchaser to create a substitute property and utility package.

Costs to the buyer include site value and all direct and indirect construction costs including the builder's overhead and profit. In considering production of a residence of like utility, it is important to consider the cost to the buyer of producing an exact replica of the subject, in the same location and condition as the subject as of the valuation date.

The cost approach assumes a market orientation. That is, the standard employed as the appraiser applies the cost approach to the subject should be the standard in the local marketplace. However, cost is not necessarily the same as market value. Cost is related to price and is based on production. If typically informed market participants relate cost to market value, there will be a strong relationship between cost and market value. The goal of the appraiser using the cost approach is to estimate this relationship utilizing individual judgment, experience and professional training.

B. Applications and Limitations of the Cost Approach

The cost approach represents a normal check-and-balance within the framework of the three approaches to value. It is most applicable in two situations—appraisals on properties with new or almost-new improvements and appraisals on unique or "no market" properties. For example, the cost approach might be very applicable for valuation of a new residence, likewise it might be equally applicable for valuation of an automobile auction (unique property). If a market has several recent sales of property similar to the subject, the cost approach has less application because market participants should gather more price information from the marketplace.

Estimation of cost new—whether reproduction or replacement—involves judgment and therefore is subject to error. Moreover, estimation of depreciation is difficult at best (properties with old improvements have the most accrued depreciation). Because it is difficult to estimate the amount of total accrued depreciation accurately, the cost approach has limited application for properties with older improvements.

C. Valuation Principles

Several valuation principles underlie the cost approach: the principles of substitution, contribution, balance, and highest and best use. The principle of substitution is most applicable because a typically informed purchaser should pay no more for a property than the cost of constructing one with similar utility, assuming no excess delay is required. The value of improvements can be measured by the amount that they add to total property value; this is related to the concept of contribution, for there is an optimal amount of improvements for each site. This optimal amount is where value is enhanced because the factors of production (land, labor, capital and entrepreneurship) are in balance. Finally, highest and best use is important in the cost approach because it serves as the basis for site valuation.

D. Steps in the Cost Approach

To estimate value using the cost approach, the appraiser should follow a logical, step-by-step sequence toward a value estimate. This sequence is as follows:

1. Estimate Site Value—Estimate the value of the site as if vacant and available for highest and best use. Site value is estimated using one of the techniques presented in Chapter 6. The preferable and most common technique for site valuation is the sales comparison approach. Other methods of site valuation include the allocation procedure, the extraction method, the land residual technique, the subdivision development technique and ground rent capitalization.

2. Estimate Cost New of Improvements—The second step in the cost approach is to estimate the cost of the improvements as if they were new. There are two types of new costs: reproduction costs and replacement costs (discussed below). However, in most instances, the appraiser will be estimating reproduction cost new.[1]

3. Estimate All Elements of Accrued Depreciation—Accrued depreciation is a loss in value from all sources due to a loss in utility. Accrued depreciation, as it relates to real estate appraisal, is economic in nature and occurs in three forms: physical deterioration, functional obsolescence and external obsolescence.

4. Subtract for Estimate of Depreciated Cost New—Subtract total accrued depreciation from cost new to get an estimate of the depreciated cost new of the improvements.

5. Add Value of Improvements to Site Value—Add estimated depreciated present worth or contribution of improvements to the value of the site. Improvements may be of two forms: those *on* the site (such as buildings) and those *to* the site (such as grading and utilities). Improvements to the site are those necessary to prepare the land for its intended use.[2]

6. Round the Estimate—*Round the resulting conclusion* to show that the number is an estimate and not a precise mathematical calculation.

E. **Estimating Cost New**

1. Reproduction versus Replacement Cost—When estimating cost new, the appraiser will either be seeking an estimate of reproduction cost new or replacement cost new. *Reproduction cost* is the cost to construct an exact replica of the subject. *Replacement cost* is the cost to construct a structure having similar or equal utility to the subject, but constructed with modern standards and materials. In most appraisals, the appraiser should estimate reproduction cost new. Replacement cost implicitly assumes that there is no functional obsolescence (except superadequacies), because it is the cost to construct a structure having similar utility but built with modern materials and to current standards.

2. Techniques for Estimating Cost New—Several techniques are commonly available for estimating the cost of new improvements: the quantity survey technique, the unit-in-place method and the comparative unit method.[3]

a. The **quantity survey method** is the most complete and detailed method of new cost estimation. Local contractors, suppliers, subcontractors, developers and others in the construction industry are surveyed to obtain detailed cost estimates by type of improvement. Although this method is the most complete and detailed method, it is seldom used in residential appraisals; it is costly and very time consuming.

b. The **unit-in-place method** asks the question, "What does it cost to put a unit, such as the roof, in place?" Each major component of the subject is estimated on the assumption that it is "in place." Published cost manuals may be used to apply this technique.

c. Many appraisers use the **comparative unit method**, which estimates a total cost per square foot or per cubic foot. These estimates are obtained from published cost manuals.[4] The cost per square foot or per cubic foot is multiplied times the number of square feet or cubic feet in the subject. Because the cost manuals are based on past cost information, the appraiser must adjust those past costs to current estimates by multiplying the published cost times a current multiplier. In that costs are based on national averages, the appraiser must adjust these costs to his or her local area by multiplying the current adjusted cost times the local multiplier.[5] Appraisers should be cautious of published cost sources because they are based on national trends and may not be indicative of the local marketplace.

3. Types of Costs—Quantity survey, comparative unit and unit in place are techniques for estimating cost new, but in some instances the appraiser must estimate the different cost components including direct cost, indirect cost, overhead and entrepreneurial or managerial profit. For example, suppose an appraiser has been hired to appraise a proposed house from a set of plans and specifications. To apply the cost approach, the appraiser should know the amount of direct cost, indirect cost and entrepreneurial (managerial) profit.

   a. **Direct costs** encompass the "hard" costs of construction, the two most common of which are materials and labor. A distinguishing characteristic of direct cost is that it can be assigned to a particular house. For example, materials and labor can be assigned to one house, but a computer needed to design the house plan cannot be assigned so easily. Computer time must be allocated between several houses.

b. **Indirect costs** cannot be assigned to a given structure but must be allocated. Some examples include architect fees, management costs and development costs common to all lots such as costs of the streets, builder's overhead and profit, surveyor and engineering fees, financing charges and fees, and selling expenses.

c. **Entrepreneurial** or **managerial profit (coordination)** is the developer's profit for undertaking the development.

II. Accrued Depreciation

Accrued depreciation is a loss in value (because of a loss in utility) from all sources, "the difference between an improvement's reproduction or replacement cost new and its market value as of the date of the appraisal."[6] In measuring accrued depreciation, the appraiser is interested in identifying and measuring the loss in utility experienced by the subject structure in its present condition, as compared to the utility it would have as a new improvement representing the highest and best use of the site.

Accrued depreciation is applied only to the improvements, never to land. The rationale is that land generally does not economically waste away and any decline in land values is the result of market forces.[7]

Accrued depreciation may be divided into three broad categories: physical deterioration, functional obsolescence and external obsolescence. Physical deterioration and functional obsolescence result within the subject's boundaries, whereas external obsolescence results outside the subject's boundaries.

A. Physical Deterioration

Physical deterioration is a loss in value as a result of the passage of time or a wasting away caused by the elements. In essence, physical deterioration is deferred maintenance. Items of physical deterioration may be curable or incurable.[8]

1. Curable—An item of physical deterioration is **curable** if the cost to cure is less than or equal to the value added by "curing" the problem.

2. Incurable—An item of physical deterioration is **incurable** if the cost to cure is greater than the value added by curing the problem. Items of incurable physical deterioration may be short-lived or long-lived.

a. **Short-lived** physical deterioration arises when the life of the item is less than the life of the structure. Examples of short-lived physical incurable deterioration items include carpeting, roofing and appliances.

b. **Long-lived** physical deterioration occurs where the economic life of the item is equal to the life of the structure. For example the foundation and exterior walls are long-lived items.

B. **Functional Obsolescence**

Functional obsolescence is a loss in value as a result of the subject not performing the function for which it was intended. Items of functional obsolescence may be curable or incurable. Functional obsolescence generally results inside the subject's property boundaries and is usually divided into three components: functional obsolescence arising from a deficiency, functional obsolescence arising from a defect and functional obsolescence arising from a superadequacy.

1. Functional Obsolescence (Deficiency)—A **deficiency** is a loss in value as a result of missing items or inadequacies, based on local market standards.

2. Functional Obsolescence (Defect)—A **defect** is a loss in value as a result of existing items not performing to local market standards.

3. Functional Obsolescence (Superadequacy)—A **superadequacy** is a loss in value as a result of existing items being far superior to local market standards.

C. **External Obsolescence**

External obsolescence is a loss in value as a result of external conditions. It is generally outside the subject's property boundaries and, as a result, is almost always incurable because the subject's owner usually can do little or nothing about the problem.[9] External obsolescence may be locational or economic in nature.

1. External obsolescence (**locational**)—The subject's proximity to a factor can cause a loss in utility. For example, a subject located near a hog farm causing noxious odors could cause a loss in utility and hence a loss in value.

2. External obsolescence (**economic**)—Economic factors can also cause external obsolescence. For example, high unemployment can cause a loss in utility for houses in a local market.

D. **Techniques for Estimating Depreciation**

Several techniques are available to the appraiser for estimating accrued depreciation. These methods include market abstraction (or market based), age-life method, the modified age-life method and the observed condition breakdown method.

1. Market Abstraction—**Market abstraction** is a technique for estimating depreciation directly from the marketplace. However, it requires several sales of properties similar to the subject. To compute an estimate of depreciation using this approach, the appraiser obtains the sales price of a similar sale in the marketplace and subtracts the site value. This "adjusted sales price" is the depreciated cost of the improvements. This depreciated cost of the improvements is then compared to the cost new of the improvements, with any difference being accrued depreciation. A major advantage of this approach is that it incorporates perceptions of market participants. However, one disadvantage of the market abstraction technique is that it does separate depreciation into its component parts.

2. Age-Life Method (Straight Line)—**The age-life method** is a very simple technique for estimating accrued depreciation. The formula for the age-life method is:

$$\frac{\text{Effective Age}}{\text{Total Economic Life}} \times \text{Cost New} = \text{Accrued Depreciation}$$

Total economic life is the time over which the improvements will contribute to value. The actual age of the property is equal to its **chronological age**. However, a property may have been well maintained. For example, a house may have an actual age of 10 years, but it may appear to be similar to 5-year-old houses because it has been well maintained. The "age" of the property considering its maintenance and preservation is its **effective age**, which, as seen, may be more (or less) than actual age.

Remaining economic life is total economic life minus effective age, or the remaining time over which the improvements will contribute to value. *Cost new* may be reproduction cost or replacement cost but is usually reproduction cost.

A major disadvantage of the age-life method is that it does not recognize curable elements independently. Curable physical and functional (and external too if curable) obsolescence are not addressed using this method.

3. Modified Age-Life Method—The **modified age-life method** is similar to the age-life method, except that curable items (physical and functional)[10] are removed before estimating the amount of depreciation. The formula for the modified age-life method is:

$$(\text{Cost New}^{11} - \text{Curable Items}) \times \frac{\text{Effective Age}}{\text{Total Economic Life}} = \text{Accrued Depreciation}$$

4. Observed Condition Breakdown—The **observed condition breakdown method** analyzes each component of depreciation and is the most detailed method for analyzing accrued depreciation. Items of depreciation are separated (or "broken down") into three components for analysis: physical components, functional components and external components.

   a. Physical deterioration is a loss in value as a result of the passage of time or a wasting away caused by the elements. In essence, physical deterioration is deferred maintenance. Items of physical deterioration may be curable or incurable.

      1) As already noted, an item is *curable* if the cost to cure is less than or equal to the value added by curing the problem. Curable physical items are those a prudent buyer would anticipate correcting upon purchase of the property. The measure of depreciation is usually the cost to cure. Examples are repair or replacement of a worn-out component (roof or floor tile); reconditioning (painting or wallpapering); repair of broken items (cracked windows or floor or wall tiles).

      2) An item is *incurable* if the cost to cure is greater than the value added by curing the problem. Items of incurable physical deterioration may be short-lived or long-lived.

         (a) A *short-lived item* of physical deterioration has a life that is less than the life of the structure. The effective age of each separate component is estimated as a percentage of the economic life of that component on a straight-line basis. The appropriate percentage is applied to the reproduction cost new of each component to estimate the amount of depreciation chargeable to incurable short-lived items.

(b) A *long-lived item* has an economic life that is equal to the life of the structure. Examples include the basic structural components (foundation, framing, partitions, subfloors) which normally have an economic life as long as that of the entire structure.

The effective age utilized in estimating incurable physical deterioration is the effective age after curable items are cured. Effecting the cure by replacing and/or rehabilitating "curable" items extends the remaining economic life of the structure, thereby reducing its effective age. The extension of remaining economic life (or reduction of effective age) resulting from effecting cures of "curable" items cannot be too long but it must be realistic in terms of what is cured, how much the cost to cure is, and the proportion of cost to cure in relation to total reproduction cost new.

b. Functional utility is the ability of the structure to perform the function for which it was intended. Lack of this ability is considered to be functional obsolescence, generally divided into three categories: functional obsolescence from a deficiency, functional obsolescence from a defect and functional obsolescence from a superadequacy. All forms of functional obsolescence may be curable or incurable.[12]

1) Functional obsolescence from a deficiency is a loss in utility due to a missing component or system—for example, a house without central air-conditioning when this was the market standard.

2) Functional obsolescence from a defect is a loss in utility arising from an existing component or system not performing to the market standard—for example the existence of a central air-conditioning unit that was too small to cool the residence sufficiently.

3) Functional obsolescence from a superadequacy is a loss in utility due to an excess over the market standard—for example a residence with three central air-conditioning units, each one capable of cooling the entire residence.

The measure of functional obsolescence is based on whether the particular item is curable or incurable. For a deficiency, the reproduction cost new of a standard item is not included in the reproduction cost of the entire structure. The measure of a curable functional deficiency is the excess of cost to cure over the reproduction cost new of a standard item installed when the structure was built. Otherwise, a charge would be made against a nonexistent item and double counting would result. If curing a functional deficiency involves replacement (e.g., modernization), then the cost to cure is the cost of installing the modern fixture less the depreciated value of the existing fixture or component (often called a defect).

The measure of curable functional obsolescence due to a defect is found in the cost to cure the defective component. This is the cost to install the component now plus any undepreciated reproduction cost new remaining in the existing component that is to be removed. A defect is a component that exists in the structure but does not meet current standards of the marketplace. The estimate of total reproduction cost new (RCN) includes the amount necessary to install the component during construction. Therefore, any part of the RCN attributable to the defective part, that has not been totally used up by physical deterioration, will add to the loss found in the excess cost to cure.

A curable functional superadequacy is measured by the reproduction cost new of the item, less any physical deterioration already charged, plus the cost to install a normally adequate or standard item.

An incurable functional deficiency can be measured by the rent loss attributed to the deficiency in comparison with "standard" residences, multiplied by the Gross Rent Multiplier as derived from Gross Rent Multiplier analysis. Alternatively, sales comparisons may be employed to measure incurable functional obsolescence if sufficient sales data are available. A comparison of otherwise similar properties, some with the deficiency and some without it, should reveal the reduction in sales price made by prudent buyers. However, this requires adequate, reliable market sales data, which are not often available.

Utility lost because of incurable functional obsolescence due to a defect is potentially more difficult to measure than loss from curable causes. Outdated components or structural features (defects) are usually intermingled with large amounts of physical deterioration and, on occasion, external obsolescence as well as other forms of functional obsolescence. Often several types of incurable obsolescence will exist at the same time, for example, excessive ceiling heights combined with a poor floor plan and oversized window and door openings in a residential structure.

Incurable functional superadequacies may be measured by the capitalized value of the rent loss or excess cost of ownership due to the condition. The Gross Rent Multiplier (GRM) is used to "capitalize" the monthly rent loss or increased cost for residential properties. In this case, rent loss is based on the added expense (e.g., extra heating cost, added taxes and such) attributable to the superadequacy; plus the excess reproduction cost new of the item over and above the cost that may be supported by an increase in market rental as a result of the existence of the item.

c. External obsolescence is a loss in utility (and value) as a result of factors outside or "external" to the subject. Technically, external obsolescence may be curable or incurable. Because the owner of the subject usually has little control of these external factors, items of external obsolescence are usually incurable. Items of external obsolescence can be divided into two components: locational and economic.

1) External obsolescence caused by locational factors is a loss in utility (value) as a result of the location of the subject. For example, the subject may be situated near an industrial plant that emits noxious odors. Locational external obsolescence is usually specific to the subject property or a very few other properties in its immediate neighborhood.

Locational obsolescence may be measured in two ways: (1) estimated directly by comparison of market sales of otherwise similar properties some of which are subject to the negative influences. This requires adequate, reliable data, which are not often available. (2) measured by capitalizing the rent loss attributable to the negative locational influence. Both rent loss and GRM used to estimate total locational obsolescence must be derived from GRM analysis. In either method, the diminished utility attributable to negative locational influences must be allocated between building and site. This is most commonly done by utilizing a ratio of site value to building value among properties competitive with the subject property.

2) External obsolescence caused by economic factors is a loss in utility (value) as a result of economic factors. For example, high unemployment tends to have a negative impact on value in that potential purchasers may be unable to afford housing. Measurement of economic obsolescence depends on the estimate of how long the negative factors may last, (for example oversupply). It may also be the difference in the present worth between normal financing and excessively high rates.

Endnotes

1. The Uniform Residential Appraisal Report, for example, specifically refers to reproduction cost in the cost section of the form.
2. Land is raw, but a site has been improved for its intended use; these improvements are called improvements to the site and typically are shown on a depreciated cost basis (net of depreciation).
3. Other techniques include the builder's or trade breakdown method and cost indexing.
4. An example of a published cost manual for residential properties is the *Marshall and Swift Residential Cost Manual* published by Marshall and Swift. Published cost manuals obtain their cost information from surveys of contractors, suppliers and others in the construction industry.
5. Both current and local multipliers may be found in published cost manuals.
6. Appraised Institute, *The Dictionary of Real Estate Appraisal,* 2nd ed. (1989), p. 4.
7. There are isolated examples where land actually does waste away. For example, land along a shoreline or beach may waste away. In addition, land along a river may waste away. The Mississippi River provides an excellent example based on erosion.
8. Appraisal Institute, *The Dictionary of Real Estate Appraisal,* 2nd ed. (1989), pp. 78, 158.
9. Technically, external obsolescence may be curable or incurable but it is usually incurable.
10. For simplicity, items of external obsolescence will be assumed to be incurable. However, if these items are curable, they would also be deducted.
11. Cost new is usually considered to be reproduction cost new.
12. The test for curability is the same test presented under physical deterioration, or cost to cure versus value added.

Cost Approach Problem

You are appraising a 10-year-old, ranch-style, 1,100-square-foot residence, containing 6 rooms, 3 bedrooms and 1 bath. Reproduction cost new is reliably estimated from a standard cost service at $30 per sq. ft. The market value of the site is estimated to be $8,250 (typically 20 percent of total new property market value). The residence needs a new hot-water tank whose cost to replace is $250 and whose reproduction cost new is $225. The ages, useful lives and reproduction cost new of all short-lived items are shown in the following tables:

Item	Reproduction Cost New	Actual Age	Useful Life
Carpet	$2,500	2	8
Roof	3,000	10	20
Appliances	950	10	15

All competitive homes in the area have either a carport or a one-car garage. The subject site is large enough to accommodate a carport within the zoning setbacks. Cost to construct a carport on the site today is $2,500, but it would cost only $2,200 if it were built during construction of a new residence. Residential properties in the area that have a carport have recently sold for $3,000 more than other similar residences with no carport.

The subject property suffers from another functional deficiency based on an estimate of rent loss arising from a crawl space and slab floor construction in lieu of a three-quarter or full basement. An analysis of similar properties with the same deficiency indicates a rent loss of $15 per month. The GRM of 127 for the subject property has been derived from the market.

The subject property is located at the intersection of a main traffic road and the entrance road to a development. Residences not exposed to this level of traffic are valued and sell for an indicated $3,750 more than do properties impacted by heavy traffic.

After curing all physical deterioration, the effective age of the structure will be 10 years. Total expected economic life new is 60 years.

The depreciated reproduction cost new of the site improvements is $4,000.

Estimate the market value of the property via the cost approach.

Suggested Solution

1. Estimate reproduction cost new:

    1,100 sq. ft. @ $30 per sq. ft. = $33,000

2. Estimate physical deterioration:
   a. Curable physical deterioration

Item	Reproduction Cost New	Cost to Cure	Depreciation Charge
Water Heater	$225	$250	$250
Total	$225	$250	$250

   b. Incurable physical deterioration, short-lived items:

Item	Reproduction Cost New	Actual Age	Useful Life	Depreciation (%)	Depreciation Charge
Carpet	$2,500	2	8	25	$ 625
Roof	3,000	10	20	50	1,500
Appliances	950	10	15	66-2/3	633
Total	$6,450				$2,758

   c. Incurable physical deterioration, long-lived items:

Total reproduction cost new	$ 33,000
Physical deterioration:	
Curable items—reproduction cost new	−225
Incurable items: short-lived reproduction cost new	−6,450
Undepreciated reproduction cost new	$ 26,325
Effective age/economic life (10 years/60 years)	× .16667
Incurable physical deterioration: long-lived items	$4,388

   d. Total physical deterioration:

Curable	$ 250
Incurable—short-lived items	2,758
Incurable—long-lived items	4,388
Total	$7,396

3. Estimate functional obsolescence
   a. Curable functional obsolescence:

Defect (substitutions and modernization)		-0-
Deficiency* (addition)		
Carport: $ 2,500	cost to install now	
−2,200	reproduction cost in new construction	
$ 300		$ 300
Superadequacy		-0-
Total curable functional obsolescence		$ 300

   b. Incurable functional obsolescence:

Defect (substitutions and modernization)	-0-
Deficiency (addition)	
(rent loss $15 × GRM 127 = $1,905)	$1,905
Superadequacy	-0-
Total incurable functional obsolescence	$1,905

   c. Total functional obsolescence

Curable	$ 300
Incurable	1,905
Total	$ 2,205

4. Estimate external obsolescence
   a. locational:

Value difference for heavy traffic:	$ 3,750
Allocation to building (80%; site value 20%)	× .80
Total locational obsolescence	$ 3,000

   b. Total external obsolescence:

Locational	$ 3,000
Total	$ 3,000

---

* Deficiency (lack of carport) is "curable" because the value added is greater than the cost to cure: $3,000 is greater than $2,500.

5. Total accrued depreciation:
   Physical deterioration $ 7,396
   Functional obsolescence 2,205
   External obsolescence 3,000
   Total $12,601

   Estimated site value: $ 8,250
   Estimated reproduction cost new of the
        main improvements: $33,000
   Less Accrued depreciation: –12,601
   Equals Depreciated reproduction cost of
        main improvements: $20,399
   Plus Depreciated reproduction cost of site
        improvements: + 4,000
   Equals Depreciated value of all improvements: $24,399

   Equals Estimated Value: $32,649
   or
   $32,500 rounded, market value via cost approach

Key Terms and Concepts

Cost approach
Utility
Techniques for cost estimation:
    quantity survey method
    comparative unit method
    unit-in-place method
Types of costs:
    direct costs
    indirect costs
    entrepreneurial or managerial profit
        (coordination)
Accrued depreciation:
    physical deterioration
        curable
        incurable
            short-lived
            long-lived
    functional obsolescence
        deficiency
        defect
        superadequacy
    external obsolescence
        locational
        economic
Techniques for estimating depreciation:
    market abstraction
    age-life method (straight-line)
    modified age-life method
    observed condition breakdown method
Total economic life
Remaining economic life
Chronological (actual) age
Effective age

Review Questions

1. The primary economic principle underlying the cost approach is the principle of:
   a. substitution.
   b. anticipation.
   c. supply and demand.
   d. liquidity.

2. When using the cost approach in residential appraisals, the appraiser will usually be estimating _____ cost.
   a. new
   b. replacement
   c. reproduction
   d. historical

3. _____ cost is the cost to construct a structure having similar utility, but built with current technology and to current standards.
   a. Reproduction
   b. Replacement
   c. Historical
   d. Relevant

4. The most detailed and time-consuming method of cost estimation is:
   a. unit-in-place.
   b. comparative unit.
   c. trade breakdown.
   d. quantity survey.

5. The cost approach is typically most applicable for:
   a. new structures or "no-market" appraisals.
   b. valuing income properties.
   c. valuing old, historic structures.
   d. accountants.

6. The cost to construct an exact replica of the subject is _____ cost.
   a. replacement
   b. reproduction
   c. limited
   d. replica

7. Direct costs:
    a. can be estimated.
    b. can be assigned to a particular house or structure.
    c. can be projected.
    d. cannot be assigned to a particular house or structure.

Refer to the following data to answer Questions 8–12.

The total reproduction cost new of the improvements was estimated to be $100,000. Total accrued depreciation from all causes was estimated to be 40 percent of reproduction cost new. The site was valued at $20,000. The subject has 1,500 square feet of living area and 1,200 additional square feet of garage and storage space.

8. What is the estimated depreciated reproduction cost new of the improvements?
    a. $ 40,000
    b. $100,000
    c. $80,000
    d. $60,000

9. What is the estimated value of the subject using the cost approach?
    a. $ 40,000
    b. $100,000
    c. $80,000
    d. $60,000

10. What is the estimated value per square foot based on square feet of living area? (round to nearest whole number)
    a. $40
    b. $53
    c. $67
    d. $72

11. What is the estimated value per square foot based on total square footage? (round to nearest whole number)
    a. $53
    b. $67
    c. $30
    d. $43

12. If a loss in value occurs as a result of forces outside a subject's property boundaries, the loss is usually considered to be:
    a. physical deterioration.
    b. functional obsolescence—deficiency.
    c. functional obsolescence—defect.
    d. external obsolescence—economic or locational.

13. An item is curable when the cost to cure is:
    a. less than the cost to repair.
    b. less than or equal to cost to repair.
    c. less than or equal to the value added.
    d. more than or equal to the value added.

14. A loss in value from all sources is:
    a. physical deterioration.
    b functional obsolescence—deficiency.
    c. accrued depreciation.
    d. functional obsolescence—superadequacy.

15. The easiest and least time-consuming method of estimating depreciation is the:
    a. age-life method.
    b modified age-life method.
    c. engineering breakdown method.
    d. quantity survey method.

16. Loss in value as a result of having 1 bathroom when the market standard is 2 bathrooms is considered:
    a. physical deterioration.
    b. functional obsolescence.
    c. external obsolescence.
    d. diminished utility.

17. Loss in value as a result of being located adjacent to a nuclear power plant is considered:

    a. external obsolescence.
    b. functional obsolescence—deficiency.
    c. functional obsolescence—defect.
    d. physical deterioration.

13 The Income Approach

Overview

This chapter reviews the income approach to value. Although the income approach has limited application for most residential properties, especially single-family residential properties, it has more application for two- to four-family residential dwellings. The gross rent multiplier may be used for single-family residential properties and may be a proxy or substitute for the income approach (in residential properties).

Learning Objectives

After completing this chapter, the student should be able to:

- Estimate potential and effective gross income

- Estimate operating expenses

- Calculate operating ratios including operating expense ratio, break-even ratio and the debt coverage ratio

- Estimate net operating income

- Estimate annual debt service

- Calculate and apply gross rent multipliers

I. The Income Approach

A. Rationale

The income approach to value is based on the premise that the purchaser buys the right to receive future cash flows. These cash inflows generally occur in two forms: periodic cash flows (such as rental income) and a reversion (proceeds of resale). Two critical questions that the appraiser must ask in the income approach are (1) what are the future cash inflows and (2) what is the appropriate rate that should be used to convert these cash inflows into a value estimate?

The income approach to value also is based on the **principle of anticipation,** where the typically informed purchaser buys a property in expectation of receiving future cash flows. The principle of anticipation is the most important economic principle underlying the income approach to value.

B. Estimation of Income and Expenses

The initial step in the income approach is to estimate the total cash flows provided by the subject. In forecasting the amount of revenue generated by the subject, the appraiser should focus on the nature of the subject. Two types of cash flows are present in income-producing real estate: **periodic income,** in the form of rental income, and a **reversion,** which occurs when the property is sold (the proceeds of resale).

1. Types of Income Estimation—**Gross market income,** also known as potential gross income, is the income that would be expected if the property was occupied 100 percent of the time. An appraiser can make several assumptions when estimating future **gross market income.** These assumptions include estimation of stabilized gross market income, changing constant dollar amounts, changing gross market income based on a constant percentage amount, and changing gross market income based on a changing percentage. Most appraisers utilize a cash flow analysis to estimate revenues, expenses and net operating income. A framework for cash flow analysis follows:

Revenues

Gross Market Income (Potential Gross Income) − Vacancy and Collection Loss = Rental Income (Rent Collections)

Rental Income + Miscellaneous Income = Effective Gross Income

Expenses

Fixed expenses + Variable Expenses + Reserves for Replacement = Total Operating Expenses

Effective Gross Income − Total Operating Expenses = Net Operating Income

Summary

Effective Gross Income − Total Operating Expenses = Net Operating Income (NOI)

Net Operating Income − Annual Debt Service (ADS) = Before-Tax Cash Flow (BTCF)

Before-Tax Cash Flow ± Taxes or Tax Savings = After-Tax Cash Flow (ATCF)

2. Contract versus Market Rent—The periodic income provided by the rental stream may be based on contract rent or market rent. **Contract rent** is the amount of rent specified in the lease contract. **Market rent** is the amount of rent that the space would command in the local market given current supply and demand conditions.[1] For example, suppose a tenant leased a building two years ago for $10 per square foot for five years. Because the building had no clause for increased rents over time, the rent remained constant at $10 per square foot for five years. If current market rents for similar properties are $12 per square foot, the contract rent would be $10 per square foot, but the current market rent would be $12 per square foot. *In general, if estimating market value, the appraiser should use market rent when estimating gross market income.*

3. Estimation of Gross Market Income—Gross market income is the total amount of revenue that the subject would generate if it were occupied 100 percent of the year.[2] Gross market income is estimated on an annual basis. For example, suppose the subject was a four-unit apartment complex that rented for $400 per unit. The gross market income would be $19,200 (4 units × $400 per month × 12 months). This is the amount of revenue that the complex would generate if all units were occupied 100 percent of the time, 24 hours per day, 365 days per year. In most situations, the occupancy rate will be less than 100 percent.

   a. The **vacancy rate** is the time (and the consequent potential lost revenue) during which the subject is not occupied. The vacancy rate can be estimated from vacancy rates of similar properties. Usually the vacancy rate is stated as a percentage of gross market income.

For example, if the vacancy rate was 5 percent in the above example, the dollar amount of vacancy would be $960 (.05 × $19,200).

    b. The **collection loss** represents loss as a result of the rental collection process. It could stem from several sources, including "bad" checks or nonpayment of rent. Collection losses are generally included with vacancy rates.

    c. Miscellaneous income is additional income not directly attributable to the rental of space. For example, a subject apartment complex may have a separate laundry facility for tenants. If the laundry generates additional revenues, this is an example of miscellaneous income; because the revenues are not directly attributable to the rental of space.

4. Effective Gross Income—**Effective gross income** can be estimated by subtracting vacancy and collection losses from gross market income, then adding miscellaneous income. This calculation will result in an estimate of net revenues from the subject based on market conditions as of the date of the value estimate.

5. Operating Expenses—Three types of operating expenses are included under the general heading "Operating Expenses": fixed expenses, variable expenses and reserves for replacement.

    a. **Fixed expenses** remain constant regardless of the level of occupancy. Examples include property taxes and fire insurance premiums.

    b. **Variable expenses** change or fluctuate based on the amount of space rented. An example is management fees.

    c. **Reserves for Replacement** items are projected to wear out before the basic structure. Therefore a reserve is established to replace these items. Examples include carpeting, appliances and roofing.

    d. **Total operating expenses** are usually shown on an annual basis. These are the sum of fixed expenses, variable expenses and reserves for replacement.

6. Net Operating Income—**Net operating income** is effective gross income less total operating expenses. In essence, this is the cash flow that the investor is purchasing in an income-producing property. In addition,

this is the cash flow that the appraiser must estimate when seeking an estimate of market value using the income approach.

7. Annual Debt Service—**Annual debt service** is the monthly mortgage payment annualized or multiplied times the number of payments in a year. For example, if the mortgage payment on the subject is $1,500 per month the annual debt service is $18,000 ($1,500 × 12). The annual debt service is the cash flow that the lender is entitled to receive. The lender is also entitled to receive the balance outstanding (payoff) on the mortgage when it is sold.[3] If the appraiser were attempting to estimate the value of the mortgage, the relevant cash flows would be the annual debt service[4] and the balance outstanding.

II. Capitalization

Capitalization is the process by which an income stream, such as net operating income, is converted into value. In most appraisal assignments, the appraiser will be seeking market value, in which case the appropriate cash flow or income stream to capitalize is net operating income. However, in some situations the appraiser will be seeking the value of the equity. The cash flows to equity can be converted into value by capitalizing the before-tax cash flow into a value estimate since this residual cash flow accrues to the equity investor. Likewise, the appraiser could be asked to estimate the value of the cash flow to the lender. This would be the value of the mortgage or the value of the annual debt service.

Regardless of the cash flow to be capitalized, there are two types of capitalization: direct capitalization and yield capitalization. This residential exam prep book will only address direct capitalization, as yield capitalization will not be required on the residential exam—although it *will* be required on the general appraisal examination.

A. Direct Capitalization

Direct capitalization is a process of converting a single year's income stream or cash flow into a value estimate through use of an overall capitalization rate. The assumption is that the forecast single year's net operating income is a stabilized forecast. Furthermore, the assumption is that the income stream will continue forever (a perpetuity) into the future. Direct capitalization is usually determined from the following formula:

$$V = \frac{I}{R_o}$$

where V = value, I = net operating income and R_o = overall capitalization rate.

The **overall capitalization rate** may be estimated from a variety of techniques including similar sales, band of investment technique, use of the debt coverage ratio, use of the operating expense ratio and use of gross income multipliers. For example, if an appraiser was assigned to value a property with a net operating income (*I*) of $50,000 and the local marketplace indicated a capitalization rate (*R*) of 10 percent, the indicated value (*V*) would be $500,000 ($50,000 ÷ .10 = $500,000).

1. Similar Sales—**Similar Sales** may be used to estimate the overall capitalization rate. If the net operating income and sales price are known, the overall capitalization rate can be estimated by dividing net operating income by sales price.

2. Debt Coverage Ratio—The **debt coverage ratio,** also known as the debt service ratio, is net operating income divided by annual debt service. The overall capitalization rate (*R*) can be estimated using the following formula:

$$R_o = DCR \times R_M \times M$$

where R_o = overall capitalization rate, R_M = the mortgage loan constant, and M = the loan-to-value ratio. (The loan-to-value ratio is the initial loan amount divided by the sales price. The loan-to-value ratio may be derived from local market conditions. Local lenders tend to have maximum loan-to-value ratios for different types of property in a given market area.)

For example, assume the following: the debt coverage ratio on the subject was 1.22; the maximum (and typical) loan-to-value ratio in the local marketplace for this type of property was 80 percent, or .80; typical loan terms were a 20 percent cash down payment, 25 year financing with monthly payments at 12 percent. The overall capitalization rate can be estimated by multiplying 1.22 × .126387 (the mortgage loan constant[5]) × .80, which equals .123354. If the subject had a net operating income of $100,000 and an overall capitalization rate of .123354, the indicated value (before rounding) using this approach to direct capitalization would be $810,677 ($100,000 ÷ .123354).

3. Band of Investment Technique—The **Band of investment technique** divides the overall rate into two components, mortgage and equity. Each component is weighted by its percentage of total property investment to estimate the overall capitalization rate as follows:

Component	Percentage		Cost		Weighted Average
Mortgage			R_M		
M	80	×	.123354	=	.098683
Equity			R_E		
(1–M)	20	×	.15		+ .030000
	100			R_o =	.128683

The mortgage component is multiplied times the cost of the mortgage funds, or the mortgage loan constant (R_M). The equity component is multiplied times the cost of equity funds, or the equity dividend rate (R_E). This produces a weighted average that, when added together, provides the appraiser with an estimate of the overall capitalization rate.

4. Operating Expense Ratio—The overall capitalization rate can be estimated using the **operating expense ratio**. The formula is:

$$R_o = \frac{(1 - \text{Operating Expense Ratio})}{\text{EGIM}}$$

where EGIM = effective gross income multiplier. The effective gross income multiplier is sales price divided by effective gross income. The operating expense ratio is total operating expenses divided by effective gross income.

B. Yield Capitalization

Yield capitalization is conversion of the appropriate cash flows into an estimate of value using the appropriate yield rate. Each cash flow component (periodic income and reversion) is valued separately based on the applicable yield rate and the investor's holding period for the asset. One technique used in yield capitalization is **discounted cash flow (DCF) analysis**. In a DCF analysis, the appraiser determines the present value of the periodic cash flow (usually the net operating income) and adds that present value to the present value of the reversion cash flow to estimate a value for the subject. Yield capitalization is beyond the scope of the residential appraisal examination and therefore is not detailed in this text.

III. Operating Ratios

In general, operating ratios are intended to measure management's ability to operate the property efficiently. There are several types of efficiency ratios, including the debt service (debt coverage)[6] ratio, the operating expense ratio, break-even ratio, equity dividend ratio and the loan-to-value ratio.

A. Debt Service Ratio

The **debt service ratio,** also known as the **debt coverage ratio**, is the ratio of net operating income to annual debt service. The formula is net operating income divided by annual debt service:

$$\text{Debt Service Ratio} = \frac{\text{NOI}}{\text{ADS}}$$

The debt service ratio is important to many lenders as it represents how many times the net operating income covers the annual debt service. For example, if the debt service ratio is 1.2, this means that the net operating income covers the annual debt service 1.2 times. Obviously, lenders would like to see a debt service ratio that is as high as possible to protect their loan.

B. Operating Expense Ratio

The **operating expense ratio** is the ratio of total operating expenses to effective gross income. It is calculated by dividing total operating expenses by effective gross income:

$$\text{Operating Expense Ratio} = \frac{\text{Total Operating Expenses}}{\text{Effective Gross Income}}$$

C. Break-Even Ratio

The **break-even ratio** is the ratio at which the property is just covering all of its costs; there are no annual profits. The formula for the break-even ratio is:

$$\text{Break-Even} = \frac{\text{Total Operating Expenses} + \text{Annual Debt Service}}{\text{Potential Gross Income}}$$

D. Equity Dividend Rate

The **equity dividend rate** is the annualized rate of return that equity investors receive. Equity investors are entitled to receive the before-tax cash flow. Debt investors (lenders) have first claim on cash flows and therefore receive the annual debt service prior to equity. The remaining cash flow, before-tax cash flow, accrues to the equity investors. This is the rate that many investors use to compare different investments. The calculation of the equity dividend rate is as follows:

$$\text{Equity Dividend Rate (EDR)} = \frac{\text{Before-Tax Cash Flow}}{\text{Equity}}$$

E. Loan-to-Value Ratio

The loan-to-value ratio is a mortgage ratio computed by dividing the mortgage or loan amount by the value. Most lenders have maximum loan-to-value ratios for different types of property. This maximum loan-to-value ratio will vary by lender and locale. For example, some lenders might have a maximum loan-to-value ratio of .75 for apartments and a maximum loan-to-value ratio of .85 for industrial properties.

IV. Gross Rent Multiplier

The gross rent multiplier (GRM) may be used as a proxy for the income approach in residential properties. Technically, the GRM is part of the sales comparison approach but is considered part of the income approach for residential properties. For residential property valuation, gross rent multipliers are used rather than an income approach using capitalization of net operating income. This is because residential properties rarely if ever produce "other" nonrental income. Residential properties typically are not purchased for investment income nor profit. Therefore, net income is not employed in estimating residential property value. The difficulty in estimating the effect on market value of amenities directly is one major reason why GRM analysis must be used with care and caution.

A. Requirements for Use of GRMs

Three conditions must be present before using gross rent multipliers in residential property appraisal: an active rental market for similar properties, properties that were rented and sold as rental properties, and rentals of similar properties on an unfurnished basis. Because of these constraints, the income approach is not applicable in many residential appraisal assignments.

B. Nature of Gross Rent Multipliers

Gross rent multipliers are simply numbers that express the ratio between the sale price of a residential property and its monthly unfurnished rental.

The ratio between sales prices and gross monthly unfurnished rentals tends to be consistent for the same type of property under the same market conditions. Value is estimated by multiplying the appropriate GRM by the estimated market rental of the subject property.

C. Gross Rent Multiplier Procedure

GRM analysis is done in three steps, the first two of which involve considerable market analysis and data gathering. The first step is to estimate the current monthly market rental of the subject. The second step is to calculate the appropriate gross rent multiplier from sales of comparable properties that were rented at the time of sale. Finally, multiply the estimated market rental of the subject property by the GRM to obtain an estimate of market value of the subject property. (See accompanying GRM example.)

D. Calculating Estimated Value

Once the market rental for the subject property and the gross rent multiplier have been estimated via comparative analysis with rental properties and sales of rental properties, the estimate of market value of the subject property is obtained by multiplying the market rental by the gross rent multiplier:

$$\text{Value} = \text{Market Rent} \times \text{Gross Rent Multiplier}$$

For example, if the monthly market rental estimation for the subject property is $160 and the GRM indicated by comparative analysis is 140, the calculated indication of market value of the subject property is $22,400 ($160 × 140 = $22,400), rounded to $22,500 (the estimate of value is rounded to show that it is not a precise calculation, but an estimate).

Gross Rent Multiplier Example

The subject is a single-family residential home in an area where tenant occupancy is dominant. In a search of the area, you have found 12 recent sales of properties quite similar to the subject property. You also have been able to obtain monthly rents associated with each sale. The sales/rentals are listed below.

Sale No.	Location	Sale Price	Monthly Rental (MR)
1	101 N. Eagle Drive	$28,000	$250
2	65 Meadewood	32,000	290
3	61 Birch Heights Road	30,500	275
4	11 Baxter	27,500	250
5	17 Willowbrook	33,000	290
6	42 Septist Drive	32,500	290
7	9 Lynnwood	30,000	270
8	85 Storys Road	29,800	270
9	30 Dogg Lane	28,500	250
10	22 Eastwood	31,360	280
11	19 Westwood	32,700	290
12	10 Fairfield	31,000	280

The subject property is located at 30 Hunting Lodge Road and is currently renting at $275 per month, which is considered to be its market rental.

Sale No.	GRM (rounded)
1	112
2	110
3	111
4	110
5	114
6	112
7	111
8	110
9	114
10	112
11	113
12	111

The GRMs indicated from the foregoing analysis range from 110 to 114. This would seem to indicate a GRM for the subject property of 112. Therefore, the indicated value of the subject property is $30,800 ($V = \text{MR} \times \text{GRM} = \$275 \times 112$), rounded to $31,000.

Endnotes

1. Appraisal Institute, *The Dictionary of Real Estate Appraisal,* 2nd ed. (1989), p. 192. Market rent is the rental income that a property most probably would command on the open market.
2. Another commonly used term for *gross market income* is *potential gross income.*
3. This assumes no assumption of the existing loan by a potential purchaser.
4. Technically, the cash flow would be the monthly mortgage payment and the balance outstanding.
5. The mortgage loan constant is the amount required each period to amortize (pay both principal and interest) the loan.
6. This may also be known as the debt service coverage ratio.

Key Terms and Concepts

Principle of anticipation
Two types of cash flow:
    periodic income
    reversion
Types of income estimation:
    gross market income
    contract rent
    market rent
Vacancy rate
Collection loss
Effective gross income
Operating expenses:
    fixed expenses
    variable expenses
    reserves for placements
    total operating expenses
Net operating income
Annual debt service
Two types of capitalization:
    direct capitalization
        overall capitalization rate
        similar sales
        debt coverage ratio
        band of investment technique
        operating expense ratio
    yield capitalization
        discounted cash flow (DCF) analysis
Operating ratios:
    debt service (debt coverage) ratio
    operating expense ratio
    break-even ratio
    equity dividend rate
    loan-to-value ratio
Gross rent multiplier

Review Questions

1. The principle of _____ forms the basis for the income approach.
   a. change
   b. substitution
   c. modification
   d. anticipation

2. Value can be estimated in the income approach by:
   a. guessing.
   b. dividing the overall capitalization rate by the net operating income.
   c. dividing the net operating income into the overall capitalization rate.
   d. dividing the net operating income by the overall capitalization rate.

3. The gross rent multiplier is really an extension of the _____ approach to value.
   a. residential
   b. income
   c. cost
   d. sales comparison approach

4. Suppose a lease contract called for rents of $10 per square foot. However, similar space rents in the market for $15 per square foot. The amount specified in the lease is the _____ rent.
   a. contract
   b. market
   c. surplus
   d. overage

5. The $15 per square foot from the preceding question is called _____ rent.
   a. contract
   b. market
   c. surplus
   d. overage

6. In gross rent multiplier analysis, the comparable rentals are assumed to be:
   a. monthly on a furnished basis.
   b. annually on a furnished basis.
   c. monthly on an unfurnished basis.
   d. annually on an unfurnished basis.

Refer to the following data to answer questions 7–13.

You have received an appraisal assignment with the following information. Your search of the market revealed seven similar sales, which were rented at the time of sale. All were unfurnished.

Sale	Sale Price	Monthly Unfurnished Rental
1	$55,000	$410
2	57,000	425
3	57,000	420
4	56,000	420
5	55,500	415
6	58,000	422
7	60,000	423

7. What is the range of rents?
   a. $410 to $425
   b. $15
   c. $10
   d. $12

8. What is the median rental?
   a. $410
   b. $415
   c. $420
   d. $422

9. What is the mean rental? (Round to **nearest dollar**.)
   a. $420
   b. $410
   c. $419
   d. $415

10. What is the range of gross rent multipliers? (Round to nearest whole number.)
    a. 118 to 142
    b. 9
    c. 18
    d. 133 to 142

11. What is the median gross rent multiplier? (Round to nearest whole number.)
    a. 134
    b. 133
    c. 136
    d. 142

12. What is the modal (or mode) gross rent multiplier? (Round to nearest whole number.)

    a. 134
    b. 133
    c. 136
    d. 142

13. What is the mean gross rent multiplier? (Round to nearest whole number.)

    a. 134
    b. 133
    c. 136
    d. 142

14. If stabilized net operating income has been forecast to be $100,000 annually and the overall capitalization rate is 12.5 percent or .125, what is the indicated value?

    a. $100,000
    b. $1,000,000
    c. $800,000
    d. $1,250,000

15. Interest received by the lender on a mortgage is termed _____ capital.

    a. expensive
    b. return of equity
    c. return on debt
    d. return of debt

16. Principal received by the lender on a mortgage is termed _____ capital.

    a. expensive
    b. return of equity
    c. return on debt
    d. return of debt

17. In discounted cash flow analysis, the value of the property is equal to:

    a. present worth of the NOI plus present worth of the potential gross income.
    b. present worth of the NOI plus present worth of the reversion.
    c. present worth of the potential gross income plus present worth of the effective gross income.
    d. future worth of the NOI plus present worth of the reversion.

Refer to the following data to answer questions 18–23.

You have been asked to appraise an apartment complex with 200 units. Included in the 200 units are 100 2-bedroom units and 100 1-bedroom units. The 1-bedroom units rent for $350 per month, and the 2-bedroom units rent for 20 percent more than 1-bedroom units. The market vacancy rate is 8 percent. Total operating expenses are 40 percent of effective gross income. The monthly mortgage payment is $20,000.

18. What is the forecast potential gross income?

    a. $ 77,000
    b. $924,000
    c. $87,000
    d. $900,000

19. What is the forecast effective gross income?

    a. $850,080
    b. $ 70,840
    c. $80,040
    d. $901,600

20. What is the forecast operating expense ratio?

    a. .6
    b. .4
    c. 2
    d. 1

21. What is the forecast net operating income?

    a. $510,048
    b. $ 42,504
    c. $73,637
    d. $429,472

22. What is the annual debt service?

    a. $ 20,000
    b. $240,000
    c. $736,000
    d. $200,000

23. If equity = $1,000,000, what is the equity dividend rate?

    a. −.07
    b. .27
    c. −.006
    d. −.05

14 Valuation of Partial Interests, Reconciliation and Final Value Estimate

Overview

This chapter addresses the major forms of partial interests and their appraisal. In many instances, the legal interests being appraised will be less than the full bundle of rights, with the property owner owning less of the bundle, or a partial interest.

Learning Objectives

After completing this chapter, the student should be able to:

- List and define the major types of partial interests

- Identify and value each type of leasehold estate

- Identify the financial arrangements on leases

- Define reconciliation and explain the objective of the reconciliation process

I. Valuation of Partial Interests

A. Undivided Interests

Fee simple **undivided interests** represent potentially the simplest of valuation assignments. Sales comparables in most local areas are fee simple undivided interests, so the appraiser usually has several similar sales. As a result, no adjustment may be necessary for property rights.

B. Life Estates

Life estates are created for the life of someone. They are of an indeterminate length because the measuring life may die at any time, thus terminating the life estate. If a party is named to receive the estate following termination of the life estate, that party is known as the *remainderman*. The valuation of life estates can be very complex. To value a life estate, appraisers typically estimate the benefits accruing to the life estate based on an average mortality age of the measuring life.

C. Easements

An **easement** is the right to use another's land. There are two general types of easements: easements in gross and easements in appurtenance. Many easements are valued on a before and after basis. The value of the fee interest before the easement, or unencumbered by the easement, is compared to the value of the fee interest burdened by the easement. The difference in value before and after is the value of the easement.

D. Time-Shares

A **time-share** may be a partial form of ownership or a lease for a specified period of time. The rights conveyed with the time-share will vary depending on the time-share agreement. Traditionally, the time-share was a conveyance of partial ownership for a given period of time. For example, a purchaser who bought a one-week time-share in a Florida vacation home would receive the right to occupy that structure 1/52nd of the time. In addition, the purchaser would own 1/52nd of the property with the other time-share owners as tenants in common.

The valuation of a time-share should include several similar sales. Sales of new time-share developments, in which the developer is the grantor and the initial purchaser is the grantee, may not be comparable to resales of existing units. Initial sales charges and commissions may affect initial sales prices. In addition, sales of time-shares in different units should be questioned, because the amenity package may differ from one time-share development to another.

E. **Cooperative**

A **cooperative** is a form of ownership in which a corporation owns the structure and residents of the building own stock in the corporation. Stock ownership in the corporation gives the stockholder the right to reside in the building. Typically, the corporation signs a proprietary lease with the tenant-stockholder. This lease requires the tenant to make a pro-rata share of the operating expenses and debt payments on the building. In general, the appraiser is valuing the proprietary lease in a cooperative, as well as one share of stock in the corporation.

F. **Leases**

A **leas**e gives the right to use or occupy specified premises for a period of time. The appraiser must analyze the financial arrangements stipulated in the lease agreement so as to value each interest created by the lease. There are two parties to a lease agreement, the *lessor* (landlord) and the *lessee* (tenant).

The lessor has a specified interest in the property prior to the lease agreement. Prior to the lease, and before the property is burdened by the agreement, the owner has an unencumbered fee estate. Once leased, two interests are created: a leased fee estate and a leasehold estate

1. Leased Fee Estate—A **leased fee estate** describes the lessor's estate under the lease. A **lessor** generally has the right to receive two cash flows: the lease payments based on the lease contract (contract rent) and the property at the end of the lease period (reversion). The value of the leased fee interest is the present value of the rental income plus the present value of the reversion to be received at the end of the lease period.

2. Leasehold Estate—The leasehold estate is the **lessee's** interest, which will have value when the market rent is greater than the contract rent. The value of the lessee's interest is the present value of the excess of market rent over contract rent for the remainder of the lease term. If

contract rent is greater than market rent, the leasehold will have a negative value.

3. Unencumbered Fee Estate—The value of the **unencumbered fee estate** is the value of the leased fee interest plus the value of the leasehold interest.

II. Financial Arrangements in Leases

Financial arrangements are defined by several types of leases. These include fixed or gross leases, net leases, percentage leases, reappraisal leases, index leases and graduated payment leases.

A. Fixed or Gross Lease

In a **fixed or gross lease** the lessee (tenant) pays a flat or constant fee for the use of the premises. The lessor (landlord) pays the costs of ownership such as the taxes and fire insurance premiums. Most apartment lease contracts are fixed leases.

B. Net Lease

In a **net lease** the tenant pays some or all of the costs of ownership. For example, a tenant may pay the property taxes, or the property taxes and the fire insurance, or all of the costs of ownership.[1] A large or corporate tenant (such as a public accounting firm) may desire a net lease.

C. Percentage Lease

A **percentage lease,** common in the retail industry, has two components: a **base rent,** which is fixed, and an **overage rent** (also called *excess rent*), which usually is based on a percentage of sales.

D. Reappraisal Lease

A **reappraisal lease** is based on the appraised value of the property. Periodically, the property is reappraised and the lease payments adjusted. For example, suppose the annual lease payments are based on 3 percent of the appraised value of the property. Every five years, the property will be reappraised and the lease payments adjusted accordingly.

E. Index Lease

An **index lease** is defined by payments that are tied to an index, such as the consumer price index (CPI), the producer price index, or some other type of index. As the index changes, the lease payments are changed to reflect changes in the index. For example, suppose an index lease was tied to the CPI with annual adjustments. If the index rose 6 percent during the year, the lease payments would be adjusted upward by 6 percent.

F. Graduated Payment Lease

A **graduated payment lease** has payments that are low during the early stages of the lease but rise during the lease term.

III. Sublease and Assignment

A. Sublease

A **sublease** is an agreement between the original lessee (tenant) and a third party (**sublessee**) whereby the lessee transfers an interest to the sublessee but retains some interest. The initial lessee (also the **sublessor**) is "sandwiched" between the lessor (landlord) and the sublessee, creating a **sandwich lease.** The lessor looks to the initial lessee (**sublessor**) for payment and has no legal relationship with the sublessee, who is bound by the terms of the initial lease agreement.

B. Assignment

An **assignment** is generally considered to be a transfer of the lessee's interests in a lease agreement. In an assignment, the lessee retains no interest.

IV. Reconciliation

The ultimate objective of any residential appraisal is to estimate defined value as of a given date. To do this, the appraiser resolves (reconciles) the estimates of value from the applicable approaches into a single, final estimate of property value as of the valuation date.[2]

The process of selecting a final value estimate involves three key procedures:

A. Review

A **review** must be undertaken of all the previous work and analyses, including a check and verification of the data, logic and application of the technique. Review is not to be confused with reconciliation. Review is preparation of the findings and indications of value for reconciliation. In the review process, particular care should be taken to check for internal consistency and compatibility of data, analyses and findings among the approaches to value.

B. Reconciliation

Once the review process is completed, the appraiser must apply judgment and logic to develop a final estimate of value. This process is known as **reconciliation,** whereby the appraiser evaluates, chooses and selects from two or more alternative conclusions or indications to reach a single answer or final value estimate. The term *reconciliation* is preferred to the traditional and still widely used term *correlation* (a long-established process of statistical analysis) because reconciliation describes accurately and precisely what the appraiser does: reconciles several value indications with one another to derive a single value estimate. Reconciliation takes place every time the appraiser makes a selection or choice from among several alternatives at any point in the appraisal process.

Appraisers must avoid a tendency simply to average two or more different numbers. For example, if the cost approach indicates a value of $90,000 and the sales comparison approach indicates a value of $95,000, there may be a temptation to average the two numbers to develop a final value estimate of $92,500 ($95,000 + $90,000 = $185,000 ÷ 2 = $92,500). *A simple mathematical calculation is incorrect.* The appraiser should develop a final value estimate based on the approach that is most applicable to the subject, its local market and market conditions. The applicability of each approach is based on the appraiser's judgment, experience and professional training.

C. Rounding

The final value estimate is precisely that: an *estimate*. As such, it must be appropriately rounded to eliminate any implication of precision or excessive accuracy. **Rounding** brings the estimate to a reasonable degree of accuracy consistent with the standards of the local market, the price level or range within which the value estimate falls and the type of property involved. Thus, $43,500 or $44,000 would be more likely as a final value estimate than $43,700, $43,800 or $43,900.

V. Assumptions, Certification and Limiting Conditions

A. Assumptions

An appraiser must make several assumptions when completing an appraisal assignment. Some of these assumptions include the appraiser's reliance on information received from third parties, information of a legal nature and information about adverse conditions. Moreover, upon completion of the report, the appraiser must designate the assumed condition of the subject. The subject may be appraised under three possible assumptions concerning its physical condition: "as is," "subject to" or "as per plans and specifications."

1. "As Is"—Most appraisals estimate value as defined assuming the subject is valued **"as is,"** or in its current condition. That is, no needed repairs are assumed to have been completed. The value of the subject is based on its condition on the date of the value estimate.

2. "Subject To"—In some appraisal assignments, the subject will require certain improvements, such as painting or roofing, for improved marketability. One assumption that the appraiser may make is a value estimate **"subject to"** (conditional on) certain specified improvements.

3. "Per Plans and Specifications"—In new construction, the appraiser will initially appraise from plans and construction specifications. Any value estimate must assume that the project has a reasonable and probable expectation of completion as shown in those plans and according to proposed specifications—value **"per plans and specifications."**

B. Certification and Limiting Conditions

1. Certification—The **certification of value** states that the appraisal has been performed by the appraiser who signs the report as appraiser, and that he or she has personally conducted the appraisal assignment. In addition, those who have rendered professional opinions, analyses and expertise on the appraisal are identified. A statement of objectivity is also usually included.

2. Limiting Conditions—**Limiting conditions** restrict the scope of the appraisal as well as the responsibility of the appraiser and client. The

identification of real estate and property rights to be appraised, the date of the value estimate, the use of the appraisal and the definition of value are examples of limiting conditions of an appraisal.

Endnotes

1. Generally, the more "nets" in the lease, the more costs of ownership that are borne by the tenants.
2. It is acceptable to provide the client with a value range if requested. However, most clients will request a single value estimate.

Key Terms and Concepts

Valuation of partial interests:
    undivided interests
    life estates
    easements
    time-shares
    cooperatives
    leases
        leased fee estate
            lessor
        leasehold estate
            lessee
        unencumbered fee estate
Financial arrangements in leases:
    fixed or gross lease
    net lease
    percentage lease
        base rent
        overage rent
    reappraisal lease
    index lease
    graduated payment lease
Sublease:
    sublessee
    sublessor
    sandwich lease
Assignment
Selecting a final value estimate:
    review
    reconciliation
    rounding
Assumptions:
    "as is"
    "subject to"
    "per plans and specifications"
Certification and limiting conditions:
    certification of value
    limiting conditions

Review Questions

1. When the original lessee gives up all rights under the lease, this is:
   a. reversion.
   b. subletting.
   c. assignment.
   d. sublease.

2. When the tenant pays no costs of ownership and pays a flat fee each period, the lease is a:
   a. fixed or gross lease.
   b. net lease.
   c. reappraisal lease.
   d. guaranteed lease.

3. The right to use another's land is a(an):
   a. time-share.
   b. cooperative.
   c. easement.
   d. profit.

4. If a property owner leases space to a tenant, the property owner's interest is a(an):
   a. unencumbered fee.
   b. leased fee.
   c. leasehold.
   d. life estate.

5. The _____ lease makes a cooperative more difficult to sell.
   a. fixed gross
   b. proprietary
   c. net
   d. percentage

6. In a life estate, the party named in the deed to receive the property after termination of the measuring life is the:
   a. measuring life.
   b. grantee.
   c. remainderman.
   d. grantor.

7. A _____ may be a special form of ownership or a lease for a specified period of time.
   a. easement
   b. license
   c. cooperative
   d. time-share

8. _____ is the financial arrangement in a type of lease usually found in retail contracts.

   a. Fixed
   b. Percentage
   c. Index
   d. Reappraisal

9. In a sublease, the lessor looks to whom for payment?

   a. Lessee
   b. Grantee
   c. Sublessee
   d. Lessor

10. The value of the unencumbered fee is equal to value of the:

    a. leasehold.
    b. leased fee plus value of the sublease.
    c. leased fee plus value of the leasehold.
    d. leased fee.

11. The final value estimate should be:

    a. precise.
    b. rounded.
    c. a mathematical calculation.
    d. unsupported.

12. The ultimate objective of any appraisal is to:

    a. estimate value as defined.
    b. estimate market value.
    c. define the problem.
    d. estimate value in exchange.

15 Appraisal Standards and Ethics

Overview

This chapter covers standards and ethics in real estate appraisal. Note that each state may address this topic from a different perspective: Some states may ask questions based on the Uniform Standards of Professional Appraisal Practice whereas others may ask questions based on that state's appraiser licensing/certification statute. Finally, some states may ask questions related to both the Uniform Standards and state statute.

Learning Objectives

After completing this chapter, the student should be:

- Able to explain basics of the Uniform Standards of Professional Appraisal Practice

- Familiar with The Appraisal Foundation and its two boards: the Appraiser Qualifications Board and the Appraisal Standards Board

I. Uniform Standards of Professional Appraisal Practice

During the last half of the 1980s, major appraisal organizations began to notice increased scrutiny of appraisals and appraisers at all levels. The issue was one of federal or self regulation. In 1987, eight major appraisal organizations formed **The Appraisal Foundation.**[1] The mission of the Foundation is to promote appraisal professionalism and competency through self regulation using the Uniform Standards of Professional Appraisal Practice (USPAP). The goal of the Uniform Standards is to promote professionalism and competency in appraisals and appraisal reporting. There are a total of ten (10) standards. The first three are related to real property appraisals. Other standards are related to real estate consulting, mass appraisal, real estate analysis, personal property appraisal and business appraisals. In addition, the standards address communication of the appraisal report. Each standard sets rules that serve to interpret, clarify and guide appraisers in application of the standards. Moreover, the Standards Board (see below) may issue (subject to an exposure draft and comment) Statements on Standards, which further interpret the Standards and Standards Rules. The Uniform Standards also contain competency and ethics provisions. The first three Standards of the Uniform Standards of Professional Appraisal Practice are presented at the end of this chapter.

The Appraisal Foundation has two boards charged with promoting appraiser professionalism, competency and appraisal standards: the **Appraisal Standards Board** and the **Appraiser Qualifications Board.** Information concerning the Foundation or its boards may be obtained by writing or telephoning the Foundation at:

> The Appraisal Foundation
> 1029 Vermont Avenue, N.W.
> Washington, DC 20005
> Telephone: 202-347-7722.

Each member organization of the Foundation has adopted the USPAP, referred to as Uniform Standards.

II. State License Law

The **Financial Institutions Reform, Recovery and Enforcement Act (FIRREA) of 1989** requires states to have a license/certification law in place as of December 31, 1991. As a result, states are enacting legislation affecting appraiser licensure and/or certification (see Chapter 1).

Each state examination, both residential and general, will test a common body of appraisal knowledge. For the residential examination, the common body of knowledge will be based on those principles, theories, problems and applications presented throughout this text.

In addition to a common body of appraisal knowledge, each state will test students on that state's appraiser license and/or certification law. Students should obtain a copy of their state law from their real estate commission or state appraisal board. Items found in most state legislation, which should be reviewed by the student, are described below.

A. **State Requirements for Licensure and/or Certification**

1. Education—Students should know how many hours of education will be required and the composition of those hours. In addition, students should know the different education requirements for residential versus general licensure and certification.

2. Experience—Students should know how many years of experience are required for licensure or certification at both the residential and general levels. The Appraiser Qualifications Board has stated that 1,000 hours of appraisal work constitutes one year of experience.

B. **State Definitions**

1. Terminology—Certain states have defined terms *by statute for that state*. For example, some states have a statutory definition of *market value*. Students should know all applicable statutory definitions as they relate to appraisal.

2. Scope of the State Statute—Students preparing to take the residential or general examinations should know what types of appraisals and/or evaluations are covered by their state's law.

Endnote

1. The eight founding organizations were (in no specific order) The American Institue of Real Estate Appraisers, The Society of Real Estate Appraisers, National Association of Real Estate Appraisers, The American Society of Farm Managers and Rural Appraisers, The International Right Way Association, The American Society of Appraisers, The International Association of Assessing Officers, and The National Association of Independent Fee Appraisers. The Foundation presently includes several "special" members representing commercial banking, mortgage banking, savings and loan and real estate educational interests. There were initially nine founding organizations, but the Appraisal Institute of Canada resigned from membership.

Excerpts From the Uniform Standards of Professional Appraisal Practice Applicable to Federally Related Transactions

(Based upon the Uniform Standards of Professional Appraisal Practice as promulgated by the Appraisal Standard Board of The Appraisal Foundation)

Table of Contents
Section I – Introduction
  Preamble
  Ethics Provision
  Competency Provision
  Jurisdictional Exception
  Supplemental Standards
  Definitions
Section II – Real Property Appraisals
  Standard 1
  Standard 2
Section III – Review Appraisals
  Standard 3

Section I – Introduction
Preamble

It is essential that a professional appraiser arrive at and communicate his or her analyses, opinions, and advice in a manner that will be meaningful to the client and will not be misleading in the marketplace. These Uniform Standard of Professional Appraisal Practice reflect the current standard of the appraisal profession.

The importance of the role of the appraiser places ethical obligations on those who serve in this capacity. These standards include explanatory comments and begin with an Ethics Provision setting forth the requirements for integrity, objectivity, independent judgement, and ethical conduct. In addition, these standards include a Competency Provision which places an immediate responsibility on the appraiser prior to acceptance of an assignment. The standards contain binding requirements, as well as specific guidelines. Definitions applicable to these standard are also included.

These standards deal with the procedures to be followed in performing an appraisal or review and the manner in which an appraisal or review is communicated. Standards 1 and 2 relate to the development and communication of a real property appraisal. Standard 3 establishes guidelines for reviewing an appraisal and reporting on that review.

These standards are for appraisers and the users of appraisal services. To maintain the highest level of professional practice, appraisers must observe these standards. The users of appraisal services should demand work performed in conformance with these standards.

Comment: Explanatory comments are an integral part of the Uniform Standard and should be viewed as extensions of the provisions, definitions, and standard rules. Comments provide interpretation from the Appraisal Standards Board concerning the background or application of certain provisions, definitions, or standards rules. There are no comments for provisions, definitions, and standards rules that are axiomatic or have not yet required further explanation; however, additional comments will be developed and others supplemented or revised as the need arises.

Ethics Provision

Because of the fiduciary responsibilities inherent in professional appraisal practice, the appraiser must observe the highest standards of professional ethics. This Ethics Provision is divided into four sections: conduct, management, confidentiality, and record keeping.

Comment: This provision emphasizes the personal obligations and responsibilities of the individual appraiser. However, it should also be emphasized that groups and organizations engaged in appraisal practice share the same ethical obligations.

Conduct. An appraiser must perform ethically and competently in accordance with these standards and not engage in conduct that is unlawful, unethical, or improper. An appraiser who could reasonably be perceived as a disinterested third party in rendering an unbiased appraisal, review, or consulting service must perform assignments with impartiality, objectivity, and independence and without accommodation of personal interests.

Comment: An appraiser is required to avoid any incident that could be considered misleading or fraudulent. In particular, it is unethical for an appraiser to use or communicate a misleading or fraudulent report or to knowingly permit an employee or other person to communicate a misleading or fraudulent report.

The development of an appraisal, review, or consulting service based upon a hypothetical condition is unethical unless:
(1) The use of the hypothesis is clearly disclosed;
(2) The assumption of the hypothetical condition is clearly required for legal purposes, for purposes of reasonable analysis, or for purposes of comparison and would not be misleading; and
(3) The report clearly describes the rationale for this assumption, the nature of the hypothetical condition, and its effect on the result of the appraisal, review, or consulting service.

An individual appraiser employed by a group or organization conducts itself in a manner that does not conform to these standards should take steps that are appropriate under the circumstances to ensure compliance with the standards.

Management. The acceptance of compensation that is contingent upon the reporting of a predetermined value or a direction in value that favors the cause of the attainment of a stipulated result, or the occurrence of a subsequent event is unethical.

The payment of undisclosed fees, commissions, or things of value in connection with the procurement of appraisal, review, or consulting assignments is unethical

Comment: Disclosure of fees, commissions, or things of value connected to the procurement of an assignment should appear in the certification of a written record and in any transmittal letter in which conclusions are stated. In groups or organizations engaged in appraisal practice, intracompany payments to employees for business development are not considered to be unethical. Competency, rather than financial incentives, should be the primary basis for awarding an assignment.

Advertising for or soliciting appraisal assignments in a manner which is false, misleading or exaggerated is unethical.

Comment: In groups or organizations engaged on appraisal practice, decisions concerning finder or referral fees, contingent compensation, and advertising may not be the responsibility of an individual appraiser, but for a particular assignment it is the responsibility of the individual appraiser to ascertain that there has been no breach of ethics, that the appraisal is prepared in accordance with these standards, and that the report can be properly certified as required by Standards Rules 2-3 or 3-2.

The restriction on contingent compensation in the first paragraph of this section does not apply to consulting assignments where the appraiser is not acting in a disinterested manner and would not reasonably be perceived as performing a service that requires impartiality. This permitted contingent compensation must be properly disclosed in the report.

Comment: The preparer of the written report of an assignment where the appraiser is not acting in a disinterested manner must certify that the compensation is contingent and must explain the basis for the contingency in the report, certification, executive summary and in any transmittal letter in which conclusions are stated.

Confidentiality. An appraiser must protect the confidential nature of the appraiser-client relationship.

Comment: A appraiser must not disclose confidential factual data obtained from a client or the result of an assignment prepared for a client to anyone other than: (1) The client and persons specifically authorized by the client; (2) such third parties as may be authorized by due process of law; and (3) a duly authorized professional peer review committee. As a corollary, it is unethical for a member of a duly authorized professional peer review committee to disclose confidential information or factual data presented to the committee.

Record Keeping. An appraiser must prepare written records of appraisal, review and consulting assignments-including oral testimony and reports-and retain such records for a period of at least five (5) years after preparation or at least two (2) years after final disposition of any judicial proceeding in which testimony was given, whichever period expires last.

Comment. Written records of assignments include true copies of written reports, written summaries of oral testimony and reports (or a transcript of testimony) all data and statements required by these standards, and other information as may be required to support the findings and conclusions of the appraiser. The term written records also includes information stored on electronic, magnetic, or other media. Such records must be made available by the appraiser when required by due process of law or by duly authorized professional peer review committee.

Competency Provision

Prior to accepting an assignment or entering into an agreement to perform any assignment, an appraiser must properly identify the problem to be addressed and have the knowledge and experience to complete the assignment competently; or alternatively:

1. Disclose the lack of knowledge and/or experience to the client before accepting the assignment; and
2. Take all steps necessary or appropriate to complete the assignment competently; and
3. Describe the lack of knowledge and/or experience and the steps taken to complete the assignment competently in the report.

Comment: The background and experience of appraisers varies widely and a lack of knowledge or experience can lead to inaccurate or inappropriate appraisal practice. The competency provision requires the appraiser to perform a specific appraisal service competently. If an appraiser is offered an opportunity to perform an appraisal service but lacks the necessary knowledge or experience to complete it competently, the appraiser must disclose his or her lack of knowledge or experience to the client before accepting the assignment and then take the necessary or appropriate steps to complete the appraisal service competently. This may be accomplished in various ways including, but not limited to, personal study by the appraiser; association with an appraiser believed to have the necessary knowledge or experience; or retention of others who possess the required knowledge or experience.

Although this provision requires an appraiser to identify the problem and disclose any deficiency in competence prior to accepting an assignment, facts or conditions uncovered during the course of an assignment could cause an appraiser to discover that he or she lacks the required knowledge or experience to complete the assignment competently. At the point of such discovery, the appraiser is obligated to notify the client and comply with items 2 and 3 of the provision.

The concept of competency also extends to appraisers who are requested or required to travel to geographic area wherein they have no recent appraisal experience. An appraiser preparing an appraisal in an unfamiliar location must spend sufficient time to understand the nuances of the local market and the supply and demand factors relating to the specific property type and the location involved. Such understanding will not be imparted solely from a consideration of specific data such as demographics, costs, sales and rentals. The necessary understanding of the local market conditions provides the bridge between a sale and a comparable sale or a rental and a comparable rental. If an appraiser is not in a position to spend the necessary amount of time in a market area to obtain this understanding, affiliation with a qualified local appraiser may be the appropriate response to ensure the development of a competent appraisal.

Jurisdictional Exception

If any part of these standards is contrary to the law or public policy of any jurisdiction, only that part shall be void and of no force or effect in that jurisdiction.

Supplemental Standards

These Uniform Standards provide the common basis for all appraisal practice. Supplemental standard applicable to appraisals prepared to specific purposes or property types may be issued by public agencies and certain client groups, e.g., regulatory agencies, eminent domain authorities, asset managers, and financial institutions. Appraiser and clients ascertain whether any supplemental standards in addition to these Uniform Standard apply to the assignment being considered.

Definitions

For the purpose of these standards, the following definitions apply:

Appraisal: (noun) The act or process of estimating value; an estimate of value. (adjective) of or pertaining to appraising and related functions, e.g. appraisal practice, appraisal services.

Appraisal practice: The work or services performed by Appraisers, defined by three terms in these standards: appraisal, review, and consulting.

Comment: These three terms are intentionally generic, and are not mutually exclusive. For example, an estimate of value may be required as a part of a review or consulting service. The use of other nomenclature by an appraiser (e.g. analyses, counseling, evaluation, study, submission, valuation) does not exempt an appraiser from adherence to these standards.

Cash Flow Analysis: A study of the anticipated movement of cash into or out of an investment.

Client: Any party for whom an appraiser performs a service.

Consulting: The act or process of providing information, analyses of real estate data, and recommendations or conclusions on diversified problems in real estate, other than estimating value.

Feasibility Analysis: A study of the cost benefit relationship of an economic endeavor.

Investment Analysis: A study that reflects the relationship between acquisition price and anticipated future benefits of a real estate investment.

Market Analysis: A study of real estate market conditions for a specific type of property.

Market Value: Market value is the major focus of most real property appraisal assignments. Both economic and legal definitions of market value have been developed and refined.

A current economic definition agreed upon by federal financial institutions in the United States of America is:

The most probable price which a property should bring in a competitive and open market under all conditions requisite to a fair sale, the buyer and the seller each acting prudently and knowledgeably, and assuming the price is not affected by undue stimulus. Implicit in this definition is the consummation of a sale as of a specified date and the passing of title from buyer to seller under conditions whereby:

1. Buyer and seller are typically motivated;
2. Both parties are well informed or well advised, and acting in what they consider their best interests;
3. A reasonable time is allowed for exposure in the open market;
4. Payment is made in the terms of cash in United States dollars or in terms of financial arrangements comparable thereto; and
5. The price represents the normal consideration for the property sold unaffected by special or creative financing or sales concessions granted by anyone associated with the sale.

Substitution of another currency for *United States dollars* in the fourth condition is appropriate in countries or in reports addressed to clients from other countries.

Persons performing appraisal services that may be subject to litigation are cautioned to seek the exact legal definition of market value in the jurisdiction in which the services are being performed.

Mass Appraisal: The process of valuing a universe of properties as of a given date utilizing standard methodology, employing common data, and allowing for statistical testing.

Mass Appraisal Model: A mathematical expression of how supply and demand factors interact in a market.

Personal Property: Identifiable portable and tangible objects which are considered by the public as being "personal," e.g. furnishings, artwork, antiques, gems and jewelry, collectibles, machinery and equipment; all property that is not classified as real estate.

Real Estate: An identifiable parcel or tract of land, including improvements, if any.

Real Property: The interests, benefits, and rights inherent in the ownership of real estate.

Comment: In some jurisdictions, the terms "real estate" and "real property" have the same legal meaning. The separate definitions recognize the traditional distinction between the two in appraisal theory.

Report: Any communication, written or oral, of an appraisal, review or analysis; the document that is transmitted to the client upon completion of an assignment.

Comment: Most reports are written and most clients mandate written reports. Oral report guidelines (See Standards Rule 2-4) and restrictions (See Ethics Provision: Record Keeping) are included to cover court testimony and other oral communications of an appraisal, review, or consulting service.

Review: The act or process of critically studying a report prepared by another.

Section II–Real Property Appraisals

Standard 1

In developing a real property appraisal, an appraiser must be aware of, understand, and correctly employ those recognized methods and techniques that are necessary to produce a credible appraisal.

Comment: Standard 1 is directed toward the substantive aspects of developing a competent appraisal. The requirements set forth in Standard Rule 1-1, the appraisal guidelines set forth in Standards Rules 1-2, 1-3, 1-4, and the requirements set forth in Standards Rule 1-5 mirror the appraisal process in the order of topics addressed and can be used by appraisers and the users of appraisal services as a convenient checklist.

Standards Rule 1-1. In developing a real property appraisal, an appraiser must:

(a) Be aware of, understand, and correctly employ those recognized methods and techniques that are necessary to produce a credible appraisal;

Comment: Departure from this binding requirement is not permitted. This rule recognizes that the principle of change continues to affect the manner in which appraisers perform appraisal services. Changes and developments in the real estate field have a substantial impact on the appraisal profession. Important changes in the cost and manner of constructing and marketing commercial, industrial, and residential real estate and changes in legal framework in which real estate property rights and interests are created, conveyed, and mortgaged have resulted in corresponding changes in appraisal theory and practice. Social change has also had an effect on appraisal theory and practice. To keep abreast of these changes and developments, the appraisal profession is constantly reviewing and revising appraisal methods and techniques and devising new methods and techniques to meet new circumstances. For this reason it is not sufficient for appraisers to simply maintain the skills and the knowledge they possess when they become appraisers. Each appraiser must continuously improve his or her skills to remain proficient in real property appraisal.

(b) Not commit a substantial error of omission or commission that significantly affects an appraisal;

Comment: Departure from this binding requirement is not permitted. In performing appraisal services an appraiser must be certain that the gathering of factual information is conducted in a manner that is sufficiently diligent to ensure that the data would have a material or significant effect on the resulting opinions or conclusions are considered. Further an appraiser must use sufficient care in analyzing such data to avoid errors that would significantly affect his or her opinions or conclusions.

(c) Not render appraisal services in a careless or negligent manner, such as a series of errors that, considered individually, may not significantly affect the results of an appraisal, but which, when considered in the aggregate, would be misleading.

Comment: Departure from this binding requirement is not permitted. Perfection is impossible to attain and competence does not require perfection. However, an appraiser must not render appraisal services in a careless of negligent manner. This rule requires an appraiser to use due diligence and due care. The fact that the carelessness and the negligence of an appraiser has not caused an error that significantly affects his or her opinions or conclusions and thereby seriously harms a client or a third party does not excuse such carelessness or negligence.

Standards Rule 1-2. In developing a real property appraisal, an appraiser must observe the following specific appraisal guidelines:

(a) Adequately define the real estate, identify the real property interest, consider the purpose and intended use of the appraisal, consider the extent of the data collection process, identify any special limiting conditions, and identify the effective date of the appraisal;

(b) Define the value being considered; if the value to be estimated is market value, the appraiser must clearly indicate whether the estimate is the most probable price:

(i) In terms of cash; or

(ii) In terms of financial arrangements equivalent to cash; or

(iii) In such other terms as may be precisely defined; if an estimate of value is based on submarket financing or financing with unusual conditions or incentives, the terms of such financing must be clearly set forth, their contributions to or negative influence on value must be described and estimated, and the market data supporting the valuation must be described and explained;

Comment: For certain types of appraisal assignments in which a legal definition of market value has been established and takes precedence, the Jurisdictional Exception may apply to this guideline.

If the concept of reasonable exposure in the open market is involved, the appraiser should be specific as to the estimate of marketing time linked to the value estimate.

(c) Consider easements, restrictions, encumbrances, leases, reservations, covenants, contracts, declarations, special assessments, ordinances, or other items of a similar nature;

(d) Consider whether an appraised fractional interest, physical segment, or partial holding contributes pro rata to the value of the whole;

Comment: This guideline does not require an appraiser to value the whole when the subject of the appraisal is a fractional interest, a physical segment, or a partial holding. However, if the value of the whole is not considered, the appraisal must clearly reflect that the value of the property being appraised cannot be used to estimate the value of the whole by mathematical extension.

(e) Identify and consider the effect on value of any personal property, trade fixtures or intangible items that are not real property but are considered in the appraisal.

Comment: This guideline requires the appraiser to recognize the inclusion of items that are not real property in an overall value estimate. Additional expertise in personal property or business appraisal may be required to allocate the overall value to its various components. Separate valuation of such items is required when they are significant to overall value.

Standards Rule 1-3. In developing a real property appraisal, an appraiser must observe the following specific appraisal guidelines:

(a) Consider the effect on use and value of the following factors: existing land use regulations, reasonably probable modifications of such land use regulations, economic demand, the physical adaptability of the real estate, neighborhood trends, and the highest and best use of the real estate;

Comment: This guideline sets forth a list of factors that affect use and value. In considering neighborhood trends, an appraiser must avoid stereotyped or biased assumptions relating to race, age, color, religion, gender, or national origin or an assumption that racial, ethnic, or religious homogeneity is necessary to maximize value in a neighborhood. Further, an appraiser must avoid making an unsupported assumption or premise about neighborhood decline, effective age, and remaining life. In considering highest and best use, an appraiser should develop the concept to the extent that is required for a proper solution of the appraisal problem being considered.

(b) Recognize that land is appraised as though vacant and available for development to its highest and best use and that the appraisal of improvements is based on their actual contribution to the site.

Comment: This guideline may be modified to reflect that, in various legal and practical situations, a site may have a contributory value that differs from the value as if vacant.

Standards Rule 1-4. In developing a real property appraisal, an appraiser must observe the following specific guidelines, when applicable:

(a) Value the site by an appropriate appraisal method or technique;

(b) Collect, verify, analyze, and reconcile: (i) Such comparable cost data as are available to estimate the cost new of the improvements (if any); (ii) Such comparable data as are available to estimate the difference between cost new and the present worth of the improvements (accrued depreciation); (iii) Such comparable sales data, adequately identified and described, as are available to indicate a value conclusion;

(iv) Such comparable rental data as are available to estimate the market rental of the property being appraised;

(v) Such comparable operating expense data as are available to estimate the operating expenses of the property being appraised;

(vi) Such comparable data as are available to estimate rates of capitalization and/or rates of discount.

Comment: This rule covers the three approaches to value. See Standards Rule 2-2 (j) for corresponding reporting requirements.

(c) Base projections of future rent and expenses on reasonably clear and appropriate evidence;

Comment: Although the value of the whole may be equal to the sum of the separate estates or parts, it also may be greater than or less than the sum of the separate estates or parts. Therefore, the value of the whole must be tested by reference to appropriate market data and supported by an appropriate analysis of such data.

A similar procedure must be followed when the value of the whole has been established and the appraiser seeks to estimate the value of a part. The value of any such part must be tested by reference to appropriate market data and supported by appropriate analysis of such data.

(f) Consider and analyze the effect on value, if any, of anticipated public or private improvements, located on or off the site, to the extent that market actions reflect such anticipated improvements as of the effective appraisal date;

Comment: In condemnation evaluation assignments in certain jurisdictions, the Jurisdictional Exception may apply to this guideline.

(g) Identify and consider the appropriate procedures and market information required to perform the appraisal, including all physical, functional, and external market factors as they may effect the appraisal;

Comment: The appraisal may require a complete market analysis.

(h) Appraise proposed improvements only after examining and having available for future examination:

(i) plans, specifications, or other documentation sufficient to identify the scope and character of the proposed improvements;

(ii) evidence indicating the probable time of completion of the proposed improvements; and

(iii) Reasonably clear and appropriate

evidence supporting development costs, anticipated earnings, occupancy projections, and the anticipated competition at the time of completion.

Comment: The evidence required to be examined and maintained under this guideline may include such items as contractor's estimates relating to cost and the time required to complete construction. Market and feasibility studies; operating cost data; and the history of recently completed similar developments. The appraisal may require a complete feasibility analysis.

(i) All pertinent data in items (a) through (h) above shall be used in the development of an appraisal.

Comment: See Standards Rule 2-2 (k) for corresponding reporting requirements.

Standards Rule 1-5. In developing a real property appraisal, an appraiser must:

(a) Consider and analyze any current Agreement of Sale, option, or listing of the property being appraised, if such information is available to the appraiser in the normal course of business;

(b) Consider and analyze any prior sales of the property being appraised that occurred in the following time periods:

(i) One year for one-to-four-family residential property; and

(ii) Three years for all other property types;

Comment: The intent of this requirement is to encourage the research and analysis of prior sales of the subject; the time frames cited are minimums.

(c) Consider and reconcile the quality and quantity of data available and analyzed within the approaches used and the applicability or suitability of the approaches used.

Comment: Departure from this binding requirement is not permitted. See Standards Rule 2-2 (k) Comment for corresponding reporting requirements.

Standard 2

In reporting the results of a real property appraisal an appraiser must communicate each analysis, opinion, and conclusion in a manner that is not misleading.

Comment: Standard 2 governs the form and content of the report that communicates the results of an appraisal to clients and third parties.

Standards Rule 2-1. Each written or oral real property appraisal report must:

(a) Clearly and accurately set forth the appraisal in a manner that will not be misleading;

Comment: Departure from this binding requirement is not permitted. Since most reports are used and relied upon by third parties, communications considered adequate by the appraiser's client may not be sufficient. An appraiser must take extreme care to make certain that his or her reports will not be misleading in the marketplace or to the public.

(b) Contain sufficient information to enable the person(s) who receive or rely on the report to understand it properly;

Comment: Departure from this binding requirement is not permitted. A failure to observe this rule could cause a client or other users of this report to make a serious error even though each analysis, opinion, and conclusion in the report is clearly and accurately stated. To avoid this problem and the dangers it presents to clients and other users of reports, this rule requires an appraiser to include in each report sufficient information to enable the reader to understand it properly. All reports, both written and oral, must clearly and accurately present the analyses, opinions, and conclusions of the appraiser in sufficient depth and detail to address adequately the significance of the particular appraisal problem.

(c) Clearly and accurately disclose any extraordinary assumption or limiting condition that directly affects the appraisal and indicate its impact on value.

Comment: Departure from this binding requirement is not permitted. Examples of extraordinary assumptions or conditions might include items such as the execution of a pending lease agreement, atypical financing, or completion of onsite or offsite improvements. In a written report the disclosure would be requires in conjunction with statements of each opinion conclusion that is affected.

Standards Rule 2-2. Each written real property appraisal report must:

(a) identify and describe the real estate being appraised;

(b) identify the real property interest being appraised;

Comment on (a) and (b): These two requirements are essential elements in any report. Identifying the real estate can be accomplished by any combination of a legal description, address, map reference, copy of a survey or map, property sketch and/or photographs. A property sketch and photographs also provide some description of the real estate in addition to written comments about the physical attributes of the real estate. Identifying the real property rights being appraised requires a direct statement substantiated as needed by copies or summaries of legal descriptions or other documents setting forth any encumbrances.

(c) State the purpose of the appraisal;

(d) Define the value to be estimated;

(e) Set forth the active date of the appraisal and the date of the report;

Comment on (c), (d), and (e): These three requirements call for clear disclosure to the reader of a report the "what, why, and when" surrounding the appraisal. The purpose of the appraisal is used generically to include both the task involved and rationale for the appraisal. Defining the value to be estimated requires both an appropriately referenced definition and any comments needed to clearly indicate to the reader how the definition is being applied [See Standards Rule 1-2 (b)]. The effective date for the appraisal establishes the context for the value estimate, while the date of the report indicates whether the perspective of the appraiser on the market conditions was prospective, current, or retrospective. Reiteration of the date of the report and the effective date of the appraisal at various stages of the report in tandem is important for the clear understanding of the reader whenever market conditions on the date of the report are different from the market conditions on the effective date of the appraisal.

(f) Describe the extent of the processes of collecting, confirming, and reporting data;

Comment: It is suggested that assumptions and limiting conditions be grouped together in an identified section of the report.

(h) Set forth the information considered, the appraisal procedures followed, and the reasoning that supports the analyses, opinions, and conclusions;

Comment: This requirement calls for the appraiser to summarize the data considered and the procedures that were followed. Each item must be addressed in the depth and detail required by its significance to the appraisal. The appraiser must be certain that sufficient information is provided so that the client, the users of the report, and the public will understand it and will not be misled or confused. The substantive content of the report, not its size, determines its compliance with this guideline.

(i) Set forth the appraiser's opinion of the highest and best use of the real estate, when such an opinion is necessary and appropriate;

Comment: This requirement calls for written report to contain a statement of the appraiser's opinion as to the highest and best use of the real estate, unless an opinion as to highest and best use is unnecessary, e.g., insurance valuation or value in use appraisals. If an opinion as to highest and best use is required; the reasoning in support of the opinion must also be included.

(j) Explain and support the exclusion of any of the usual valuation approaches;

(k) set forth any additional information that may be appropriate to show compliance with, or clearly identify and explain permitted departures from, the requirements of Standard 1;

Comment: This requirement calls for a written appraisal report or other written communication concerning the results of an appraisal to contain sufficient information to indicate that the appraiser complied with requirements of Standard 1, including the requirements governing any permitted departure from the appraisal guidelines. The amount of detail required will vary with the significance of the information to the appraisal.

Information considered and analyzed in compliance with Standards Rule 1-5 is significant information that deserves comment in any report. If such information is unattainable, comment on the efforts undertaken by the appraiser to obtain the information required.

(l) include a signed certification in accordance with Standards Rule 2-3.

Comment: Departure from binding requirements (a) through (l) above is not permitted.

Standards Rule 2-3. Each written real property appraisal report must contain a certification that is similar in content to the following form:

I certify that, to the best of my knowledge and belief:
- The statements of fact contained in this report are true and correct.
- The reported analyses, opinions, and conclusions are limited only by the supporting assumptions and limiting conditions, and are my personal, unbiased professional analyses, opinions, and conclusions.
- I have no (or the specified) present or prospective interest in the property that is the subject of this report, and I have no (or the specified) personal interest or bias with respect to the parties involved.
- My compensation is not contingent upon the reporting of a predetermined value or direction in that value that favors the cause of the client, the amount of the value estimate, the attainment of a stipulated result, or the occurrence of a subsequent event.
- My analyses, opinions, and conclusions were developed, and this report has been prepared, in conformity with the Uniform Standards of Professional Appraisal Practice.
- I have (or have not) made a personal inspection of the property that is the subject of this report. (If more than one person signs the report, this certification must clearly specify which individuals did and which individuals did not make a personal inspection of the appraised property.)
- No one provided significant professional assistance to the person signing this report. (If there are exceptions, the name of each individual providing significant professional assistance must be stated.)

Comment: Departure from this binding requirement is not permitted.

Standards Rule 2-4. To the extent that it is both possible and appropriate, each oral real property appraisal report (including expert testimony) must address the substantive matters set forth in Standards Rule 2-2.

Comment: In addition to complying with the requirements of Standards Rule 2-1, an appraiser making an oral report must use his or her best efforts to address each of the substantive matters in Standards Rule 2-2.

Testimony of an appraiser concerning his or her analyses, opinions, or conclusions is an oral report in which the appraiser must comply with the requirements of this Standards Rule.

See *Record Keeping* under the ETHICS PROVISION for corresponding requirements.

Standards Rule 2-5. An appraiser who signs a real property appraisal report prepared by another, even under the label of "review appraiser," must accept full responsibility for the contents of the report.

Comment: Departure from this binding requirement is not permitted. This requirement is directed to the employer or supervisor signing the report of an employee or subcontractor. The employer or the supervisor is as responsible as the individual preparing the appraisal for the content and the conclusions of the appraisal and the report. Using a conditional label next to the signature of the employer or supervisor or signing a form report on the line over the words "review appraiser" does not exempt that individual from adherence to these standards.

This requirement does not address the responsibilities of the review appraiser, the subject of Standard 3.

Section III–Review Appraisals

Standard 3

In reviewing an appraisal and reporting the results of that review, an appraiser must form an opinion as to the adequacy and appropriateness of the report being reviewed and must clearly disclose the nature of the review process taken.

Comment: The function of reviewing an appraisal requires the preparation of a separate report or a file memorandum by the appraiser performing the review setting forth results of the review process. Review appraisers go beyond checking for a level of completeness and consistency in the report under review by providing comment on the content and conclusions of the report. They may or may not have first-hand knowledge of the subject property or of data in the report. The COMPETENCY PROVISION applies to the appraiser performing the review as well as the appraiser who prepared the report under review.

Reviewing is a distinctly different function from that addressed Standards Rule 2-5. To avoid confusion in the marketplace between these two functions, review appraisers should not sign the report under responsibility of a cosigner.

Review appraisers must take appropriate steps to indicate to third parties the precise extent of the review process. A separate report or letter is one method. Another appropriate method is a form or checklist prepared and signed by the appraiser conducting the review and attached to the report under review. It is also possible that stamped impression on the appraisal report under review, signed or initialed by the reviewing appraiser, may be an appropriate method for separating the review function from the actual signing of the report. To be effective, however, the stamp must briefly indicate the extent of the review process and refer to a file memorandum that clearly outlines the review process conducted.

The review appraiser must exercise extreme care in clearly distinguishing between the review process and the appraisal or consulting process. Original work by the review appraiser may be governed by STANDARD 1 rather than this standard. A misleading or fraudulent review and/or report violates the ETHICS PROVISION.

Standards Rule 3-1. In interviewing an appraisal, an appraiser must:

(a) Identify the report under review, the real estate and real property interest being appraised, the effective date of the opinion in the report under review, and the date of the review;

(b) Identify the extent of the review process to be conducted;

(c) Form an opinion as to the completeness of the report under review in light of the requirements in these standards;

Comment: The review should be conducted in the context of market conditions as of the effective date of the opinion in the report being reviewed.

(d) Form an opinion as to the apparent adequacy and relevance of the data and the propriety of any adjustments to the data:

(e) Form an opinion as to the appropriateness of the appraisal methods and techniques used and develop the reasons for any disagreement;

(f) Form an opinion as to whether the analyses, opinions, and conclusions in the report under review are appropriate and reasonable, and develop the reasons for any disagreement.

Comment: Departure from binding requirements (a) through (f) above is not permitted. An opinion of a different estimate of value from that in the report under review may be expressed, provided the review appraiser:

1. Satisfies the requirements of STANDARD 1;

2. Identifies and sets forth any additional data relied upon and the reasoning and basis for the different estimate of value; and

3. Clearly identifies and discloses all assumptions and limitations connected with the different estimate of value to avoid confusion in the marketplace.

Standards Rule 3-2. In reporting the results of an appraisal review, an appraiser must: (a) Disclose the nature, extent, and detail of the review process undertaken;

(b) Disclose the information that must be considered in Standards Rule 3-1(a) and ((b);

(c) Set forth the opinions, reasons, and conclusions required in Standards Rule 3-1 (c), (d), (e) and (f);

(d) Include all known pertinent information;

(e) Include a signed certification similar in content to the following:

I certify that, to the best of my knowledge and belief:

-The facts and data reported by the review appraiser and used in the review process are true and correct.

-The analyses, opinions, and conclusions in this review report are limited only by the assumptions and limiting conditions stated in this review report, and are my personal, unbiased professional analyses, opinions and conclusions.

-I have no (or the specified) present or prospective interest in the property that is the subject of this report and I have no (or the specified) personal interest or bias with respect to the parties involved.

-My compensation is not contingent on an action or event resulting from the analyses, opinions, or conclusions in, or the use of this review report.

-My analyses, opinions, and conclusions were developed and this review report was prepared in conformity with the Uniform Standards of Professional Appraisal Practice.

-I did not (did) personally inspect the subject property of the report under review.

-No one provided significant professional assistance to the person signing this review report. (If there are exceptions, the name of each individual providing significant professional assistance must be stated.)

Comment: Departure from binding requirements (a) through (e) above is not permitted.

(Excerpted from the *Federal Register,* Vol. 55, No. 251, December 31, 1990)

Key Terms and Concepts

The Appraisal Foundation:
    Appraisal Standards Board
    Appraiser Qualifications Board
    Uniform Standards of Professional Appraisal
        Practice (USPAP)
Financial Institutions Reform, Recovery and Enforcement
    Act (FIRREA) of 1989

Review Questions

1. Under the USPAP, how long must an appraiser retain copies of an appraisal report following preparation (assuming the report was not used in a lawsuit)?

    a. Three years
    b. Five years
    c. Two years
    d. One year

2. Which Standard(s) cover(s) review appraisers?

    a. Standard 1
    b. Standard 2
    c. Standard 3
    d. All of the above

3. A review appraiser who signs the report under review, even under the heading of "review appraiser" must take _____ for the contents of the report.

    a. full responsibility
    b. no responsibility
    c. partial responsibility
    d. limited responsibility

4. Under the USPAP, an appraiser must research the sales history of the subject (for prior sales) for what minimum time period for residential properties (one- to four-family)?

    a. Past three years
    b. Past two years
    c. Past one year
    d. Past five years

5. Advisory opinions _____ have a binding effect on practicing appraisers.

    a. do not
    b. do
    c. may
    d. must

6. Under the USPAP, an appraiser must research the sales history of the subject (for prior sales) for what minimum time period for nonresidential properties?

    a. Past three years
    b. Past two years
    c. Past one year
    d. Past five years

7. The Ethics Provision of the USPAP is divided into four sections. These are:

    a. conduct, management, advertising and record keeping.
    b. conduct, management, confidentiality and record keeping.
    c. ethics, management, advertising and record keeping.
    d. ethics, management, confidentiality and record keeping.

8. The minimum number of hours for one (1) year of appraisal experience, as established by the Appraiser Qualifications Board, is:

    a. 500 hours.
    b. 1,000 hours.
    c. 2,000 hours.
    d. 2,500 hours.

9. Standard 1 of the USPAP is primarily concerned with the:

    a. appraisal process.
    b. appraisal report.
    c. appraiser's ethics.
    d. appraiser's competence.

10. According to the USPAP, if an appraiser lacks the experience or knowledge to complete an assignment, he or she must take certain steps prior to accepting the assignment. These steps include:

    a. disclosing the lack of experience or knowledge; taking the necessary steps to become competent; describing what steps were taken in the report.
    b. associating with another appraiser.
    c. undertaking personal study.
    d. employing someone who knows how to complete the assignment.

16 Practice Examinations

Overview

This chapter prepares the student for the type of questions presented on a state residential appraisal examination. Two practice examinations are presented in this chapter. Each exam contains 100 questions covering key topics related to residential appraisal.

Learning Objectives

After completing this chapter, the student should be able to:

- Identify subject areas or specific topics in which he or she is weak

- Review that material in greater detail and depth

Practice Exam I

Practice Exam I consists of 100 multiple-choice questions. Four possible answers are presented for each question. Some answers may be correct in unique or special situations, or they may be partially correct. The student should choose the BEST answer to each question.

1. Appraisers usually:
   a. set or establish value.
   b. set or establish price.
   c. estimate price.
   d. estimate value.

2. Three distinguishing physical characteristics of real estate are:
   a. homogeneity, immobility and durability.
   b. heterogeneity, mobility and durability.
   c. durability, heterogeneity and immobility.
   d. appreciation, location and long life.

3. The highest or fullest estate in land is the:
   a. fee tail.
   b. fee simple.
   c. fee simple determinable.
   d. life estate.

4. The typical value sought in an appraisal is:
   a. value in use.
   b. investment value.
   c. market value.
   d. cost of production.

5. When estimating market value, the appraiser takes the viewpoint of:
   a. any buyer.
   b. any seller.
   c. typically informed buyers.
   d. typically informed sellers.

6. Tangible and intangible benefits generated by a property that are not received in money are called:
   a. pleasantries.
   b. niceties.
   c. bonuses.
   d. amenities.

7. Market value is typically based on:

   a. highest price paid by any purchaser.
   b. lowest price paid by any purchaser.
   c. most probable price paid by any purchaser.
   d. most probable price paid by a typically informed purchaser.

8. What is the compound rate of growth for two years if property values are growing at 9 percent annually?

   a. 9 percent
   b. 18 percent
   c. 19.18 percent
   d. 18.18 percent

9. At the beginning of the year a depositor places $1,000 in a bank for exactly one year. The bank pays the depositor $1,125 at the end of the year. What annual rate of compounding is indicated?

   a. 10 percent
   b. 25 percent
   c. 12.50 percent
   d. 1.25 percent

10. Assume lots in a certain subdivision sold for an average of $10,000 one year ago. Today those lots sell for an average of $12,500. What is the indicated percentage change in value?

    a. 10 percent
    b. 25 percent
    c. 12.5 percent
    d. 1.25 percent

11. Title to real property is transferred with a:

    a. bill of sale.
    b. mortgage.
    c. deed.
    d. contract.

12. Ownership of real estate by only one owner is called:

    a. joint tenancy.
    b. tenancy by the entireties.
    c. sole proprietorship.
    d. ownership in severalty.

13. Title to personal property is transferred by a:

    a. deed.
    b. bill of sale.
    c. mortgage.
    d. deed of trust.

14. Four governmental restrictions on private ownership rights include:
    a. escheat, police power, zoning and building codes.
    b. escheat, police power, zoning and taxation.
    c. escheat, police power, eminent domain and taxation.
    d. escheat, police power, eminent domain and zoning.

15. Title to real estate generally passes with:
    a. signature of the deed.
    b. delivery and acceptance of the deed.
    c. recording of the deed.
    d. writing of the deed.

16. Parties to a deed are called:
    a. testator and testatrix.
    b. mortgagor and mortgagee.
    c. grantor and grantee.
    d. buyer and purchaser.

17. A section of land contains:
    a. 320 acres.
    b. 43,560 square feet.
    c. 36 townships.
    d. 640 acres.

18. One acre contains _____ square feet.
    a. 43,650
    b. 42,560
    c. 44,560
    d. 43,560

19. The principle of _____ holds that a purchaser is buying the right to receive future benefits.
    a. substitution
    b. supply and demand
    c. change
    d. anticipation

20. The value of a property to a particular owner or user is:
    a. market value.
    b. value in exchange.
    c. value in use.
    d. leasehold value.

21. To have value, an item must possess which economic characteristics?

    a. Land, labor, capital and entrepreneurship
    b. Social, legal/political, environmental and economic
    c. Location, location and location
    d. Utility, scarcity, effective demand and transferability

22. The reasonable and probable use that supports highest present value is:

    a. highest and best use.   c. marginal productivity.
    b. change.   d. substitution.

23. The added value of a pool to a residence could be estimated using the economic principle of:

    a. change.   c. marginal productivity.
    b. supply and demand.   d. regression analysis.

24. A good's capacity to satisfy human desires or needs is described as:

    a. usefulness.   c. functional obsolescence.
    b. utility.   d. external utility

25. A mortgage that covers more than one parcel of real estate is called a:

    a. chattel mortgage.   c. blanket mortgage.
    b. personal mortgage.   d. joint venture mortgage.

26. Sometimes the seller will take back a mortgage as part of the purchase price. Such a mortgage is a:

    a. blanket mortgage.   c. negotiable mortgage.
    b. purchase-money mortgage.   d. chattel mortgage.

27. Two components of a mortgage payment are:

    a. principal and time.   c. principal and interest.
    b. interest and time.   d. interest and term.

28. Holding all other factors constant, increasing the term on a mortgage will:

    a. lower the monthly payment.
    b. raise the monthly payment.
    c. not affect the monthly payment.
    d. lower the interest rate.

29. The process of systematic repayment of principal is referred to as:

    a. payoff.
    b. balance outstanding.
    c. amortization.
    d. negative amortization.

30. If the borrower fails to meet the interest component of the payment, the lender typically adds this deficiency to the original loan amount. This amortization process is:

    a. positive amortization.
    b. full amortization.
    c. partial amortization.
    d. negative amortization.

Use the following data to answer questions 31–35.

Suppose you purchased a house for $120,000. The lender allowed a maximum loan-to-value ratio of 90 percent. To close the loan, the lender charged a discount fee of 1 point and an origination fee of 1 point. At loan closing, the current market interest rate was 12 percent. Typical mortgage terms are 30 years with monthly payments.

31. What is the maximum amount that could be borrowed on the mortgage?

    a. $100,000
    b. $110,000
    c. $108,000
    d. $102,000

32. Assuming these are the only settlement costs and the buyer borrowed the maximum amount, what is the total dollar amount of settlement or closing costs?

    a. $2,000
    b. $3,000
    c. $2,060
    d. $2,160

33. Given a mortgage loan constant of 0.010286, what is the monthly payment on the loan at 12 percent, assuming the borrower obtained the maximum amount?

    a. $1,110.89
    b. $1,200.00
    c. $1,080.89
    d. $1,075.89

34. The four stages in the life cycle of a neighborhood are:

    a. change, supply and demand, elasticity, and purchasing power.
    b. growth, stability or maturity, decline and renewal.
    c. introduction, growth, maturity and decline.
    d. growth, decline, renewal and revitalization.

35. Four factors affecting market analysis are:

    a. legal, social, economic and environmental.
    b. sociological, legal, financial and international.
    c. regional, international, local and city.
    d. physical, economic/financial, political/governmental and sociological.

Use the following data to answer questions 36–37.

The city of East Lake has a total population of 96,000; 34,000 of its population is employed. Total basic employment in the city is 17,000. The transportation industry in East Lake employs 3,400 workers. The transportation industry employs 10 million persons throughout the United States. The United States has 150 million workers. Fax Express (part of the transportation industry) is expanding its operations in East Lake and will hire 1,600 additional people this year.

36. How much of local employment is represented by the transportation industry?

    a. 15 percent
    b. 12 percent
    c. 10 percent
    d. 50 percent

37. What is the location quotient for the transportation industry for East Lake?

    a. 2.5
    b. 1.5
    c. 15
    d. 25

38. _____ is the distance abutting a street or public way.

   a. Right of way
   b. Frontage ✓
   c. Easement
   d. Zoning

39. Effective age can be calculated as:

   a. total economic life.
   b. total economic life minus total economic life.
   c. total economic life minus remaining economic life. ✓
   d. remaining economic life minus total economic life.

40. A lot is 150' × 200'. How many acres does this lot contain?

   a. .69
   b. .60
   c. .59
   d. .50

150 × 200 = 30,000 ÷ 43,560 = .6887 rd .69

41. The standard lot size in a local market is one acre. Suppose a subject parcel contained five acres. The additional four acres are:

   a. waste.
   b. functional obsolescence—superadequacy.
   c. excess land. ✓
   d. highest and best use.

42. The total period of time the improvements contribute to value is the:

   a. remaining economic life.
   b. remaining physical life.
   c. actual age.
   d. total economic life. ✓

43. When the appraiser is seeking market value, the site is valued:

   a. as if vacant and available to be put to highest and best use.
   b. as if currently improved and at its highest and best use.
   c. as if currently improved.
   d. as time permits.

44. Four considerations or constraints on highest and best use are:
    a. permissible, okay, fluent and acceptable.
    b. physically possible, legally permissible, feasible or appropriate use and produces highest land value.
    c. legal use, environmental use, zoning use and aesthetic use.
    d. aesthetic use, legal use, sociological use and environmental use.

45. For residential properties, the sales comparison approach is based on the principle of:
    a. change.
    b. conformity.
    c. externalities.
    d. substitution.

46. One major requirement or limitation of the sales comparison approach is:
    a. several new constructions.
    b. an active market of competitive properties.
    c. accurate cost information.
    d. accurate information on investor expectations.

47. The most detailed and time-consuming method of cost estimation is:
    a. unit-in-place.
    b. comparative unit.
    c. trade breakdown.
    d. quantity survey.

48. The cost approach is typically most applicable for:
    a. new structures or "no-market" appraisals.
    b. valuing income properties.
    c. valuing old, historic structures.
    d. farms.

49. The cost to construct an exact replica of the subject is:
    a. replacement cost.
    b. reproduction cost.
    c. limited cost.
    d. historical cost.

Use the following data to answer questions 50–51.

The total reproduction cost new of the improvements was estimated to be $100,000. Total accrued depreciation from all causes was estimated to be 40 percent of reproduction cost new. The site was valued at $20,000. The subject has 1,500 square feet of living area and 1,200 additional square feet of garage and storage space.

50. What is the estimated depreciated reproduction cost new of the improvements?
    a. $40,000
    b. $100,000
    c. $80,000
    d. $60,000

51. What is the estimated value of the subject using the cost approach?
    a. $40,000
    b. $100,000
    c. $80,000
    d. $60,000

52. In the cost approach an item is curable if the cost to cure is:
    a. less than the cost to repair.
    b. less than or equal to the cost to repair.
    c. less than or equal to the value added.
    d. greater than or equal to the value added.

53. A loss in value from all sources is:
    a. physical deterioration.
    b. functional obsolescence—deficiency.
    c. accrued depreciation.
    d. functional obsolescence—superadequacy.

54. The easiest and least time-consuming method of estimating depreciation is the:
    a. age-life method.
    b. modified age-life method.
    c. engineering breakdown method.
    d. quantity survey method.

55. Loss in value as a result of having one bathroom when the market standard is two bathrooms is considered:

   a. physical deterioration.
   b. functional obsolescence.
   c. external obsolescence.
   d. functional obsolescence—superadequacy.

Use the following data to answer questions 56–62.

You have been asked to appraise a subject that is 13 years old. The estimated reproduction cost new of the improvements is $200,000 with a typical economic life of 60 years. You have determined that effective age is approximately equal to actual age. However, you notice several items that appear to contribute to a value loss. The subject is in need of exterior and interior painting. Exterior painting will cost $2,000, and interior painting will be 40 percent of the exterior painting cost. Other items in need of repair are shown below.

Item	Reproduction cost new	Effective age, years	Total economic life, years
Roof	$10,000	10	25
Carpeting	12,000	5	10
Vinyl	8,000	10	20

The subject has only one bathroom; similar houses have two and one-half bathrooms. Furthermore, you notice that the property is adjacent to a sanitary landfill. In-depth research reveals that properties located around noxious odors typically rent for $600 less per year. Gross rent multiplier analysis has suggested a GRM of 120 for similar properties. An additional full bathroom adds $5,000 to value, whereas a half-bathroom adds $3,500 to value. One bathroom would cost $4,000 to add now, but this cost estimate would have been $1,000 less had the bathroom been added when the structure was first built. A half-bathroom costs $250 more if added today than when the structure was initially completed. Curing the curable items will reduce effective age by one year.

56. What is your estimate of physical depreciation—curable?

   a. $32,800
   b. $2,000
   c. $3,800
   d. $2,800

57. What is your estimate of physical depreciation—incurable short-lived?

   a. $32,800
   b. $12,000
   c. $23,800
   d. $14,000

58. What is your estimate of physical depreciation—incurable long-lived?

   a. $32,440
   b. $12,340
   c. $33,440
   d. $2,440

59. What is your estimate of total physical deterioration from all sources?

   a. $50,240
   b. $33,440
   c. $24,300
   d. $42,300

60. What is your estimate of total functional obsolescence?

   a. $32,440
   b. $1,250
   c. $33,440
   d. $42,300

61. What is your estimate of total external obsolescence?

   a. $32,440
   b. $12,340
   c. $72,000
   d. $6,000

62. What is your estimate of total accrued depreciation?

   a. $50,240
   b. $33,440
   c. $39,440
   d. $57,490

63. The most frequently occurring value in a distribution or a sample is the:

   a. mean.
   b. median.
   c. mode.
   d. standard deviation.

64. The measure of central tendency that can be defined as the 50th percentile, or "the one in the middle," is the:

   a. mean.
   b. median.
   c. mode.
   d. standard deviation.

Use the following data to answer questions 65–67.

Suppose you are appraising a house with three bedrooms and two bathrooms. Analysis of the market reveals ten similar sales. These sales and their sales prices are as follows:

No. of sales	Price
1	$55,000
2	$60,000
3	$57,000
2	$58,000
2	$62,000

65. What is the median sales price?

   a. $55,000
   b. $60,000
   c. $57,000
   d. $58,000

66. What is the mean sales price?

   a. $55,000
   b. $60,000
   c. $57,000
   d. $58,600

67. What is the range?

   a. $55,000 to $62,000
   b. $60,000 to $60,000
   c. $7,000
   d. $58,000

68. In a normal distribution, _____ percent of the observations lie between the mean and plus or minus one standard deviation.

   a. 34.13
   b. 95.44
   c. 68.26
   d. 99.74

69. In a normal distribution, _____ percent of the observations lie between the mean and plus or minus two standard deviations.

   a. 34.13
   b. 95.44
   c. 68.26
   d. 99.74

Use the following data to answer question 70.

Suppose you have taken a sample of 32 residences in your local market to determine a pricing equation using regression analysis. You estimate sales prices (Y_c) to be based on the following equation:

$$Y_c = 40{,}900 + 5{,}000(X_1) + 2{,}500(X_2) + 500(X_3) + 3{,}000(X_4)$$

where X_1 is the number of bedrooms, X_2 is the number of bathrooms, X_3 is the number of cars the garage will hold and X_4 is the overall condition of the improvements. The condition variable, X_4, can range from 1 to 4 with 4 being the best and 1 being the worst overall condition. The subject is a four-bedroom, three-bathroom house with a three-car garage. The subject, in your opinion, is in the very best condition.

70. Using this regression equation, what is your estimate of sales price?
    a. $41,900
    b. $81,900
    c. $82,000
    d. $80,000

71. The final value estimate should:
    a. be very precise.
    b. be rounded to allow the lender to make the loan.
    c. be rounded to show that the number is an estimate and not an exact or extremely precise calculation.
    d. never be rounded.

72. The process by which the appraiser evaluates, chooses and selects a final value estimate is called:
    a. review.
    b. reconciliation.
    c. recalculation.
    d. data manipulation.

73. The preparation of the findings and indications of value for reconciliation is called:
    a. review.
    b. reconciliation.
    c. recalculation.
    d. data manipulation.

74. Which of the following is NOT an appraisal?

   a. Certified market analysis report.
   b. Letter report
   c. Narrative appraisal report
   d. Form appraisal report

75. According to the Uniform Standards of Professional Appraisal Practice, highest and best use _____ considered in all appraisals, if applicable.

   a. must be
   b. does not have to be
   c. does not merit to be
   d. is not important enough to be

76. You recently had the opportunity to appraise a unique property. However, you received assistance in your analyses, opinions and conclusions from a peer in your office. Should you disclose to your client that your peer also worked on the report?

   a. No. After all, your name is on the report.
   b. Yes. You must limit your liability.
   c. Yes. You must conform to the USPAP.
   d. It really depends on the situation and the client.

77. As a young, aggressive appraiser, you placed an advertisement that stated "I am competent to perform any and all types of appraisals. I will give you the value you need and want. Call me today for the best price." This advertisement probably:

   a. does not violate any rules, standards or code of ethics.
   b. is merely "puffing" in an effort to obtain business.
   c. is a violation of the USPAP.
   d. is just being aggressive.

78. A change in the number of members of a household is an example of _____ influences.

   a. physical/environmental   c. governmental/legal
   b. economic   d. social

79. In a condominium, the homeowner owns the common areas as a tenant in common and a particular unit as:

   a. fee simple.
   b. a tenant in common.
   c. a joint tenant.
   d. a tenant by the entireties.

80. If stabilized net operating income has been forecast to be $100,000 annually and the overall capitalization rate is 12.5 percent or .125, what is the indicated value?

   a. $ 100,000
   b. $1,000,000
   c. $800,000
   d. $1,250,000

81. In discounted cash flow analysis, the value of the property is equal to present worth of the:

   a. NOI plus present worth of the potential gross income.
   b. NOI plus present worth of the reversion.
   c. potential gross income plus present worth of the effective gross income.
   d. NOI plus future worth of the reversion.

82. One technique used for making adjustments is based on estimating the amount of adjustment for the presence or absence of a factor. This technique is called:

   a. regression analysis.
   b. grid analysis.
   c. paired sales analysis.
   d. cost analysis.

83. If a parcel of land has a value of $1,000,000 for assessment purposes and the assessment ratio is 20 percent, what is the property tax assuming the millage rate is 60 mills ($6 per $100)?

   a. $120,000
   b. $200,000
   c. $12,000
   d. $20,000

84. If a municipality has an assessment ratio of 40 percent and a taxing or millage rate of 40 mills ($4 per $100), what is the effective tax rate?

   a. 40 percent
   b. 4 percent
   c. 16 percent
   d. 1.6 percent

85. The excess or additional value from combining two or more smaller parcels into one parcel is called:

    a. incremental value.
    b. plottage value.
    c. assemblage.
    d. excess land.

86. If a landowner leased a site to a tenant, the tenant's interest would be called a(an):

    a. unencumbered fee.
    b. fee simple.
    c. leasehold.
    d. leased fee.

87. A site is typically valued:

    a. as if currently used.
    b. as if vacant and available to be put to its highest and best use.
    c. as if currently improved.
    d. as if the owner desires.

88. The principle of _____ forms the basis for the income approach.

    a. change
    b. substitution
    c. modification.
    d. anticipation.

89. In gross rent multiplier analysis, the comparable rentals are assumed to be:

    a. monthly on a furnished basis.
    b. annual on a furnished basis.
    c. monthly on an unfurnished basis.
    d. annual on an unfurnished basis.

90. The primary economic principle underlying the cost approach is the principle of:

    a. substitution.
    b. anticipation.
    c. supply and demand.
    d. liquidity.

91. _____ cost is the cost to construct a structure having similar utility but built with current technology and to current market standards.

    a. Reproduction
    b. Replacement
    c. Historical
    d. Relevant

92. When a sublease is created, the original tenant has a(an):

    a. leased fee.
    b. sandwich lease.
    c. percentage lease.
    d. assignment.

Use the following data to answer Questions 93–94.

Two comparables were (almost identical, except for the date of sale. Comparable 1 sold 18 months ago for $100,000. Comparable 2 sold yesterday for $112,000.

93. What annual rate of appreciation is indicated?

    a. 12 percent
    b. 10 percent
    c. 8 percent
    d. 11.2 percent

94. What is the dollar amount of adjustment to comparable 1 for date of sale?

    a. 0
    b. +$10,000
    c. −$12,000
    d. +$12,000

95. A lease specifies a base rent of $2,000 per month and an overage rent based on 3 percent of monthly net sales in excess of $200,000. ZeeZee Corporation had average monthly sales last year of $300,000. What was the total amount ZeeZee paid in lease payments for the year?

    a. $24,000
    b. $36,000
    c. $48,000
    d. $60,000

96. The tax rate for the subject is $2.00 per $100. The annual property tax is $1,000, while the assessment ratio is 40 percent of value. What is the market value for tax purposes?

    a. $800
    b. $2,000
    c. $125,000
    d. $20,000

97. The local government is taking a parcel of land from Sam and Mary Smith for the purpose of installing an airport runway. The right of the government to take the Smith's property is:

    a. escheat.
    b. police power.
    c. eminent domain.
    d. taxation.

98. Refer to question 97. The actual taking or the process of taking of the Smith's property is:

    a. condemnation.
    b. adverse possession.
    c. taking by prescription.
    d. escheat.

99. The noncompensable right of the government to regulate land use for the general welfare of the public is:

    a. escheat.
    b. police power.
    c. eminent domain.
    d. taxation.

100. Zoning laws, building codes and environmental regulations are examples of:

    a. escheat.
    b. police power.
    c. eminent domain.
    d. taxation.

Practice Examination II

Practice Exam II consists of 100 multiple-choice questions. Four possible answers are presented for each question. Some answers may be correct in unique or special situations, or they may be partially correct. The student should choose the BEST answer to each question.

1. Land and all the improvements on and to the land are termed:
   a. real property.
   b. real estate.
   c. personal property.
   d. fixtures.

2. The right or permission to use another's land is a(an):
   a. profit.
   b. emblement.
   c. easement.
   d. conveyance.

3. In a lease, the _____ has the right to receive periodic rents and the reversion.
   a. lessee
   b. tenant
   c. unencumbered fee owner
   d. lessor

4. The right of a municipality to regulate land use for potential environmental hazards is:
   a. police power.
   b. eminent domain.
   c. escheat.
   d. taxation.

5. Governmental entities have the right to take private property for the public good, a process called:
   a. eminent domain.
   b. condemnation.
   c. escheat.
   d. police power.

6. The typical financial arrangement in residential leases is a(n):
   a. net lease.
   b. percentage lease.
   c. index lease.
   d. fixed or gross lease.

7. In statistics, the range is computed as the:
   a. highest observation plus the lowest observation.
   b. highest observation minus the lowest observation.
   c. middle of the observations.
   d. highest plus the lowest observations divided by 2.

8. A type of multiple ownership whereby the surviving owner takes all remaining interests (outside of the deceased's estate) is:
   a. joint tenancy.
   b. tenancy in common.
   c. life estate.
   d. ownership in severalty.

9. In a condominium form of ownership, the owner of one unit owns that unit in fee simple and the common areas as a:
   a. fee simple owner.
   b. joint tenant owner.
   c. tenant in common owner.
   d. tenant by the entirety owner.

10. An appraiser hired to appraise a cooperative unit is acutally appraising:
    a. real estate.
    b. personal property.
    c. real property.
    d. fixtures.

11. The type of deed in which the seller (grantor) makes the most guarantees or representations is a:
    a. special warranty deed.
    b. quitclaim deed.
    c. general warranty deed.
    d. bargain and sale deed.

12. Assume that an investor required an annual return of 12 percent on a property whose market return was 10 percent annually. The appraiser prepared an appraisal report using the investor's required return of 12 percent. The appraiser estimated:
    a. value in use.
    b. market value.
    c. investment value.
    d. going-concern value.

13. The city of Mirage has a millage rate of 93 mills, or $9.30 per $100. The subject is an apartment complex assessed at $1,000,000. The annual property tax is:

    a. $93,000.
    b. $9,300.
    c. $930.
    d. $100.

14. The city of Mirage also taxes convenience stores at the same millage rate of 93 mills. The assessment ratio on convenience stores is 20 percent. The subject convenience store has been estimated to have a market value of $200,000. What is the effective property tax rate?

    a. 20 percent
    b. 18.6 percent
    c. 1.86 percent
    d. 9.3 percent

15. *Value in exchange* is a term used interchangeably, or synonymously, with the term:

    a. *market value.*
    b. *value in use.*
    c. *investment value.*
    d. *exchange value.*

16. According to the USPAP, market value presumes that the typical purchaser is:

    a. fully informed or fully advised.
    b. well informed or well advised.
    c. uniformed or unadvised.
    d. ignorant of market conditions.

17. The subject is situated atop a mountain and has a gorgeous view. Based on market data, the amenities that accrue as a result of the subject's location would be worth $5,000 to a typical purchaser. However, one purchaser recently paid $20,000 just to have a scenic mountain view. The $20,000 is the:

    a. market value.
    b. value in exchange.
    c. investment value.
    d. value in use.

18. Sam's house recently sold for $150,000, but similar houses on Sam's street have sold for $135,000. The appraisal on Sam's house, performed by an SRA, estimated the market value at $135,000. The $150,000 is the:

    a. price.
    b. cost.
    c. market value.
    d. investment value.

19. Susan, a local residential contractor, incurred direct costs of $35 per square foot on a recently completed house. She also had indirect costs including overhead of $15 per square foot. Susan estimated a 20 percent profit on total cost per square foot for her risk-taking function. What is her estimated total cost per square foot of the improvements?

    a. $60.00
    b. $62.50
    c. $50.00
    d. $35.00

20. According to the USPAP, market value is stated in terms of:

    a. cash or financing terms equivalent to cash.
    b. gold bouillon.
    c. nonmarket financing
    d. financial market conditions on the date of report completion.

21. The quantity of a good offered for sale at a given price is characterized as:

    a. quantity demanded.
    b. supply.
    c. demand.
    d. exchange.

22. The economic principle that forms the basis for adjustments in the sales comparison approach is the principle of:

    a. contribution.
    b. substitution.
    c. anticipation.
    d. competition.

23. The economic concept that holds that land is a residual claim or the last paid of the factors of production is known as:

    a. surplus productivity.
    b. competition.
    c. supply and demand.
    d. variable proportions.

24. The primary economic principle underlying the income approach is the principle of:

    a. contribution.
    b. substitution.
    c. anticipation.
    d. competition.

25. Analysis of highest and best use of a site is typically performed in two steps:

    a. as if vacant and under its current use.
    b. as improved and under its current use.
    c. as if vacant and as improved.
    d. as improved and as proposed.

26. Valuation of the site assuming one use and the improvements assuming a different use violates the principle of:

    a. highest and best use.
    b. supply and demand.
    c. conformity.
    d. consistent use.

27. The economic principle that serves as a rationale for the life cycle of neighborhoods is the principle of:

    a. balance.
    b. conformity.
    c. change.
    d. substitution.

28. The principle of _____ holds that value is enhanced when the subject is surrounded by similar or conforming land uses.

    a. balance
    b. conformity
    c. change
    d. substitution

29. Types of costs include direct costs, indirect costs and:

    a. overhead.
    b. materials.
    c. labor.
    d. entrepreneurial profit.

30. Which statement is true about the relationship between the market value of a property and market price at the time the property is sold?

    a. Both market value and market price are the same.
    b. Market price will always exceed market value.
    c. Market value will always exceed market price.
    d. The market price could be more or less than the market value depending on the underlying motivations of the buyer and seller, details of the transaction and other market circumstances.

31. An appraisal for a quick sale would be estimating what type of value?

  a. Value in use
  b. Use value
  c. Market value
  ✓d. Liquidation value

32. An appraisal description meaning the legally and physically possible use that, at the time of appraisal, is likely to produce the greatest land or site value is known as:

  ✓a. highest and best use.
  b. investment value.
  c. going-concern value.
  d. fee simple use.

33. The outcome of the act or process of estimating value is a(n):

  ✓a. appraisal report.
  b. appraisal.
  c. investment analysis.
  d. feasibility analysis.

34. Which of the following economic principles is the foundation on which estimating accrued depreciation is based?

  a. Change
  b. Consistent use
  ✓c. Contribution
  d. Substitution

35. In the rectangular survey method of land description, an area one mile by one mile is referred to as a:

  a. range line.
  b. township line.
  ✓c. section.
  d. township.

36. The extension of an improvement or object, such as a building or driveway, across the legal boundary of an adjoining tract of land is referred to as a(an):

  a. easement in gross.
  b. license.
  ✓c. encroachment.
  d. easement appurtenant.

37. That portion of a condominium owned in severalty by the owner is referred to as a:

  a. common element.
  b. town house.
  ✓c. unit.
  d. cooperative.

38. Which of the following applies to an item that originally was personal property but has become real property as a result of how it was used or attached to a building?

    a. Real property
    ✓b. Fixture
    c. Trade fixture
    d. Personal property

39. The right of a lessor to possess leased property when the lease terminates is the right of:

    a. termination.
    b. repossession.
    c. remainder.
    ✓d. reversion.

40. What type of accrued depreciation is generally NOT curable?

    a. Functional
    b. Straight line
    ✓c. External
    d. Physical

41. Most sales transactions occur in an open and competitive market where each party is acting in their own best interest. This is called a(an):

    a. distorted sale.
    ✓b. arm's length sale.
    c. negotiated sale.
    d. foreclosure sale.

42. John constructed a swimming pool that extended 5' across the city's draining easement. This is a(an):

    a. easement.
    ✓b. encroachment.
    c. emblements.
    d. license.

43. The estimated remaining economic life of a structure is the:

    a. total period of time over which real estate improvements contribute to property value.
    ✓b. estimated remaining period of time over which improvements (the structure) will add or contribute to property value.
    c. number of years since completion.
    d. estimated period of time remaining until repairs will have to be made.

44. Which of the following methods is NOT an acceptable technique of estimating cost new of the improvements?

   a. Quantity survey technique
   b. Unit-in-place method
   c. Breakdown method
   d. Comparative unit method

45. What term refers to the loss of value from all causes outside the subject's property boundaries?

   a. External depreciation
   b. Functional deterioration
   c. Physical deterioration
   d. Functional obsolescence—superadequacy

46. A residence may decline in value if a waste disposal plant is built nearby. This is an example of what form of depreciation?

   a. Functional depreciation
   b. External depreciation
   c. Physical depreciation
   d. Incurable functional obsolescence

47. The age of a property based on the amount of wear and tear it has sustained is referred to as:

   a. effective age.
   b. chronological age.
   c. physical age.
   d. physical life.

48. The difference between a building's total economic life and its remaining economic life is the:

   a. effective age.
   b. chronological age.
   c. physical age.
   d. physical life.

49. What is the total area of a parcel of land that measures 100 feet by 60 feet?

   a. 6,000 feet
   b. 6,000 square feet
   c. 6,000 cubic feet
   d. 6,000 square miles

50. The age of a building as indicated by its physical condition and utility compared to the building's useful life is referred to as:

   a. effective age.
   b. chronological age.
   c. physical age.
   d. physical life.

51. The difference between the reproduction cost new of the improvements and their present value is known as:

   a. accounting depreciation.
   b. accrued depreciation.
   c. physical depreciation.
   d. incurable physical depreciation.

52. An industrial building needs improved modern lighting, which costs $50,000. If the improvement would result in an increase in value to the building of $55,000, the depreciation is referred to as:

   a. functional obsolescence—incurable.
   b. functional obsolescence—curable.
   c. locational obsolescence—curable.
   d. physical obsolescence—incurable.

53. A superadequacy is defined as:

   a. a site used more efficiently than its highest and best use.
   b. a structural feature that is more than the market standard and not fully valued by the marketplace.
   c. a site whose effective age is less than its actual age.
   d. a property generating excess income.

54. The basic equation used in the income approach to value is:

   a. overall rate divided by net operating income equals value.
   b. net operating income divided by an overall capitalization rate equals value.
   c. overall rate times net operating income equals value.
   d. overall rate minus net operating income equals value.

55. The income approach to value:

    a. is based on the principle of substitution.
    b. translates the ability of property to generate income into an indication of value.
    c. requires an estimate of before-tax cash flow.
    d. All of the above

56. When a property's vacancy and collection loss are subtracted from potential gross income, which of the following is derived?

    a. Effective gross income
    b. Net operating income
    c. Rent collections
    d. Taxable income

57. A small apartment complex valued at $400,000 earns a monthly net income of $3,000. What is the overall capitalization rate?

    a. .75 percent
    b. 9 percent
    c. 12 percent
    d. 20 percent

58. Net operating income less annual debt service equals:

    a. potential gross income.
    b. effective gross income.
    c. before-tax cash flow.
    d. net income after debt subtraction.

59. Capitalization is the process used to:

    a. establish cap rates.
    b. established reasonable rates of return.
    c. establish a depreciation schedule.
    d. convert one year's income into an estimate of value.

Use the following data to answer questions 60–66.

An apartment complex is the subject of an appraisal assignment. Recent sales of similar apartments reveal the following:

Sale 1: 2 units; gross monthly rent $720; gross building area 1,900 sq. ft.; sales price $144,000

Sale 2: 4 units; gross monthly rent $1,250; gross building area 3,800 sq. ft.; sales price $262,500

Sale 3: 5 units; gross monthly rent $1,700; gross building area 4,625 sq. ft.; sales price $348,500

Sale 4: 2 units; gross monthly rent $975; gross building area 2,500 sq. ft.; sales price $195,000

60. What is the range of the gross rent multipliers?

   a. 20
   b. 200–210
   c. 250
   d. 10

61. What is the range of the indicated sales price per square foot, rounded to the nearest dollar?

   a. $6
   b. $5
   c. $69–$78
   d. $9

62. What is the mean sales price per unit to the nearest thousand?

   a. $75,000
   b. $76,000
   c. $88,000
   d. $73,000

63. What is the mean gross rent multiplier?

   a. 200
   b. 215
   c. 205
   d. 204

64. What is the median gross rent multiplier?

   a. 200
   b. 205
   c. 210
   d. 203

65. What is the modal (mode) gross rent multiplier?

a. 200
b. 205
c. 210
d. 215

66. If the property being appraised is most comparable to sale 4, what is the indicated value by the GRM of the subject property with a gross rent of $850 per month?

a. $200,500
b. $170,000
c. $200,000
d. $150,000

67. What legal interest in real estate is valued by adding the present worth of the contract rent and the present worth of the reversion?

a. The fee simple estate
b. The leasehold estate
c. The leased fee estate
d. The reversion

68. In collecting and analyzing market data, an appraiser discovers that the market rent exceeds the contract rent for the subject property. Who benefits directly from this difference?

a. Lessor
b. Leasehold estate
c. Leased fee estate
d. Mortgagee

69. According to the Uniform Standards of Professional Appraisal Practice, an appraiser must consider and analyze any prior sales of residential property (one- to four-family) bieng appraised (subject) that occurred within what time period?

a. Two years
b. One year
c. Three years
d. Five years

70. Which of the following terms describes a study that reflects the relationship between acquisition price and anticipated future benefits of a real estate investment?

a. Feasibility analysis
b. Investment analysis
c. Economic base analysis
d. Market analysis

71. Which standard of the USPAP states that in developing a real estate appraisal, an appraiser must be aware of, understand and correctly apply those recognized methods and techniques that are necessary to produce a credible appraisal?

    a. Standard 1
    b. Standard 5
    c. Standard 2
    d. Standard 3

72. What term describes a study of real estate market conditions for a specific type of property?

    a. Feasibility analysis
    b. Investment analysis
    c. Economic base analysis
    d. Market analysis

73. The purpose of the Uniform Standards of Professional Appraisal Practice is to:

    a. promote professionalism in appraisers and lenders.
    b. avoid additional regulation.
    c. present information that will be meaningful to clients and not be misleading in the marketplace.
    d. present information that will be useful to appraisers.

74. What term defines the act or process of critically studying a report prepared by another?

    a. Review
    b. Investment analysis
    c. Economic base analysis
    d. Market analysis

75. What term denotes the time and distance relationships between a subject property and other possible destinations?

    a. Linkages
    b. Egress
    c. Ingress
    d. Access

76. The appraisal process consists of many steps, the first of which is to:

    a. define the problem.
    b. collect and analyze data.
    c. analyze highest and best use.
    d. make initial estimate of value.

77. Typically, the "as of" date in an appraisal report refers to the date:

    a. the appraisal assignment was accepted.
    b. the appraisal report was delivered.
    c. of the last inspection.
    d. the loan is to be closed.

78. The objective of undertaking an appraisal of real estate is to:

    a. estimate market value.
    b. estimate value as defined.
    c. establish loan value.
    d. estimate value in exchange.

79. In applying the sales comparison approach, the appraiser determines that one of the comparables is superior to the subject property in terms of location. What adjustment should be made?

    a. The comparable should be adjusted up.
    b. The comparable should be adjusted down.
    c. The subject property should be adjusted up.
    d. The subject property should be adjusted down.

80. If comparable 1 sold for $300,000 and has a two-car garage that adds $15,000 to the value, and the subject property does not have a garage, the indicated value of the subject property would be found by:

    a. adding $15,000 to the comparable sale.
    b. subtracting $15,000 from the comparable sale.
    c. adding $15,000 to the subject property.
    d. subtracting $15,000 form the subject property.

81. The dollar amount of rent received from a parcel of real estate when rented in an open competitive market is referred to as:

    a. economic rent.   c. cash received.
    b. contract rent.   d. market rent.

82. A reversion is one benefit that accrues to the lessor. It typically follows which of the following types of legal estates?

   a. Leased fee estate
   b. Fee simple absolute
   c. Net lease
   d. Fee simple absolute

83. Which of the following leases does NOT provide at least some protection to the lessor against inflation?

   a. Fixed or gross lease
   b. Step-up lease
   c. Index lease
   d. Graduated lease

84. In collecting data, an appraiser concludes that comparable properties have increased in value at a 7 percent annual compound rate during the previous two years. A comparable sold two years ago for $20,000. The proper time adjustment is:

   a. $2,800.
   b. $2,898.
   c. $1,400.
   d. $2,500.

85. In appraising new or proposed improvements, which of the following statements is true, according to the Uniform Standards of Professional Appraisal Practice?

   a. The appraiser must examine plans and specifications or other documentation sufficient in scope to identify the character of the proposed improvements.
   b. The appraiser does not have to examine plans and specifications to identify the character of the proposed improvements if they are available to him or her.
   c. The appraiser must have the plans and specifications reviewed by an engineer or architect to see if they adhere to local building codes.
   d. The appraiser must be sure that no hazardous waste exists on the site.

86. Which provision or standard states that in reporting the results of a real estate appraisal, an appraiser must communicate each analysis, opinion and conclusion in a manner that is not misleading?

   a. Standard 3
   b. The departure provision
   c. Standard 2
   d. Standard 1

87. When a parcel of real estate is used as the collateral for a loan, the borrower is referred to as the:

   a. mortgagor.
   b. mortgagee.
   c. offeror.
   d. offeree.

88. When a parcel of real estate is used as the collateral for a loan, the lender is referred to as the:

   a. mortgagor.
   b. mortgagee.
   c. offeror.
   d. offeree.

89. In a deed, the grantee is the:

   a. seller.
   b. buyer.
   c. lender.
   d. broker.

90. The term *real estate* is generally used to refer to the physical land and improvements, whereas the term *real property* denotes:

   a. air and surface rights.
   b. subsurface and air rights only.
   c. machinery and equipment.
   d. rights, interests and benefits inherent in real estate ownership.

91. A current land use that exists prior to the establishment of a zoning district or current zoning regulations and is not consistent with current restrictions imposed on land uses in that district is called a (an):

   a. interim use.
   b. legally nonconforming use.
   c. variance use.
   d. transitional use.

92. In using the sales comparison approach, the appraiser determines that in terms of location, sale 1 is superior to the subject property but the subject is inferior to sale 2. The correct procedure should be to:

   a. adjust both sales down to the subject.
   b. adjust both sales up to the subject property.
   c. adjust sale 1 down and sale 2 up to the subject.
   d. adjust sale 1 up and sale 2 down to the subject.

93. The term *frontage* refers to the:
    a. perimeter of a property.
    b. depth of a site.
    c. distance abutting a street or public way.
    d. distance between the front of a site and the back of the site.

94. A tract of land containing five acres recently sold for $7 per square foot. What is the estimated land value?
    a. $43,560
    b. $2,661,360
    c. $5,922,720
    d. $1,524,600

95. A house with exterior dimensions of 80 feet by 50 feet has an area of:
    a. 2,490 square feet.
    b. 4,000 square feet.
    c. 4,000 feet square.
    d. 4,000 cubic feet

96. The sales comparison approach is most reliable when which of the following markets exists?
    a. Active market
    b. Inactive market
    c. Active market of similar sales
    d. Seller's market

Refer to the following data to answer questions 97–99.

A comparable property sold six months ago for $225,000. Market investigation indicates the following:

Location adjustment:	+$5,000
Time adjustment:	+$10,000
Age adjustment:	–$15,000

97. What is the indicated net adjustment to the comparable property?
    a. $0
    b. $5,000
    c. $10,000
    d. $30,000

98. What is the amount of total gross adjustments?
    a. $0
    b. $5,000
    c. $10,000
    d. $30,000

99. What is the adjusted sales price of the comparable?
    a. $225,000
    b. $230,000
    c. $240,000
    d. $220,000

100. The subject is 10 percent superior to comparable 1 but 5 percent inferior to comparable 2. What should the adjustment be to comparable 2?
    a. +5 percent
    b. −5 percent
    c. +10 percent
    d. −10 percent

Answer Key

Chapter 2

1. b. The fee simple is the highest estate in land.
2. d. Ownership by one party is termed ownership in severalty.
3. c. Four governmental restrictions on the ownership of private property are: escheat, police power, eminent domain and taxation.
4. c. Parties to a deed are called grantor and grantee.
5. b. A lease is a contract for the use of specified premises in exchange for rent.
6. d. Physical, economic or financial, political or governmental and social factors influence value.
7. d. The owner's interest is termed a leased fee estate.
8. a. An individual unit in a condominium is owned in fee simple.
9. a. In a cooperative, the owner owns stock in a corporation.
10. c. Co-tenancy is not a legal form of ownership.
11. c. Joint tenancy is co-ownership with right of survivorship.
12. c. In most states, title to real property passes with delivery and acceptance of the deed.
13. b. The conveyance "To John for life" is an example of a life estate.

Chapter 3

1. d. Most appraisals seek to estimate value.
2. c. Market value is the type of value typically sought in an appraisal.
3. c. An appraiser takes the viewpoint of a typically informed buyer.
4. d. Market value is based on most probable price paid by a typically informed purchaser.
5. c. Market value is synonymous with value in exchange.
6. c. The value to a particular user is termed value in use.
7. b. $2,000,000 × .50 = $1,000,000 × .070 = $70,000.
8. d. .40 × .080 = .032 or 3.2%.
9. c. Going-concern value is the value of an operating entity.
10. b. Investment value is the value to a particular investor.
11. b. Liquidation value is the value of a property assuming quick conversion to cash.
12. b. Market value is not the same as cost.
13. d. Both the seller and the purchaser are typically (or well) informed.
14. a. Market value may or may not be market price.

Chapter 4

1. c. Durability, heterogeneity and immobility are three distinguishing characteristics of real estate.
2. b. Real estate is land and all the improvements on and to that land.
3. b. Real property is rights in real estate.
4. d. Amenities are tangible and intangible non-monetary benefits of ownership.
5. c. Title to real property is transferred with a deed.
6. b. Title to personal property is transferred with a bill of sale.
7. b. Land, labor, capital and entrepreneurship are the four factors of production.
8. a. In a purely competitive market, all participants base decision-making on price.
9. d. The principle of anticipation holds that a purchaser is buying the right to receive future benefits.
10. d. Expected future benefits are called amenities in residential properties.
11. d. To have value, an item must have utility, scarcity, demand and transferability.
12. a. Highest present value is supported by highest and best use.
13. c. The principle of marginal productivity (or contribution) could be used to estimate the value of a pool.
14. b. Utility is the ability of a good to satisfy human needs and desires.

Chapter 5

1. b. Interest is the price of money.
2. d. The Federal Reserve system has responsibility for monetary policy.
3. a. Fractional reserve banking describes a banking system wherein banks retain only a small portion of deposits and loan the majority to customers.
4. b. Leverage is the use of debt to finance assets.
5. b. A purchase money mortgage is one in which a seller takes back part of the purchase in the form of a mortgage.
6. c. Principal and interest are two components of a mortgage payment.
7. a. Increasing the term on a mortgage typically will lower the monthly payment.
8. c. Amortization is the systematic repayment of principal.
9. b. Interest is satisfied first from each payment of an amortized mortgage.
10. d. Negative amortization is the process whereby a certain portion of a payment is added to the original loan amount if the payment is insufficient to meet the interest.
11. c. A balloon payment is the amount remaining at the end of a partially amortized loan.
12. b. Real estate is characterized by a high degree of debt financing.

13. c. A package mortgage may be secured by both real and personal property.
14. a. Market analysis is the study of a local market for a given type of property.
15. d. Appraisal firms are not sources of real estate capital.

Chapter 6

1. b. The date of the value estimate establishes its market conditions.
2. c. Every appraisal should consider the three approaches to value.
3. b. An appraiser typically values the site to estimate market value.
4. a. Description of the real estate (both physical and legal) occurs during the definition of the problem.
5. a. During the definition of the problem, identification of the property interest occurs.
6. c. The first step in the appraisal process is to define the problem.
7. b. The final step in the appraisal process is to write the report and provide the findings to the client.
8. c. Reconciliation is performed after application of the approaches to value.
9. c. The final estimate is rounded to show that it is an estimate and not a precise calculation.
10. c. The date of the value estimate identifies market and environmental conditions in effect at that time.
11. d. A narrative report is a detailed, comprehensive appraisal report.
12. c. Expert testimony is an example of an oral report.
13. a. Assumptions and limiting conditions are typically addressed during the definition of the problem.
14. a. Certification of value is typically addressed during the definition of the problem.
15. b. Data verification should occur during the data collection and analysis step.

Chapter 7

1. c. Excess land is additional land over the market standard.
2. b. Sites include land and any improvements to the land.
3. a. Functional utility is the sum of the attractiveness and usefulness of a property.
4. c. Platform construction is a type of construction where, theoretically, each floor supports itself.
5. c. Amenities are non-monetary pleasantries of ownership.
6. d. The adequacy of a structure is measured in terms of market standards.
7. a. A site is typically estimated to determine market value.
8. b. Front feet or frontage is the distance abutting a street or public way.

9. c. Depth is the distance from front to rear of a site.
10. c. The foundation is the major part of the structure below grade (or below the ground).
11. b. Modernization is the process of bringing a property up to current market standards.
12. d. Rehabilitation is changing a structure's form or style to correct functional deficiencies.
13. a. Repair is placing the property in a suitable condition.
14. c. The frame is the skeleton of a structure.

Chapter 8

1. b. A site is valued as if vacant and available to be put to its highest and best use.
2. c. The highest and best use of a site may be different from the highest and best use of a property as improved.
3. a. Physically possible, legally permissible, financially feasible and most profitable use are four tests of best use.
4. a. Highest and best use is the perfect use.
5. c. Non-conformity to governmental regulations fails the test of legal permissibility.
6. c. Legal non-conforming use refers to an improvement that does not conform to current regulations.
7. d. An interim use is one where highest and best use is expected to change.
8. b. A variance allows the legal construction of a non-conforming structure.
9. d. Functional obsolescence results when improvements are less than ideal.
10. a. To be the most profitable use, a site must provide the highest cash to the land.

Chapter 9

1. c. The mode is the most frequently occurring value in a distribution or sample.
2. b. The median is the 50th percentile.
3. b. The range is the difference between the high and low values.
4. b. Description and inference are two uses of statistics.
5. d. $58,000 is the median sales price.
6. d. The mean is the average or the sum of the observations divided by the number of observations; in this case, $58,600.
7. c. The range is $7,000 (the difference between the highest and lowest values).
8. d. *a* is the Y intercept.
9. c. *b* is the slope of the line.

10. c. 68.26 percent of the observations lie between the mean and plus or minus one standard deviation.
11. b. 95.44 percent of the observations lie between the mean and plus or minus two standard deviations.

Chapter 10

1. d. The sales comparison is based primarily on the principle of substitution.
2. a. Market value estimates are through the eyes of typically informed purchasers.
3. b. The direct sales comparison approach requires an active market of competitive properties.
4. b. Primary data is data that has not been previously collected.
5. b. Adjustments are made to the comparables to make them similar to the subject.
6. c. Paired sales analysis is based on the amount that a factor contributes to value in its presence or detracts from value in its absence.
7. b. The sales comparison approach is typically the most applicable for appraising residential properties.
8. d. Dollar and percentage are two generally accepted types of adjustments.
9. b. The sequence of adjustments is the proper order of adjustments.
10. b. All adjustments should be market-justified when using paired sales analysis.
11. c. The objective of any appraisal is to estimate value as defined.
12. d. No set minimum number of sales is required in the sales comparison approach.
13. a. The comparables do not need a financing adjustment because they are financed at market terms.
14. d. Never adjust the subject, only the comparables.
15. d. 5% per year, or for comparable 1, $175,000 × .05 = $8,750; for comparable 2, $180,000 × .05 = $9,000; comparable 3 sold last week, and needs no time adjustment.
16. b. The adjusted sales price for comparable 1 is $189,000 ($180,000 + $9,000 for time = $189,000); comparable 2, when adjusted for time, is similar to comparable 3 except for a basement. The difference between the adjusted sales price for comparable 2 and the sales price for comparable 3 is $11,000, the amount of the adjustment for basement. The subject is better than comparable 1, so add $11,000 to comparable 1 for a basement; the subject is better than comparable 2, so add $11,000 to comparable 2 for a basement; comparable 3 has a basement and needs no adjustment.
17. d. **Comparables 2 and 3** have 2-car garages and need no adjustment; comparable 1 has a one-car garage and requires a $3,000 adjustment.

18. d. Comparables 2 and 3 both have 2,000 square feet and require no adjustment; $2,250 is obtained by adjusting the sales price of comparable 1 for time, basement and garage and comparing this figure to comparables 2 and 3 ($200,000 − $197,500 = $2,250).
19. c. The total adjustments for comparables 1, 2 and 3 are +$25,000, +$20,000 and $0.
20. d. The adjusted sales prices are estimated by taking the sales price of each comparable and adding the total adjustments.

Chapter 11

1. c. Plottage value is the added value from combining two or more sites into one larger parcel.
2. a. Assemblage is the process of combining two or more parcels into one ownership.
3. c. The extraction technique estimates site value by subtracting the depreciated cost of improvements from the sales price of the total property.
4. c. The subdivision (development) technique is used for new developments.
5. b. Site value is typically estimated as if vacant and available to be put to its highest and best use.
6. d. The sales comparison technique is the preferred technique for site valuation if similar sales are available.
7. c. The indicated unit of comparison is price per square foot or price per acre.
8. a. $1.53; $1.60; $2.00 per square foot.
9. c. The indicated *dollar* adjustment is +1,800; +1,320; 0.

Chapter 12

1. a. Substitution is the primary principle underlying the cost approach.
2. c. Reproduction cost is usually estimated in residential appraisals.
3. b. Replacement cost is the cost to construct using current technology and design standards.
4. d. The quantity survey technique is the most detailed method of cost estimation.
5. a. The cost approach is typically most applicable for new structures or "no-market" appraisals.
6. b. Reproduction cost is the cost to construct an exact replica of a structure.
7. b. Direct costs can be assigned.
8. d. The estimated depreciated reproduction cost new is $60,000.
9. c. $60,000 depreciated cost new + site value of $20,000 = $80,000.
10. b. $53 ($80,000 ÷ $1,500).

11. c. $80,000 ÷ 2,700 = $30.
12. d. External obsolescence occurs outside the subject's property boundaries.
13. c. An item is curable when the cost to cure is less than or equal to the value added.
14. c. Accrued depreciation is a loss in value from all sources.
15. a. The age-life method is the least time-consuming method of estimating depreciation.
16. b. Functional obsolescence is a loss due to a missing component of the market standard; here, a second bathroom.
17. a. Here, external obsolescence is due to the undesirability of the site's location.

Chapter 13

1. d. The principle of anticipation forms the basis for the income approach.
2. d. Value can be estimated by dividing net operating income by the overall capitalization rate.
3. d. GRM is an extension of the sales comparison approach.
4. a. Contract rent is the amount of rent specified in a lease.
5. b. Market rent is the amount that rental space could command in the open market.
6. c. In GRM, comparables are assumed to be monthly on an unfurnished basis.
7. b. The range is $15 ($425 – $410).
8. c. $420 is the median.
9. c. $419 is the mean (the sum of the rents divided by the number of rents, or $2,935 ÷ 7 = $419, rounded).
10. b. The range is the highest observation minus the lowest observation, or 142 – 133 = 9.
11. a. The median is 134.
12. a. The mode is the most frequently occurring (134).
13. c. The mean gross rent multiplier is 136 (the sum of the gross rent multipliers divided by the number of gross multipliers).
14. c. Indicated value equals net operating income divided by the overall capitalization rate, or $100,000 ÷ .125 = $800,000.
15. c. Interest received by the lender is termed return on debt capital.
16. d. Principal received by the lender is termed return of debt capital.
17. b. Using discounted cash flow, the value of the property is equal to the present value of the NOI plus the present value of the reversion.
18. b. 100 units multiplied by $350 × 12 months plus 100 units × $420 × 12 months = 924,000 (100 × $350 = $35,000 × 12 = $420,000; 100 × $420 = $42,000 × 12 = $504,000; $420,000 + $504,000 = $924,000).
19. a. $924,000 – 8% = $924,000 × .92 = $850,080.

20. b. The operating expense ratio is total operating expenses divided by effective gross income (40%).
21. a. Effective gross income of $850,080 minus operating expenses of $340,032 equals $510,048.
22. b. $240,000 (annual debt service is equal to the monthly mortgage payment multiplied by 12 or, $20,000 × 12).
23. b. Before tax cash flow divided by the equity investment equals the equity dividend rate or, $270,048 ÷ $1,000,000 = .27.

Chapter 14

1. c. An assignment occurs when the original lessee gives up all rights under the lease.
2. a. A fixed or gross lease is where the tenant pays a flat or fixed amount each period and pays none of the costs of ownership.
3. c. An easement is the right to use land belonging to another.
4. b. A landowner's interest is termed a leased fee if the owner leases space to a tenant.
5. b. A proprietary lease makes a cooperative harder to sell.
6. c. A remainderman receives property after the death of the measuring life (life tenant).
7. d. A time-share may be a lease or conveyance of ownership for a specified period of time.
8. b. Retail leases are typically percentage leases.
9. a. In a sublease, the lessor typically looks to the original lessee for payment.
10. c. The value of the unencumbered fee is equal to the value of the leased fee plus the value of the leasehold.
11. b. The final value estimate should be rounded.
12. a. The objective of any appraisal is to estimate value as defined.

Chapter 15

1. b. According to the USPAP, an appraiser must retain copies of an appraisal report for 5 years following preparation.
2. c. Standard 3 of the USPAP covers review appraisers.
3. a. A review appraiser who signs the report under review must accept full responsibility for the contents of the report.
4. c. For one- to four-family residential properties, the USPAP requires the appraiser to research prior sales of the subject for the past year.
5. a. Advisory opinions of the Appraisal Standards Board of The Appraisal Foundation have no binding effect on appraisers.

6. a. The USPAP requires an appraiser to research prior sales of a subject non-residential property for the past three years.
7. b. The Ethics Provision is divided into four sections: conduct; management; confidentiality; and record keeping.
8. b. The minimum number of hours for one year of appraisal experience is 1,000 hours.
9. a. Standard 1 of the USPAP is primarily concerned with the appraisal process.
10. a. The Competency Provision requires an appraiser who lacks knowledge or experience to disclose this fact; take the necessary steps to become competent; and describe the steps taken in the report.

Practice Exam I

1. d. Appraisers estimate value, not price.
2. c. Durability, heterogeneity and immobility are three distinguishing characteristics of real estate.
3. b. The fee simple estate is the highest estate in land.
4. c. Market value is the value typically sought or estimated in an appraisal.
5. c. The appraiser takes the viewpoint of typically or well informed purchasers or buyers when estimating market value.
6. d. Amenities are non-monetary pleasantries of ownership.
7. d. Market value is based on the most probable price paid by a typically informed purchaser.
8. d. $1.09 \times 1.09 = 1.1818$, or a 18.18% growth rate.
9. c. 12.5% ($1,125 − $1,000) ÷ 1,000 = 125 ÷ 1,000 = .125 or 12.5%.
10. b. 25% ($12,500 − $10,000) ÷ 10,000 = 2,500 ÷ 10,000 = .25 or 25%.
11. c. A deed is a document used to transfer title to real property.
12. d. Ownership in severalty is ownership by only one party.
13. b. A bill of sale transfers title to personal property.
14. c. Four governmental restrictions on ownership of real property are escheat, police power, eminent domain and taxation.
15. b. Title to real estate generally passes with delivery and acceptance of the deed; recording is not required in many states for a valid conveyance.
16. c. The parties to a deed are termed the grantor and grantee.
17. d. One section contains 640 acres.
18. d. One acre contains 43,560 square feet.
19. d. The principle of anticipation asserts that a purchaser is buying the right to receive future benefits.
20. c. Value in use is the value to a particular user or owner.
21. d. Utility, scarcity, effective demand and transferability are required for an item to have value.

22.	a.	Highest and best use is that reasonable and probable use which support highest present value of a site.
23.	c.	The principle of marginal productivity (or contribution) is used to estimate the value that an item, such as a pool, adds to value in its presence or detracts from value in its absence.
24.	b.	Utility is the ability of a good to satisfy human needs or desires.
25.	c.	A blanket mortgage covers more than one parcel of real estate.
26.	b.	A purchase-money mortgage is one in which the seller takes back part of the purchase price in the form of a mortgage.
27.	c.	Principal and interest are two components of a mortgage payment.
28.	a.	Increasing the term on a mortgage will lower the monthly payment.
29.	c.	Amortization is the systematic repayment of principal.
30.	d.	Negative amortization occurs when the borrower's periodic payment is insufficient to cover the interest component of a mortgage.
31.	c.	$120,000 × .90 = $108,000 (purchase price multiplied by maximum loan-to-value ratio).
32.	d.	$108,000 (maximum mortgage) × .01 (origination fee) = $1,080 $108,000 × .01 (discount fee) = $1,080 Total settlement costs = $2,160
33.	a.	$108,000 × 0.010286 = 1,110.89.
34.	b.	The four stages in the life cycle of a neighborhood are: growth, maturity or stability, decline, and renewal or revitalization.
35.	d.	Physical, economic or financial, political or governmental, and sociological factors affect market analysis.
36.	c.	3,400 ÷ 34,000 = .10 or 10 percent.
37.	b.	(3,400 ÷ 34,000) ÷ (10,000,000 ÷ 150,000,000) = .10 ÷ 0.0667 = 1.5.
38.	b.	Frontage or front footage is the distance abutting a street or public way.
39.	c.	Effective age is total economic life minus remaining economic life.
40.	a.	(150' × 200') ÷ 43,560' = 30,000' ÷ 43,560' = .69 acres.
41.	c.	A parcel of land in excess of the market standard is termed excess land.
42.	d.	Total economic life is the total time over which the improvements contribute to value.
43.	a.	A site is typically valued as if it were vacant and available to be put to its highest and best use.
44.	b.	The four constraints or tests on highest and best use are: physically possible; legally permissible; economically feasible; and most profitable use.
45.	d.	The sales comparison approach for residential properties is based on the principle of substitution.
46.	b.	The sales comparison approach requires an active market of similar sales of competitive properties.

47. **d.** The quantity survey technique is the most detailed method of cost estimation.

48. **a.** In most appraisal assignments, the cost approach is most applicable for new structures or those properties where no—or a very limited—market exists.

49. **b.** Reproduction cost is the cost to construct an exact replica.

50. **d.** $100,000 × .40 = $40,000 accrued depreciation;
$100,000 − $40,000 = $60,000 estimated depreciated reproduction cost new.

51. **c.** $60,000 estimated depreciated reproduction cost new plus $20,000 site value = $80,000.

52. **c.** An item is curable when the cost to cure is less than or equal to the value added.

53. **c.** Accrued depreciation is a loss in value from all sources.

54. **a.** The age-life method is the simplest and least time-consuming method of estimating depreciation.

55. **b.** Functional obsolescence occurs when the subject has less than the market standard of a particular item or feature.

56. **d.** $2,000 for exterior painting plus interior painting ($2,000 × .40 = $800) equals $2,800.

57. **d.**
Roof: $10,000 × (10 ÷ 25) = $10,000 × .40	$ 4,000
Carpeting: $12,000 × (5/10) = $12,000 × .50	$ 6,000
Vinyl: $8,000 × (10 ÷ 20) = $8,000 × .50	$ 4,000
Total physical deterioration incurable short-lived	$14,000

58. **c.**
Total reproduction cost new:	$200,000
Less physical curable	−2,800
Less reproduction cost new of those items in physical incurable short-lived	−30,000
Total reproduction cost new allocated to structure (long-lived components)	$167,200
Times part of structure "wasted away" or Effective Age/Total Economic Life equals 12/60	× .20
Total physical incurable long-lived	$ 33,440

59. **a.** $2,800 physical curable + $14,000 physical incurable short-lived + $33,440 physical incurable long-lived = $50,240.

60. **b.** There is an excess cost if installed now of $1,000 for a full bath plus $250 for a half bath for a total excess cost of $1,250.

61. **d.** $600 annual rent loss divided by 12 months equals $50 rent loss per month multiplied by 120 GRM equals a value loss of $6,000.

62. **d.** Total accrued depreciation is physical plus functional plus external, or ($2,800 + 14,000 + 33,440) + $1,250 + $6,000 = $57,490.

63. **c.** The mode is the most frequently occurring value or observation in a sample.

64. **b.** The median is the 50th percentile.

Answer Key

65. d. If the data are arranged (smallest to largest value), the observation in the middle is $58,000.

66. d. $58,600 (the mean is the average).

67. c. The range is the highest observation minus the lowest observation or $62,000 − $55,000 = $7,000.

68. c. 68.26 percent of the observation in a normal distribution lie between plus or minus 1 standard deviation.

69. b. 95.44 percent of the observation in a normal distribution occur between plus or minus 2 standard deviations.

70. b. $Y_c = \$40,900 + \$5,000(X_1) + \$2,500(X_2) + \$500(X_3) + \$3,000(X_4)$
$Y_c = \$40,900 + (\$5,000 \times 4 = \$20,000) + (\$2,500 \times 3 = \$7,500) + (\$500 \times 3 = \$1,500) + (\$3,000 \times 4 = \$12,000) = \$81,900$.
These figures are obtained by multiplying each coefficient by its respective variable values.

71. b. A value estimate is rounded to show it is an estimate and not a precise mathematical calculation.

72. b. Reconciliation includes the selection of a final value estimate.

73. a. Review is the preparation of data and analyses for reconciliation.

74. a. A certified market analysis report is not an appraisal.

75. a. Highest and best use must be considered in every appraisal if applicable; in some assignments, highest and best use will not be applicable such as in the estimation of value in use.

76. c. According to USPAP, anyone who renders professional appraisal assistance including analyses, opinions or conclusions must be disclosed in the report.

77. c. This would be a violation of the management section of the Ethics provision of the USPAP.

78. d. This is an example of social factors that influence value.

79. a. The owner owns the unit in fee simple and the common areas as tenants in common.

80. c. Value equals the NOI divided by the overall capitalization rate (100,000 ÷ .125 = 800,000).

81. b. Value is equal to present worth of the NOI plus present worth of the reversion.

82. c. The paired sales analysis estimates the amount of an adjustment for a factor's presence or absence.

83. c. $1,000,000 (value) × .20 (assessment ratio) = $200,000 × .06 (millage rate) = $12,000.

84. d. Effective tax rate equals assessment ratio times millage rate, or .40 × .04 = .016 or 1.6 percent.

85. b. Plottage value is the excess value from combining two or more parcels into a larger parcel.

86. c. A tenant's interest is termed a leasehold.
87. b. Sites are typically valued as if vacant and available to be put to highest and best use.
88. d. The income approach is based on the principle of anticipation.
89. c. Rentals are monthly on an unfurnished basis in GMR analysis.
90. a. Substitution is the primary principle underlying the cost approach.
91. b. Replacement cost is the cost to construct similar improvements having similar utility.
92. b. In a sublease, the original tenant has what is commonly termed a sandwich lease.
93. c. The annual dollar amount of appreciation is $8,000; ($112,000 − $100,000 = $12,000 for 18 months; 12,000 ÷ 1.5 years = $8,000 per year). The annual rate is $8,000 ÷ $100,000 = .08 or 8 percent.
94. d. +$12,000 is the adjustment for date of sale.
95. d. Base rent of $2,000 multiplied by 12 months equals $24,000. Excess rent based on $100,000 ($300,000 − $200,000) multiplied by .03 (3%) equals $3,000 per month. Total monthly rent of $2,000 base rent plus $3,000 excess rent equals $5,000 per month multiplied by 12 months equals $60,000.
96. c. The $1,000 property tax divided by a tax rate of 0.02 equals $50,000 assessed value; $50,000 divided by assessment ratio of .40 equals $125,000, or market value for tax purposes.
97. c. Eminent domain is the right of the government to take private property for the public good.
98. a. The process of taking private property for the public good is termed condemnation.
99. b. Police power is the right of the government to regulate land use for the public welfare and is generally noncompensatory.
100. b. Police power includes zoning laws, building codes and environmental regulations.

Practice Exam II

1. b. Real estate is land and all the improvements on and to the land.
2. c. An easement is the right to use the land of another.
3. d. A lessor (landlord) has the right to receive rent and a reversion upon expiration of the lease.
4. a. Police power is the right of a government to regulate land use for public safety.
5. b. The *right* to take private property for the public good is termed eminent domain, but the *process* is termed condemnation.

6. d. In a residential lease, the typical financial arrangement is a fixed or gross lease.
7. b. The range is the highest observation minus the lowest observation.
8. a. A joint tenant's interest does not pass through his or her estate; it goes to the surviving joint tenant(s).
9. c. In a condominium, the owner typically owns the common areas as a tenant in common with other owners of individual units in the complex.
10. b. The appraiser is actually appraising personal property (a share of stock) in a cooperative.
11. c. The grantor makes the most warranties or representations in a general warranty deed.
12. c. Investment value is the value to a particular or given investor using that investor's constraints or requirements.
13. a. $1,000,000 (assessed value) multiplied by 0.093 (millage rate) equals $93,000.
14. c. The effective tax rate is 1.86 percent or .0186 (.20 assessment ratio multiplied by .093 millage rate equals .0186).
15. a. *Value in exchange* is used as a synomyn for *market value*.
16. b. The USPAP assumes that the typical purchaser is well-informed or well-advised.
17. d. Value to a particular user is termed value in use.
18. a. $150,000 is price, not market value.
19. b. Three types of cost are direct, indirect and entrepreneurial profit. Here, direct costs are $35 per square foot and indirect costs were $15 per square foot, for a total cost per square foot (before entrepreneurial profit) of $50 per square foot. This $50 represents 80 percent of total costs because entrepreneurial profit represents 20 percent. $50 divided by .80 equals a total cost of $62.50 (for proof, $62.50 × .20 = $12.50).
20. a. Market value is typically stated in terms of cash or financing terms equivalent to cash.
21. b. Supply is the quantity offered at a given price.
22. a. The principle of contribution forms the basis for adjustments in the sales comparison approach.
23. a. The concept of surplus productivity holds that land is paid as a residual claim.
24. c. Anticipation is the primary principle underlying the income approach.
25. c. Highest and best use of a site is typically performed assuming the site is vacant, or "as if vacant," and as improved.
26. d. The principle of consistent use holds that the site and improvements must be valued assuming the same use.

27. c. The principle of change holds that all neighborhoods undergo change, causing a life cycle effect.
28. b. The principle of conformity holds that value is enhanced when land uses are in conformity.
29. d. The three major categories of cost are direct, indirect and entrepreneurial profit.
30. d. Market price and market value may be different, depending on several factors.
31. d. Liquidation value assumes a rapid conversion to cash or a quick sale.
32. a. Highest and best use assumes a maximally productive or most profitable use resulting in highest land value.
33. a. An appraisal report is the outcome of the process or act of estimating value.
34. c. Accrued depreciation is based on the principal of contribution.
35. c. A section of land is one mile square (one mile on each side).
36. c. An encroachment is a protrusion of an improvement or other object across the land of another.
37. c. A unit is owned in fee simple by a condominium owner.
38. b. A fixture is an item that was formerly considered to be personal property, but has become real property because of its permanent attachment and use.
39. d. The lessor has the right to the reversion at the end of the lease.
40. c. External depreciation is generally not curable.
41. b. An arm's length sale is one in which the parties are acting in what they perceive to be their best interests.
42. b. An encroachment is trespassing on the domain of an another.
43. b. Remaining economic life is the estimated remaining period of time over which improvements will contribute to value.
44. c. The breakdown method is a method of estimating depreciation and not cost new.
45. a. External depreciation is a loss in value from all sources outside the subject's boundaries.
46. b. This is an example of external obsolescence.
47. a. Effective age is the age of a property taking into account its maintenance, upkeep and general wear and tear.
48. a. Effective age is computed by taking total economic life of the structure and subtracting remaining economic life.
49. b. 100' × 60' = 6,000 sq ft.
50. a. Effective age takes into account physical condition compared to similar structures.
51. b. Accrued depreciation is the difference between cost new and the present value of the improvements.

52. b. Functional obsolescence-curable, because the value added is equal to or greater than the cost to cure.
53. b. A superadequacy is a structural feature more than the market standard.
54. b. Value using direct capitalization in the income approach is estimated by taking NOI and dividing by an overall capitalization rate.
55. b. The income approach translates the ability of a property to generate income into an indication of value.
56. c. Potential gross income (or gross market income) minus vacancy and collection loss equals rent collections.
57. b. $3,000 × 12 months = $36,000; $36,000 ÷ $400,000 = .09 or 9 percent.
58. c. Before-tax cash flow equals NOI minus annual debt service.
59. d. Capitalization is a process to convert one year's income into value.
60. d. The range is the highest observation minus the lowest observation, or 210 minus 200 equals 10.
61. d. $78 − $69 = $9.
62. d. Sale prices per unit are: #1, $144,000; #2, $262,500; #3, $348,500; #4, $195,000. The mean sale price per unit is the sum of the sale prices per unit divided by the number of units, which is $950,000 ÷ 13 units, or $73,076, or rounded $73,000.
63. d. GRMs are as follows: #1, 200; #2, 210; #3, 205; #4, 200. The sum of the GRMs divided by the number (815 ÷ 4) is 203.75, or rounded to 204.
64. d. The median is the 50th percentile, or the one in the middle. When the terms are arranged from smallest to largest, the two in the middle are 200 and 205; 200 + 205 = 405 ÷ 2 = 202.5, or rounded to 203.
65. a. The mode is the most frequently occurring observation; 200 is the most frequently occurring GRM.
66. b. Value using the GRM is the market rent times the GRM. Assuming $850 to be the market rent, the value is $850 × 200, or $170,000.
67. c. The leased fee estate is the present value of the contract rental stream plus the present value of the reversion.
68. b. A leasehold estate benefits when the market rent is greater than contract rent because others in the marketplace are paying more for similar space.
69. b. An appraiser must consider prior sales of the subject within the previous year for one- to four-family residential properties.
70. b. Investment analysis is the relationship between acquisition price and anticipated future benefits.
71. a. Standard 1 of the USPAP covers a credible real estate appraisal.
72. d. Market analysis is a study of market conditions for a specific type of property.

73. c. The purpose of USPAP is to present information in appraisal reports that will be meaningful to clients and not be misleading in the marketplace.
74. a. The process of critically studying a report prepared by another is termed review.
75. a. Linkages denote time and distance relationships.
76. a. Defining the problem is the first step in the appraisal process.
77. c. Typically, the as-of date is the date of last or final inspection.
78. b. The objective of an appraisal is to estimate value as defined.
79. b. The comparable is better or superior to the subject; when the comparable is better, subtract or adjust the comparable down.
80. b. Subtract $15,000 from the comparable.
81. d. Market rent is the amount that the space would bring in an open and competitive environment.
82. a. A reversion typically follows the leased fee estate; a net lease is a financial arrangement and not a legal interest.
83. a. A fixed or gross lease provides no protection to the lessor.
84. b. $2,898 (20,000 × 1.07 × 1.07 − 20,000 = 2,898).
85. a. The USPAP requires the appraiser, when appraising proposed improvements, to examine plans, specifications or other documentation sufficient in scope to identify the character of the proposed improvements.
86. c. Standard 2 of the USPAP states that an appraiser must communicate each analysis, opinion and conclusion in a manner that is not misleading.
87. a. The borrower is the mortgagor; the lender is the mortgagee.
88. b. The lender is the mortgagee; the borrower is the mortgagor.
89. b. The grantee is typically the purchaser or buyer.
90. d. *Real property* is the rights, interests and benefits inherent in the ownership of real estate.
91. b. Legally non-conforming uses are those which existed prior to a zoning change or establishment of a zoning district.
92. a. Both sales should be adjusted to the subject; sale 1 is superior to the subject; the subject is inferior to sale 2 (sale 2 is superior to the subject).
93. c. Frontage is the distance abutting a street or public way.
94. d. 43,560 square feet per acre times 5 acres equals 217,800 square feet times $7 per square foot equals 1,524,600.
95. b. 80' × 50' = 4,000 sq ft.
96. a. The sales comparison approach is most reliable when there is an active market.
97. a. The net adjustment is +5,000, +10,000, −15,000 or 0.
98. d. Total gross adjustments are $30,000 (15,000 negative adjustments and 15,000 positive adjustments): Note that gross adjustments ignore arithmetic signs.

99. a. The adjusted sales prices of the comparables is $225,000.
100. b. The subject is inferior to comparable 2, meaning that comparable 2 is superior to the subject (deduct 5%).

Glossary

absorption rate The rate at which properties for sale or lease have been, or are expected to be, successfully marketed in a given area; usually used in forecasting sales or leasing activity.

accrued depreciation *1.* The difference between an improvement's reproduction or replacement cost and its market value as of the appraisal date. *2.* In accounting, the amount reserved each year or accumulated to date in the accounting system for replacement of a building or other asset.

actual age The number of years that have elapsed since construction of an improvement was completed; *also called* chronological age.

adjustable-rate mortgage A mortgage loan in which the interest rate is adjusted periodically based on a specified index or formula.

adverse possession The actual, exclusive, open, notorious, hostile and continuous possession and occupation of real property under an evident claim of right or title. The time required to obtain title legally by adverse possession varies from state to state.

age-life method The method of estimating accrued depreciation in which the ratio of a building's effective age to its total economic life is applied to the current cost of the improvements to obtain a lump-sum deduction.

allocation A method used to estimate land value in which an appraiser analyzes sales of improved properties to establish a typical ratio of site value to total property value and applies this ratio to a property being appraised or to a comparable sale being analyzed.

amenity *1.* A pleasant quality. *2.* A tangible or intangible benefit of real property that enhances its attractiveness or increases the satisfaction of the user, but is not essential to its use. Natural amenities may include a pleasant location near water or a scenic view of the surrounding area; man-made amenities include swimming pools, tennis courts, community buildings and other recreational facilities.

amortization The process of retiring a debt or recovering a capital investment through scheduled repayment of principal; a program of periodic contribution to a sinking fund or debt retirement fund.

anticipation The perception that value is created by the expectation of benefits to be derived in the future.

area The surface extent of a building, site, neighborhood, city section, tract or region that is measured in square units.

arm's-length transaction A transaction arrived at by unrelated parties, neither of whom is under duress.

assemblage The combining of two or more parcels, usually (but not necessarily) contiguous, into one ownership or use.

assessed value The value according to the tax rolls in ad valorem taxation.

assignment A written transfer of the rights of use and occupancy of the property to be held by another legal entity or to be used for the benefit of creditors.

assumptions and limiting conditions A list of assumptions and limitations on which the value estimate is based.

balance The principle holding that real property value is created and sustained when contrasting, opposing or interacting elements are in a state of equilibrium.

balloon mortgage A mortgage that is not fully amortized at maturity and thus requires a lump-sum, or balloon, payment of the outstanding balance.

balloon payment The outstanding balance due at the maturity of a balloon mortgage.

band of investment A technique in which cash flow rates attributable to components of a capital investment are weighted and combined to derive a weighted average rate attributable to the total investment.

blanket mortgage A mortgage that covers more than one property; common in subdivision development and in situations where the equity in one property is insufficient to satisfy loan policy. Usually, individual properties are released from the blanket mortgage as they are sold.

bundle of rights The concept that compares property ownership to a bundle of sticks, with each stick representing a distinct and separate right of the property owner. For example, the right to use real estate, to sell it, to lease it, to give it away or to choose to exercise all or none of these rights.

capital *1.* Accumulated wealth; a sum of money available for investment. *2.* In building construction, the uppermost part of a column, usually ornamented.

capitalization The conversion of income into value.

capital market The interaction of buyers and sellers trading long-term or intermediate-term money instruments.

cash equivalent A price expressed in terms of cash, as distinguished from a price expressed totally or partly in terms of the face amounts of notes or other securities that cannot be sold at their amounts.

change The result of the relationship between cause and effect that affects real property value.

chattel A legal term for personal property.

chattel mortgage A lien on chattels.

coefficient of correlation In statistics, a measure of the degree of relationship between variables and the way in which they change together. The correlation coefficient can range in value from -1 (perfect negative correlation) to "zero" (independence) to $+1$ (perfect positive correlation).

coefficient of determination In statistics, the proportion of the total variance in the dependent variable that is explained by the independent variables; the proportion of total variance explained by the regression; in business and economics, preferred to the term *coefficient of correlation* because coefficient of determination states the proportion of the variance in the dependent variable more clearly.

coefficient of variation In statistics, the standard error of the estimate divided by the mean value of the dependent variable; a measure of the relative chance for error in a forecast or estimate of the dependent variable.

commercial bank A privately owned institution that offers businesses and individuals a variety of financial services; may be state or federally chartered and is subject to government regulation; managed by a board of directors who are selected by stockholders.

comparables A term that describes similar property sales, rentals or operating expenses used for comparison in the valuation process; *also called* comps.

comparative-unit method The cost-estimating method used to derive a cost estimate in terms of dollars per unit of area or volume, based on known costs of similar structures and adjusted for time and physical differences.

competition Between purchasers or tenants, the interactive efforts of two or more potential purchasers or tenants to secure a purchase or lease; between sellers or landlords, the interactive efforts of two or more potential sellers or landlords to complete a sale or lease.

conformity The appraisal principle holding that real property value is created and sustained when a property's characteristics conform to the demands of its market.

consistent use The concept that the land cannot be valued on the basis of one use and the improvements valued on the basis of another use.

contribution The concept that the value of a particular component is measured in terms of its contribution to the value of the whole property, or as the amount that its absence would detract from the value of the whole.

cooperative ownership A form of ownership in which each owner of stock in a cooperative apartment building or housing corporation receives a proprietary lease on a specific apartment and is obligated to pay a rental that represents the proportionate share of operating expenses and debt service on the underlying mortgage, which is paid by the corporation. This proportionate share is based on the proportion of the total stock owned.

cost approach Approach through which an appraiser derives a value indication of the fee simple interest in a property by estimating the current cost to construct a reproduction of or replacement for the existing structure, deducting for all evidence of accrued depreciation from the cost new of the reproduction or replacement structure, and adding the estimated land value plus an entrepreneurial profit. Adjustments may be made to the indicated fee simple value of the subject property to reflect the value indication of the property interest being appraised.

curable functional obsolescence An element of accrued depreciation; a curable defect caused by a defect in the structure, materials or design.

curable physical deterioration An element of accrued depreciation; a curable defect caused by deferred maintenance.

debt coverage ratio (DCR) The ratio of net operating income (NOI) to annual debt service (ADS): DCR = NOI ÷ ADS.

debt service The periodic payment that covers interest on and retirement of the outstanding principal of the mortgage loan.

decline A stage of diminishing demand in a neighborhood's life cycle.

deed restriction A limitation that passes with land regardless of the owner; usually limits the real estate's type of use or intensity of use.

deficiency An inadequacy in a structure or one of its components.

demand The desire and ability to purchase or lease goods or services; in real estate, the quantity of a type of real estate desired for purchase or rent at various prices.

depreciation *1.* In appraising, a loss in property value from any cause; any difference between reproduction cost or replacement cost and market value as of the appraisal date. *2.* In regard to improvements, depreciation measures deterioration and obsolescence. *3.* In accounting, an allowance made against the loss in value of an asset for a defined purpose and computed using a specified method.

direct capitalization *1.* The method used to convert an estimate of a single year's income expectancy or an average of several years' income expectancies into an indication of value in one direct step, either by dividing the income estimate by an appropriate rate or by multiplying the income estimate by an appropriate factor. *2.* A capitalization technique that utilizes capitalization rates and multipliers extracted from sales. Only the first year's income is considered. Yield and value change are implied but not identified.

direct cost Expenditures for the labor and materials necessary to construct a new improvement.

discounted cash flow analysis A set of procedures in which the quantity, variability, timing and duration of periodic income, as well as the quantity and timing of reversions, are specified and discounted to a present value at a specified yield rate.

easement An interest in real property that conveys use, but not ownership, of a portion of an owner's property.

easements in appurtenance An easement that is attached to, benefits and passes with the conveyance of the dominant estate; runs with the land for the benefit of the dominant estate and continues to burden the servient estate, although such estates may be conveyed to new owners.

easements in gross An easement that is not attached or appurtenant to any particular estate; neither runs with the land nor is it transferred through the conveyance of title.

effective age The age indicated by the condition and utility of a structure.

effective gross income multiplier (EGIM) The ratio between sales price or value (V) and effective gross income (EGI); a single year's EGI expectancy or an annual average of several years' EGI expectancies: (EGIM = V ÷ EGI).

eminent domain The right of government to take private property for public use upon the payment of just compensation.

encroachment 1. Trespassing on the domain of another. 2. Partial or gradual displacement of an existing use by another use, for example, locating commercial or industrial improvements in a residential district.

entrepreneur One who assumes the risk and management of a business or enterprise; a promoter who initiates development.

entrepreneurial profit A market-derived figure that represents the amount an entrepreneur expects to receive in addition to costs; the difference between total cost and market value.

equity One of two characteristics of investment, the other being debt. Equity investors assume greater risk, and their earnings are subordinate to operating expenses and debt service. Equity investors are compensated with dividends and the possible appreciation in the value of their investments. With regard to a specific property, equity also refers to the net value of the property, obtained by subtracting from its total value all liens or other charges against it, or the value of an owner's interest in property in excess of all claims and liens.

equity capitalization rate (R_E)   An income rate that reflects the relationship between a single year's pretax cash flow expectancy, or an annual average of several years' pretax cash flow expectancies, and the equity investment; used in direct capitalization to convert pretax cash flow into an equity value indication: RE = pretax cash flow ÷ equity. *Also called* equity dividend rate, cash on cash rate, and cash flow rate.

escheat   The right of government that gives the state titular ownership of a property when its owner dies without a will or any ascertainable heirs.

excess land   For an improved site, the surplus land not needed to serve or support the existing improvement; for a vacant site or site considered as though vacant, the land not needed to accommodate the site's primary highest and best use. Excess land may have its own highest and best use or may allow for future expansion of the existing or anticipated improvement.

external obsolescence   An element of accrued depreciation; a defect, usually incurable, caused by negative influences outside a site.

extraction   A method of estimating land value by estimating the depreciated cost of the improvements on the improved property and deducting this amount from the total sales price to arrive at an estimated sale price for the land; most effective when the improvements contribute little to the total sales price of the property.

factors of production   The elements of labor, capital, coordination and land; together these factors create wealth, income or services.

feasibility study   The analysis that determines whether a project will fulfill the objectives of the party for whom the study is done; an analysis of the profitability of a specific real estate undertaking in terms of the criteria of a specific market or investor.

Federal Reserve Bank   One of 12 banks created and regulated by the Federal Reserve system.

Federal Reserve System (the Fed)   The central banking system of the United States that regulates money supply, determines the legal reserve of member banks, oversees the mint, effects transfers of funds, promotes and facilitates the clearance and collection of checks, examines member banks and serves other functions; consists of 12 Federal Reserve Banks, their 24 branches and national and state banks that are members of the system. Each national bank is a stockholding member of the Federal Reserve Bank in its district; membership for state banks and trust companies is optional.

fee simple estate   Absolute ownership unencumbered by any other interest or estate, subject only to the powers of government.

final value estimate A range of values or final single amount that an appraiser derives in the reconciliation of value indications and states in the appraisal report.

fixed expenses The operating expenses that generally do not vary with occupancy and have to be paid whether the property is occupied or vacant.

fixed-rate mortgage A conventional mortgage with an interest rate that does not vary over the life of the loan.

form report An appraisal report presented on a standard form, as required by financial institutions, insurance companies and government agencies. The reporting requirements for form reports, which are the same as for other types or reports, are set forth in the USPAP Standards Rules (Standards 2 and 5) and in the Appraisal Institute's Guide Note 3.

frontage The measured footage of a site or water that abuts a street.

front foot A land measure, one foot in width, taken along the road or water frontage of a property.

fully amortizing mortgage loan A loan with equal periodic payments, usually on a monthly basis, that provide for both a return *on* investment, or interest, and a return *of* investment, or recovery of principle, over the term of the loan.

functional utility The ability of a property or a building to be useful and to perform the function for which it is intended according to current market taste and standards, as well as the efficiency of a building's use in terms of architectural style, design and layout, traffic patterns, and size and types of rooms.

general warranty deed A covenant of warranty inserted in a deed that binds the grantor and heirs to defend the title conveyed to the grantee and heirs against the lawful claims of all persons.

going-concern value The value created by a proven property operation; going-concern value is considered as a separate entity to be valued with an established business.

graduated payment lease A lease that provides for specified changes, either step-up or step-down, in the rent at one or more points during the lease term.

grantee A person to whom property is transferred by deed or to whom property rights are granted by a trust instrument or other document.

grantor A person who transfers property by deed or grants property rights through a trust instrument or other document.

gross lease A lease in which the landlord receives stipulated rent and is obligated to pay all or most of the fixed and operating expenses attributable to the real estate.

gross rent multiplier (GRM) The relationship (or ratio) between sale price (or value) and gross rental income.

ground rent Rent paid for the right to use and occupy land; the portion of the total rent allocated to the underlying land.

growth A stage in a neighborhood's life cycle in which a neighborhood gains public favor and acceptance.

highest and best use The reasonably probable and legal use of vacant land or an improved property that is physically possible, appropriately supported, financially feasible and results in the highest value. The four criteria the highest and best use must meet are legal permissibility, physical possibility, financial feasibility and maximum profitability.

highest and best use of property (as improved) The use that should be made of a property as it exists.

highest and best use of site (as vacant) The use of a property based on the assumption that a parcel of land is vacant or can be made vacant through demolition of any improvements.

improvements Buildings or other relatively permanent structures or developments located on, or attached to, land.

income capitalization approach Approach through which an appraiser derives a value indication for income-producing property by converting anticipated benefits, for example, cash flows and reversions, into property value. This conversion can be accomplished in two ways: (1) One year's income expectancy or an annual average of several years' income expectancies may be capitalized at a market-derived capitalization rate or a capitalization rate that reflects a specified income pattern, return on investment and change in the value of the investment or (2) the annual cash flows may be discounted for the holding period and the reversion at a specified yield rate.

incurable functional obsolescence An element of accrued depreciation; a defect caused by a deficiency or a superadequacy in the structure, materials, or design that is not financially feasible or practical to correct.

incurable physical deterioration An element of accrued depreciation; a defect caused by physical deterioration that is impractical or uneconomic to correct.

index lease A lease that provides for periodic rent adjustments based on the change in a specific index, for example, the cost of living index.

indirect cost In construction, expenditures for items other than labor and materials, for example, administrative costs; professional fees; financing costs and interest paid on permanent and construction loans; taxes and builder's or developer's all-risk insurance during construction; and marketing, sales, and lease-up costs incurred in achieving occupancy or sale.

insurable value That portion of the value of an asset or asset group that is acknowledged or recognized under the provisions of an applicable loss insurance policy.

interest Money paid for, or earned by, the use of capital as distinguished from a return of capital.

interim use The temporary use to which a site or improved property is put until it is ready to be put to its highest and best use.

investment value The specific value of an investment to a particular investor or class of investors based on individual requirements; different from market value, which is impersonal and detached.

joint tenancy Joint ownership by two or more persons with right of survivorship.

land *1.* The earth's surface, both land and water, and anything that is attached to it; all natural resources in their original state, that is, mineral deposits, wildlife, timber, fish, water, coal deposits, soil. *2.* In law, the solid surface on the earth, as distinguished from water.

lease A written document in which the rights to use and occupancy of land or structures are transferred by the owner to another for a specified period of time in return for a specified rent.

leased fee estate An ownership interest held by a landlord with the right of use and occupancy conveyed by lease to others; the rights of lessor or the leased fee owner and the leased fee are specified by contract terms in the lease.

leasehold estate The right to use and occupy real estate for a stated term and under certain conditions; conveyed by a lease.

legally nonconforming use That use that was lawfully established but no longer conforms to the use regulations of the zone in which it is located.

letter report A brief appraisal report that contains only the conclusions reached in the appraiser's investigation and analysis. The reporting requirements for letter reports, which are the same as for other types of reports, are set forth in the USPAP Standards Rules (Standards 2 and 5).

leverage The effect of borrowed funds on the rate of return on equity investment.

license *1.* A formal agreement from a lawful source that allows a business or profession to be conducted, for example, a franchise. *2.* Government permission to conduct an activity.

lien A charge against property in which the property is the security for payment of the debt.

life estates Total rights to use, occupancy, and control; limited to the lifetime of a designated party, often known as the life tenant.

liquidation 1. Forced or voluntary cash realization; the selling of real estate, stocks, bonds, or other investments, either to take profits or in anticipation of declining prices. 2. The termination or conclusion of a business or real estate operation by the conversion of its assets into cash; the proceeds are distributed first to creditors in order of preference, and the remainder, if any, is allocated to the owners in proportion to their holdings.

loan-to-value ratio The ratio of a mortgage loan and the value of the security pledged; usually expressed as a percentage.

long-lived item A component with an expected remaining economic life that is the same as the remaining economic life of the entire structure.

market value The most probable price, as of a specified date, in cash, or in terms equivalent to cash, or in other precisely revealed terms for which the specified property rights should sell after reasonable exposure in a competitive market under all conditions requisite to a fair sale, with the buyer and seller each acting prudently, knowledgeably, and for self-interest, and assuming that neither is under undue duress.

Many of the legal definitions of market value are based on the following:

The highest price estimated in terms of money that the land would bring if exposed for sale in the open market, with reasonable time allowed in which to find a purchaser, buying with knowledge of all of the uses and purposes to which it was adapted and for which it was capable of being used. [*Sacramento Southern R. R. Co.* v. *Heilbron* 156 Cal. 408, 104 P. 979 (1909).]

Persons performing appraisal services that may be subject to litigation are cautioned to seek the exact definition of market value in the jurisdiction in which the services are being performed.

As defined in the Uniform Standards of Professional Appraisal Practice (USPAP), market value is "the most probable price which a property should bring in a competitive and open market under all conditions requisite to a fair sale, the buyer and the seller each acting prudently and knowledgeably, and assuming the price is not affected by undue stimulus."

mean A measure of central tendency. The sum of the values of a set divided by the number of values.

median A measure of central tendency. The value of the middle item in an uneven number of items arranged or arrayed according to size; the arithmetic average of the two central items in an even number of items similarly arranged; a positional average that is not affected by the size of extreme values.

mode A measure of central tendency. The most frequent, or typical, value in an array of numbers; a positional average that is not affected by extreme items. It is the most descriptive average and easily identified when the number of items is small; however, if the sample is too small, and none of the values are repeated, no mode exists.

modernization A type of renovation in which worn or outdated elements are replaced with their current counterparts.

money market The interaction of buyers and sellers who trade short-term money instruments.

mortgage A legal document pledging a described property for the repayment of a loan under certain terms and conditions.

mortgage banker A person or company that makes mortgage loans with its own funds on its own behalf, usually in expectation of reselling the loans to lenders at a profit and then servicing the loans.

mortgage broker One who places mortgages, that is, finds appropriate borrowers or willing lenders for a fee, which is usually a percentage of the loan amount.

narrative report An appraisal report in which the appraiser supports and explains the opinions and conclusions presented and demonstrates the soundness of the final value estimate. The reporting requirements for narrative reports, which are the same as for other types of reports, are set forth in the USPAP Standards Rules (Standards 2 and 5).

net lease A lease in which the tenant pays all property changes, in addition to the stipulated rent.

net operating income The actual or anticipated net income remaining after deducting all operating expenses from effective gross income, but before deducting mortgage debt service and book depreciation; may be calculated before or after deducting replacement reserves.

operating expense The periodic expenditures necessary to maintain the real property and to continue the production of the effective gross income.

operating expense ratio The ratio of total operating expenses to effective gross income; the complement of the net income ratio.

oral report An unwritten appraisal report that includes a property description and all facts, assumptions, conditions and reasoning on which the conclusion is based. The reporting requirements for oral reports, which are the same as for written reports, are set forth in the USPAP Standards Rules (Standards 2 and 5).

overhead Expenses of direction and administration that are necessary to conduct a business.

paired data analysis A procedure in which sales are compared in pairs to identify the effect of specific differences on sales price.

partially amortizing mortgage loan A loan that is not fully amortized at maturity; the outstanding principal must be repaid in one lump sum; often created by writing a loan for one maturity and calculating debt service payments based on a longer amortization period.

pension fund Contributions from an employer and the employee that are placed with a trustee, who must invest and reinvest prudently, accumulate funds and pay benefits to retirees.

percentage lease A lease in which the rent, or some portion of it, represents a specified percentage of the volume of business, productivity or use achieved by the tenant.

plottage The increment of value when two or more sites are assembled or created to produce greater utility.

police power The right of government to regulate property use to protect public safety, health, morals and general welfare.

post and beam framing In construction, a type of framing in which beams are spaced up to eight feet apart and supported on post and exterior walls; framing members are much larger and heavier than those used in other framing systems.

potential gross income The total income attributable to real property at full occupancy before deduction for vacancy and operating expenses.

price The amount a particular purchaser agrees to pay and a particular seller agrees to accept under the circumstances surrounding their transaction.

principal A capital sum invested; a payment that represents partial or full repayment of the capital loaned or invested, as distinguished from the payment of interest; the unrecovered capital remaining in a loan or investment.

profit *1.* The amount by which the proceeds of a transaction exceed its cost. *2.* In theoretical economics, the residual share of the product of enterprise that accrues to the entrepreneur after interest for capital, rent for land, and wages for labor and management. *3.* In accounting, an increase in wealth that results from the operation of an enterprise. Gross profit usually is the selling price minus cost; items such as selling and operating expenses are deducted from the gross profit to indicate net profit.

purchase-money mortgage   A mortgage that is given by a purchaser to a seller as partial payment for the purchase of real property; an alternative to an institutional loan.

quantity survey method   The cost-estimating method that is a computation of the quantity and quality of all materials used and all categories of labor required, to which unit cost figures are applied to arrive at a total cost estimate for materials and labor.

quitclaim deed   A form of conveyance in which any interest the grantor possesses in the property described in the deed is conveyed to the grantee without warranty of title.

range   The largest sample observation minus the smallest observation.

reconciliation   The step in the valuation process in which an appraiser analyzes alternate value indications to arrive at a final value estimate.

remainderman   A person entitled to an estate after a prior estate or interest has expired.

remodeling   A type of renovation that changes property use or configuration by changing property design.

renovation   The process in which older structures or historic buildings are modernized, remodeled or restored.

replacement cost   The cost of construction, at current prices, of a building having utility equivalent to the building being appraised but built with modern materials and according to current standards, design and layout.

reproduction cost   The cost of construction, at current prices, of an exact duplicate or replica using the same materials, construction standards, design, layout and quality of workmanship, and embodying all the deficiencies, superadequacies and obsolescence of the subject building.

reserve for replacement   An allowance that provides for the periodic replacement of building components that deteriorate and must be replaced during the building's economic life.

reversion   A lump-sum benefit that an investor receives or expects to receive at the termination of an investment or lease.

revitalization A stage of renewal, modernization and increasing demand in a neighborhood's life cycle.

rounding The expression of a number, increased or decreased by a relatively small amount, for simplicity or to reflect the precision of its source.

sales comparison approach Approach through which an appraiser derives a value indication by comparing the property being appraised to similar properties that sold recently, applying appropriate units of comparison and making adjustments, based on the elements of comparison, to the sale prices of the comparables.

sandwich lease A lease in which an intermediate leaseholder is the lessee of one party and the lessor of another ("sandwiched"). The owner of the sandwich lease is neither the fee owner nor the user of the property; he or she may be a leaseholder in a chain of leases, excluding the ultimate sublessee.

savings and loan association A financial intermediary that receives savings deposits, lends money at interest and distributes dividends to depositors after paying operating expenses and establishing appropriate reserves.

scarcity The present or anticipated undersupply of an item relative to the demand for it.

secondary mortgage market A market created by government and private agencies for the purchase and sale of existing mortgages; it provides greater liquidity for mortgages.

sequence of adjustments The order in which adjustments are applied to comparable sales prices: property rights conveyed, financing (cash equivalency), conditions of sale (motivation) and market conditions (time).

short-lived item A component with an expected remaining physical life that is shorter than the remaining physical life of the entire structure.

single-family house A dwelling designed for occupancy by one family.

site Land that is improved so that it is ready to be used for a specific purpose.

special warranty deed A warranty clause in a deed of lands in which the grantor covenants that he and his heirs will defend title to the land against legal claims created by the actions or omissions of the grantor or his heirs. If the warranty is against the claims of all persons, it is a general warranty.

stability A stage in a neighborhood's life cycle in which the neighborhood experiences equilibrium without marked gains or losses.

standard deviation In statistics, a measure of the extent of absolute dispersion, variability or scatter in a frequency distribution; obtained by extracting the square root of the arithmetic mean of the squares of the deviations from the arithmetic mean of the frequency distribution.

subdivision A tract of land that has been divided into blocks or plots with streets, roadways, open areas, and other facilities appropriate to its development as residential, commercial, or industrial sites.

sublease An agreement in which the lessee in a prior lease conveys the right of use and occupancy of a property to another, the sublessee.

substitution The appraisal principle that states when several similar or commensurate commodities, goods or services are available, the one with the lowest price will attract the greatest demand and widest distribution.

superadequacy An excess in the capacity or quality of a structure or structural component; determinable by market standards.

supply The quantity of a type of real estate available for sale or lease at various prices.

supply and demand *1.* In economic theory, the principle that states the price of a commodity, good or service varies directly, but not necessarily proportionately, with demand and inversely, but not necessarily proportionately, with supply. *2.* In real estate, the appraisal principle that states that the price of real property varies directly, but not necessarily proportionately, with demand and inversely, but not necessarily proportionately, with supply.

taxation The right of government to raise revenue through assessment on valuable goods, products and rights.

tenancy by the entirety An estate held by a husband and wife in which neither has a disposable interest in the property during the other's lifetime, except through joint action.

tenancy in common An estate held by two or more persons, each of whom has an undivided interest.

terms of sale Conditions and agreements in a contract of sale.

time-sharing The sale of limited ownership interests in residential apartments or hotel rooms; there are two forms of time-sharing: time-share, time-span, or tenancy in common ownership; and interval ownership.

total operating expense The sum of the fixed and variable expenses and the replacement allowance cited in an appraiser's operating expense estimate.

unit-in-place method The cost-estimating method used to establish total building cost by employing unit costs for the various building components as installed.

units of comparison The components into which a property may be divided for comparison purposes, such as price per square foot, per front foot, per cubic foot, per room, per bed, per seat or per apartment unit.

utility The ability of a product to satisfy a human want, need or desire.

vacancy rate *1.* The relationship between the amount of vacancy space and the total space in a building. *2.* The relationship between the rent estimated for vacant building space and the total rent estimated for all space in the building.

value in use The value a specific property has for a specific use.

variable expenses All operating expenses that vary generally with the level of occupancy or the extent of services provided.

variance *1.* In statistics, a measure of the degree of spread among a set of values; a measure of the tendency of individual values to vary from the mean value. *See also* zoning variance.

yield capitalization The capitalization method used to convert future benefits to present value by discounting each future benefit at an appropriate yield rate or by developing an overall rate that explicitly reflects the investment's income pattern, value change and yield rate.

zoning variance A legally authorized modification in the use of property at a particular location that does not conform to the regulated use set forth in the zoning ordinance for the surrounding area; not an exception or change in the legally applicable zoning.

Index

Absorption, 54–55, 268
Access, 85
Accrued depreciation: categories of, 150–151; definition of, 150, 268; physical deterioration, 150–151; techniques for estimating, 152–157
Actual age, 152, 268
Adjustable-rate mortgage, 61, 268
Adjustments, 121, 126
Adverse possession, 16, 268
Age-life method, 152–153, 268
Allocation, 268
Amenity, 86, 268
Amortization, 61, 268
Annual property taxes, 34, 35
Anticipation, 42, 170, 268
Appraisal: complex, 4; definition of, 4; legal considerations in, 12–22, noncomplex, 4
Appraisal Foundation, 200, 201
Appraisal of Real Estate, 5
Appraisal process: defining problem, 72, 73–74; steps, 72–76
Appraisal report, 75–76
Appraisal Standards Board, 200
Appraiser licensure/certification, 4
Appraiser Qualifications Board, 3, 5, 200
Area, 85, 268
Arm's-length transaction, 269
Assemblage, 138, 269
Assessed value, 33, 34, 269
Assignment, 191, 269
Assumptions and limiting conditions, 193–194, 269

Balance, 42, 269
Balloon mortgage, 269
Balloon payment, 61, 269
Band of investment, 174–175, 269
Basic construction and design, 88–89
Basic mathematical skills, 111–112
Blanket mortgage, 62, 269
Break-even ratio, 176
Bundle of rights, 11, 17, 269
Buydown, 61

Capital, 60, 269
Capitalization, 173, 174, 269
Capital market, 59, 269
Cash equivalent, 269
Cash flow, 170
Central tendency, 106–108

Certification of value, 193
Change, 43, 269
Chattel, 270
Chattel mortgage, 63, 270
Chronological age, 152, 269
Coefficient of correlation, 111, 270
Coefficient of determination, 110, 270
Coefficient of variation, 109, 270
Collection loss, 172
Commercial bank, 60, 270
Comparables, 120–123, 270
Comparable sales data, 121
Comparative unit method, 149, 270
Comparison, elements of, 125
Competition, 43, 270
Condemnation, 16
Condominium, 19
Conformity, 43, 96, 270
Consistent use, 43, 270
Contract rent, 171
Contribution, 45, 270
Cooperative, 20, 189, 270–271
Cost, 32, 149–150
Cost approach: application and limitations of, 146–147; definition of, 271; rationale for, 146; sample problem, 158–161; steps, 147–148; types of costs, 149–150; valuation principles, 147
Cost new: definition of, 152, 157; estimating, 147–149
Curable functional obsolescence, 271
Curable physical deterioration, 150, 271

Data, 72–73
Debt coverage ratio (DCR), 174, 271
Debt service, 173, 274
Debt service ratio, 176. *See also* Debt coverage ratio.
Decline, 55, 271
Deed, 13, 21–22
Deed recordation, 22
Deed restriction, 274
Defect, 151, 154
Deficiency, 151, 154, 155, 274
Demand, 43, 54, 274
Depreciation, 274; techniques for estimating, 152–157
Dictionary of Real Estate Appraisal, 5
Direct capitalization, 173, 271
Direct cost, 149–150, 271

Discounted cash flow (DCF) analysis, 175, 272
Dispersion, 108–109
Dollar adjustments, 124

Easement, 15, 188, 272
Easements in appurtenance, 15, 272
Easements in gross, 15, 272
Effective age, 152, 154, 272
Effective demand, 46
Effective gross income, 172
Effective gross income multiplier (EGIM), 175, 272
Effective (property) tax rate, 34, 35
Emblement, 18
Eminent domain, 16–17, 272
Encroachment, 16, 22, 272
Entrepreneur, 272
Entrepreneurial profit, 150, 272
Equity, 272
Equity capitalization rate, 273. *See also* Equity dividend rate.
Equity dividend rate (EDR), 176–177, 273
Escheat, 16, 273
Exam content weights, 7–8
Excess land, 273
External obsolescence, 151–152, 156–157, 273
Extraction, 273

Factors of production, 42, 273
Feasibility study, 54, 273
Federal Financial Institutions Examination Council (FFIEC), 4
Federal Open Market Committee (FOMC), 59, 63
Federal Reserve Bank, 273
Federal Reserve System, 58, 273
Fee simple estate, 17, 188, 273
Final value estimate, 192–194, 274
Financial Institutions Reform, Recovery and Enforcement Act (FIRREA) of 1989, 4, 5, 200
Finish, 89
Fiscal policy, 59
Fixed expenses, 172, 274
Fixed lease, 190
Fixed-rate mortgage, 61, 274
Fixture, 13
Forecasts, 55
Form report, 75, 274
Foundation, 89
Fractional reserve banking, 58
Frame, 89
Frontage, 274
Front foot, 274
Fully amortizing mortgage, 61, 274

Functional adequacy, 88
Functional obsolescence, 151, 154–156
Functional utility, 88, 154, 274

General warranty deed, 21–22, 274
Going-concern value, 33–34, 274
Governmental survey, 20–21
Graduated payment lease, 191, 274
Grantee, 13, 274
Grantor, 13, 274
Gross lease, 190, 274
Gross market income, 170, 171–172
Gross Rent Multiplier (GRM): definition of, 155, 177, 275; calculating estimated value, 178; example, 179; nature of, 177–178; procedure, 178; use of, 156, 177
Ground rent, 275
Growth, 55, 275

Highest and best use: definition of, 44, 74, 96, 275; analysis, 96–100; application of, 98–100; cost approach, 147; establishing, 87; tests (constraints), 96–98
Highest and best use of property as improved, 99–100, 275
Highest and best use of site as vacant, 98–99, 275

Improvement, 84, 275
Improvement description, 87–88
Income approach: anticipation in, 170; definition of, 76, 275; estimating income and expenses, 170–173; rationale for, 170
Incurable functional obsolescence, 275
Incurable physical deterioration, 150, 275
Index lease, 191, 275
Indirect cost, 150, 275–276
Insurable value, 33, 35, 276
Interest, 61, 276
Interim use, 100, 276
Investment value, 33, 276

Joint tenancy, 276
Joint tenants, 19

Land, 84, 276
Lease: definition of, 13, 189, 276; financial arrangements in, 190–191; interest in, 14; leased fee estate, 189; leasehold estate, 189–190; parties to, 13–14; rights created by, 14; types of, 190–191; unencumbered fee estate, 190
Leased fee estate, 14, 18, 189, 276
Leasehold estate, 14, 18, 189–190, 276
Legal description, 20–21
Legally nonconforming use, 100, 276

Legal rights and interests, 17–18
Lessee, 13, 189
Lessor, 13, 189
Letter of opinion, 75, 76
Letter report, 75, 276
Leverage, 62, 276
License, 18, 276
Lien, 15, 277
Life estate: definition of, 17, 188, 277; grantee of, 22, kinds of, 17–18
Life estate, conventional, 17–18
Life estate pur autre vie, 17–18
Liquidation, 33, 277
Loan-to-value ratio, 62, 177, 277
Long-lived item, 151, 153–154, 277
Lot and block, 21

Market, 54, 56
Marketability, 54, 63, 88
Market abstraction, 152
Market analysis, 54–55
Market price, 32
Market rent, 171, 180
Market value: assumptions, 30–31; definition of, 30, 277; distinctions, 31–32; estimate, 73–74
Mean, 106–107, 113, 277
Measuring life, 17
Median, 107–108, 278
Metes and bounds, 20
Mode, 108, 278
Modernization, 88–89, 278
Modified age-life method, 153
Monetary policy, 58
Money and capital markets, role of, 58–60
Money market, 59, 278
Monuments, 21
Mortgage: definition of, 14, 59, 278; payment plans, 61–62; terms, 60–61; types of, 62–63
Mortgage banker, 60, 278
Mortgage broker, 60, 278
Mortgage loan constant, 174, 180
Mortgage markets, 59–60
Mortgage payment plans, 61–62
Most probable sales price, 31–32
Most probable use, 96

Narrative report, 75, 278
Negative amortization, 61
Neighborhood, 55
Neighborhood analysis, 55
Neighborhood boundaries, 55
Neighborhood life cycle, 55
Net lease, 190, 278
Net operating income, 172–173, 278
Nontraditional property analysis, 100

Observed condition breakdown: definition of, 153; external obsolescence, 156–157; functional obsolescence, 151, 154–156; physical deterioration, 153–154
Operating expense, 172, 278
Operating expense ratio, 175, 176, 278
Operating ratios, 176–177
Oral report, 75, 279
Overall capitalization rate, 174–175
Overhead, 279

Package mortgage, 63
Paired data analysis, 126, 279
Partial interests, valuation of, 188–190
Partially amortizing mortgage, 61, 279
Pension fund, 60, 279
Percentage adjustments, 112, 124
Percentage change, 111–112
Percentage lease, 190, 279
Personal property, 12
Physical deterioration, 150–151, 153–154
Plottage value, 138, 139, 279
Police power, 16, 57, 279
Post and beam frame, 89, 279
Potential gross income, 279. See also Gross market income.
Price, 279
Price per acre, 123, 124, 137
Price per front foot, 123, 124, 137
Price per gross rent, 123, 124
Price per lot or building site, 137
Price per room, 123, 124
Price per square foot, 123–124, 137
Primary mortgage market, 59–60
Principal, 60–61, 279
Private limitations, 13–16
Private mortgage insurance, 62, 63
Profit, 18, 279–280
Public limitations, 16
Published cost manuals, 157
Purchase money mortgage, 62–63, 280

Quantity survey method, 149, 280
Quitclaim deed, 22, 280

Range, 108–109, 280
Real estate, 12, 22
Real estate markets, 56–58
Real estate ownership: limitations on, private, 13–16, public, 16–17; multiple forms of, 18–19; special forms of, 19–20
Real estate value, influences on, 12
Real property, 12
Real property valuation, 42–45
Reappraisal lease, 190
Reconciliation, 75, 191–192, 280

Rectangular survey. *See* Governmental survey.
Regression analysis, 109–111, 113
Rehabilitation, 89
Remainderman, 17, 188, 280
Remaining economic life, 152
Remodeling, 89, 280
Renovation, 280
Replacement cost, 148, 280
Reproduction cost, 148, 280
Reserve for replacement, 172, 280
Reversion, 170, 280
Reversionary right, 22
Revitalization, 55, 281
Rounding, 148, 192–193, 281

Sales comparison approach: conditions of sale, 123; definition of, 76, 281; economic principles, 120; elements of comparison, 125; sequence of adjustments, 125–126; steps, 121–127; types of adjustments, 124; units of comparison, 123–124
Sandwich lease, 191, 281
Savings and loan association, 60, 281
Scarcity, 46, 281
Secondary mortgage market, 60, 281
Segmented markets, 57
Sequence of adjustments, 125–126, 281
Severalty, 18
Short-lived item, 151, 153, 281
Simple regression, 113
Single-family house, 281
Site, 84, 281
Site analysis, 84–87
Site improvements, 85
Site valuation, 136–139
Size, 85
Special warranty deed, 22, 281
Stability, 281
Standard deviation, 109, 281–282
State license law, 200–201
Statistical concepts in appraisal: basic mathematical skills, 111–113; regression analysis, 109–111; specific quantitative skills, 106–109
Subdivision, 282
Subject property, 120
Sublease, 191, 282

Substitution, 44–45, 120, 147, 282
Superadequacy, 151, 154, 155, 282
Superstructure, 89, 90
Supply, 43, 54, 282
Supply and demand, 43, 56, 120, 282

Taxation, 17, 282
Tenancy by the entirety, 19, 282
Tenancy in common, 19, 282
Terms of sale, 282
Test-taking strategies, 5–7
Time-share, 20, 188–189
Time-sharing, 282
Topography, 85
Total economic life, 152
Total operating expenses, 172, 282
Transferability, 46
Transfer of title, 21–22

Unencumbered fee estate, 14, 190
Uniform content outlines, 3
Uniform Residential Appraisal Report (URAR), 75
Uniform Standards of Professional Appraisal Practice (USPAP), 3, 30, 200; excerpt, Section I, 202–204; Section II, 204–207; Section III, 207–208
Unit-in-place method, 149, 282
Units of comparison, 123–124, 136–137, 283
U.S. financial markets, 59–60
Utilities, types of, 84–85
Utility, 46, 156, 283

Vacancy rate, 171–172, 283
Valuation process. *See* Appraisal process.
Value: approaches to, 75; economic characteristics of, 46; types of, 30–34
Value estimate, date of, 72
Value in exchange, 33
Value in use, 33, 283
Variable expense, 172, 283
Variable proportions and increasing/decreasing returns, 45
Variance, 190, 283. *See also* Zoning variance.

Yield capitalization, 175, 283

Zoning variance, 97, 283